CHARLOTTE
SALOMON

COLORS OF THE SOUL

Text by Ilaria Ferramosca

Illustrations by Gian Marco De Francisco

FANFARE · PONENT MON

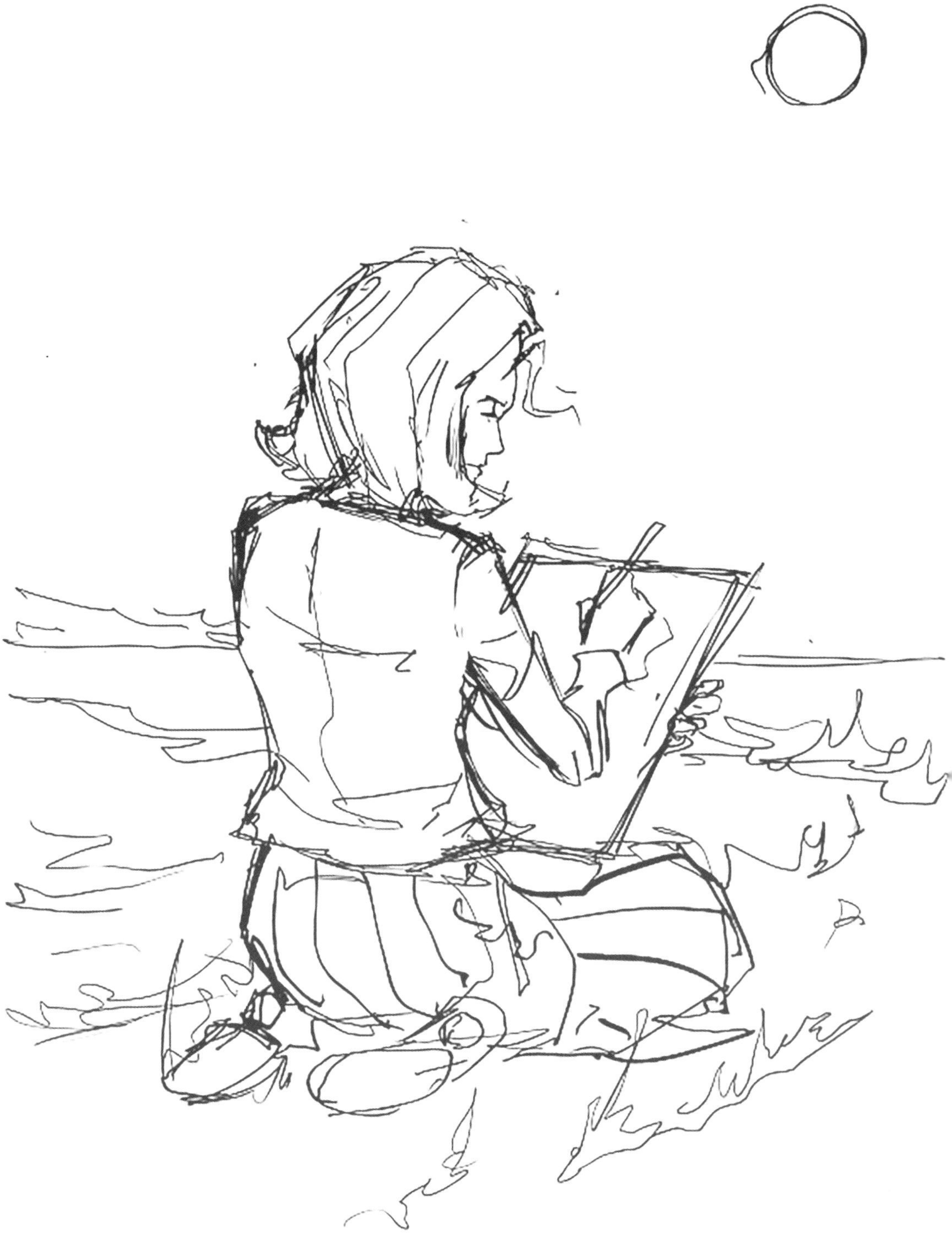

Index

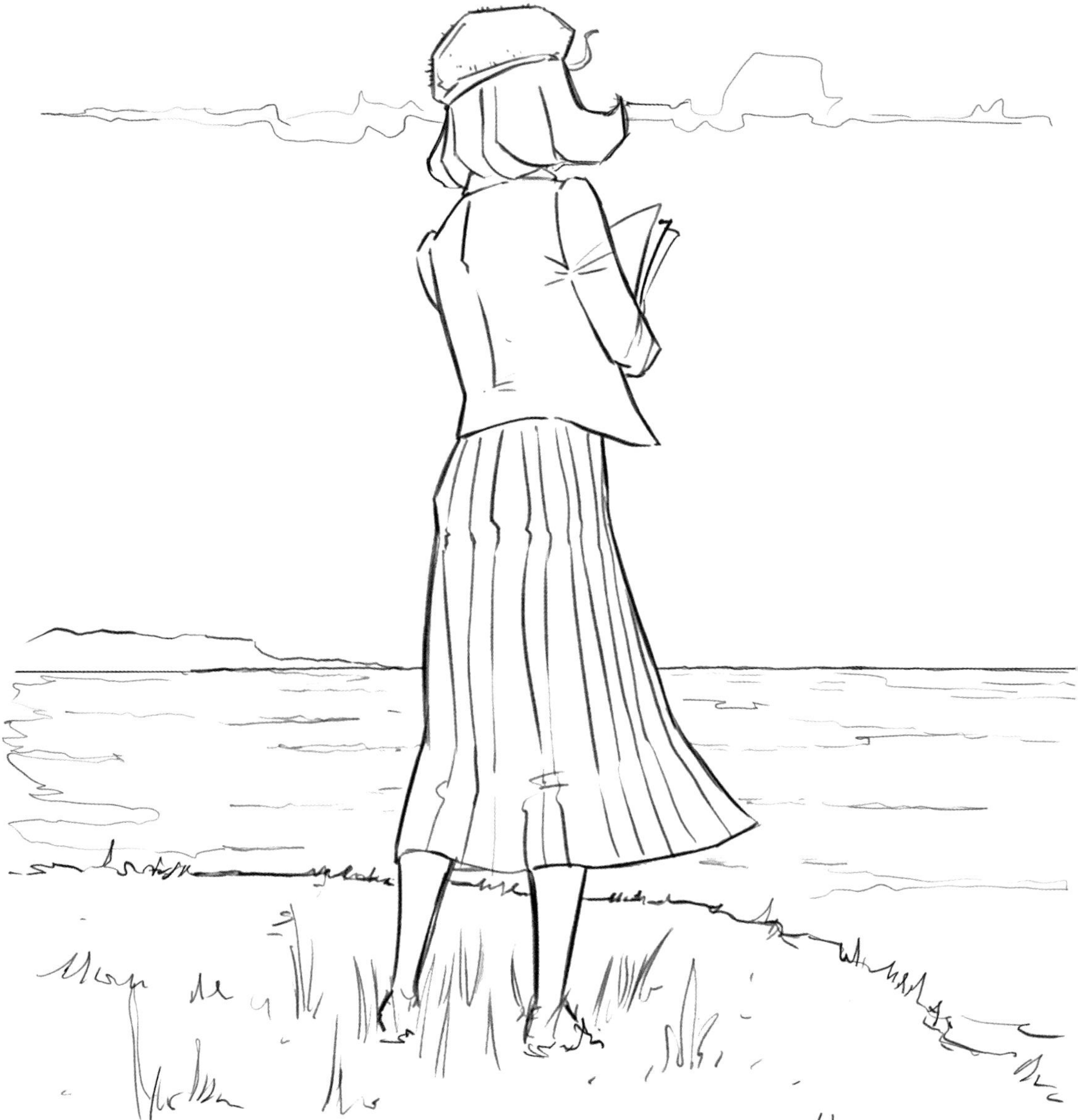

The Heritage of Charlotte

By Claudia Bourdin

To talk about Charlotte Salomon's life isn't easy, after all she did that very well through her own works. Whoever tries to talk about her under narrative form, or through a critique of her opera, won't be fully effective because the opera itself is her life. Fiction or not, that's how she represented it and we don't need to resort to useless words to add something to what she left to us, through colors, musical codes and writing.

In fact, Charlotte's opera can be considered a multi-media work. Her gouaches are a condensation of historical and cultural information, they can be read on a single medium that catches the eye. It's a direct communication that facilitates and holds the interest of people of all ages.

Just as our daily life is made up of an almost uninterrupted flow of images, so is Charlotte's work. Its richness and variety allow you to imagine a pedagogical approach even in the age of multi-media and the Internet. It is an ideal "instrument" to attract students' attention, in order to guide them towards an analysis of the progressive mechanism of the marginalization of individuality and of the dramatic consequences of this type of policy. It is a complex and complete means of expression, within which there is a whole life's story. From a moving and tragic side, due to the historical context in which it takes place and the family's vicissitudes that overwhelmed the young painter from an early age, to the other, a story that exudes courage and determination, the desire to cling to life to defeat destiny through art and love.

It's for this reason that a multitude of artists, directors and writers have been touched and inspired by the opera of Charlotte Salomon. In 1980 the Dutch filmmaker Frans Weisz made a dramatical fiction, Charlotte, followed by the documentary *Life? Or Theater?* thirty years later.

Then there have been theatrical scripts, musical operas, ballets, university researches, a remarkable biography by Mary Felstiner (a historian who studied the life and works of Charlotte Salomon. We owe to her all the information we have about Charlotte), educational initiatives and literary texts.

Thirty exhibitions of her pictorial production have been made in Germany, ten in the United States and the Netherlands with others in Israel, Japan, Canada, the United Kingdom, Denmark, Austria, Switzerland, Norway, Belgium, France and for the first time, in 2017, in Italy, where a part of her gouaches were exposed at the Palazzo Reale in Milan.

What she left us is so important, both from an artistic and experimental point of view, and from the emotional and historical one, that to preserve its memory has become crucial.

Alain Kleinmann (artist and painter) summed up the reason why remembering Charlotte is so fundamental: "Art is at the service of history, memory is at the service of art", and in some way this is the soul of the mission of the project of the *RectoVerso* association, dedicated to Charlotte Salomon and to the studies on the Shoah.

As president of this association, I therefore enthusiastically accepted the idea of supporting a new initiative to protect Charlotte's memory. Especially since, through this graphic novel it is the first time that someone dares to use her own narrative language to tell us about her, so we are faced with an absolutely innovative work compared to previous productions.

Comics are an art form that follow its own precise composition rules, constant over time. This is why it is also called "sequential art". On the contrary, Charlotte did not take into account any of these rules; the reader enters into her artistic production directly by following her choices of graphic design. Today the authors of this new and uniquely designed publication have been able to give us back the living and effective testimony of Charlotte, trying to keep her narrative modalities unchanged by using a structure without grids (as the typical comic division would require) and resorting to many free flowing levels of sequences.

For this reason I invite you to read the book carefully, paying attention to its many levels: the artistic, emotional and the merely historical and biographical ones. Because from the whole of these tiles, as in a mosaic, the opera and the complex figure of Charlotte Salomon comes back to life.

Claudia Bourdin is president of *RectoVerso*,
European Association of Art, History and Memory
dedicated to Charlotte Salomon.

CHARLOTTE
SALOMON

COLORS OF THE SOUL

To Maddalena, primary inspirer of this work and a precious support; to Claudia, indispensable reference point on Charlotte; to my family and friends who have always supported me.
Ilaria

To my father's honesty and my mother's determination. Thanks.
Gian Marco

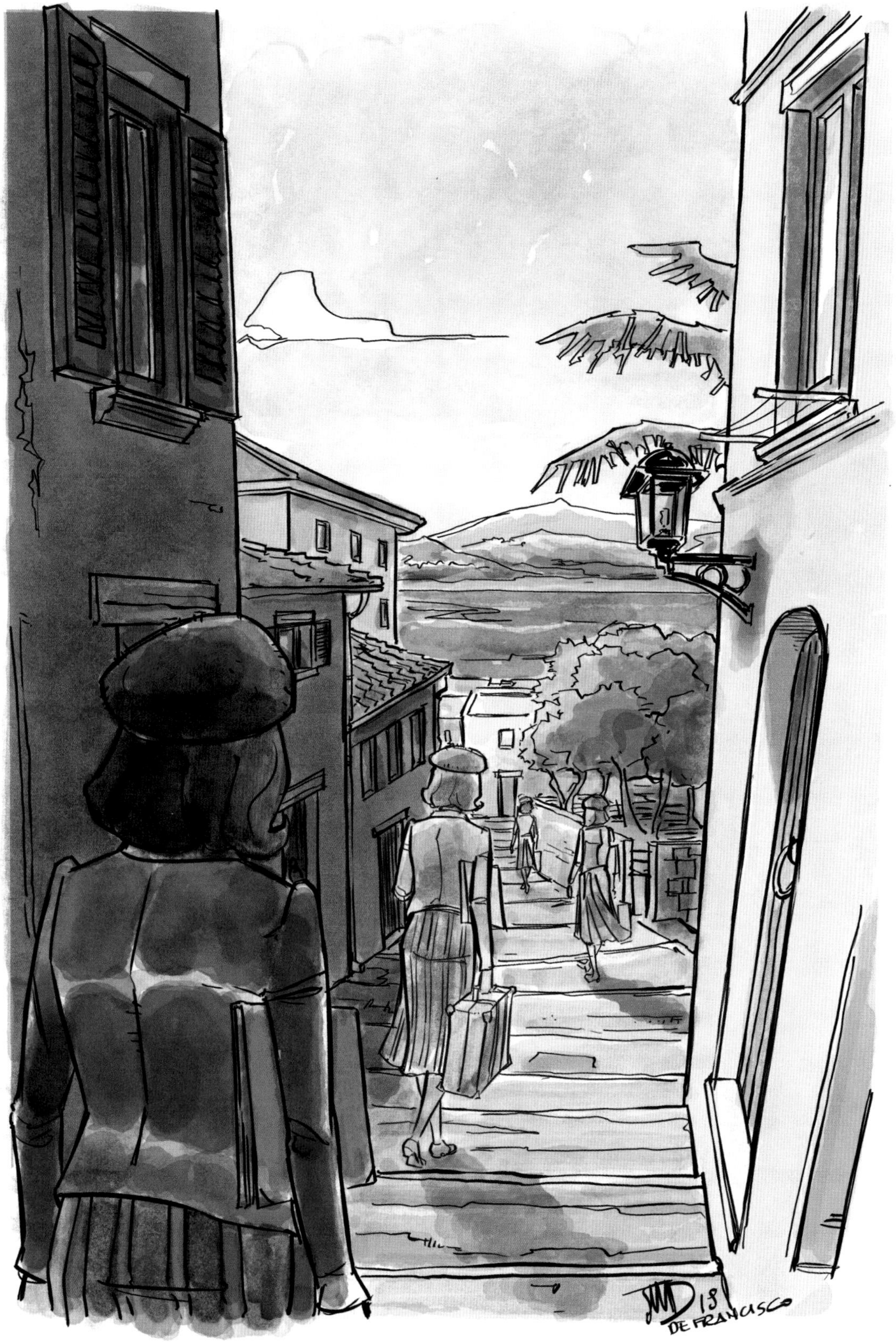
18
DE FRANCISCO

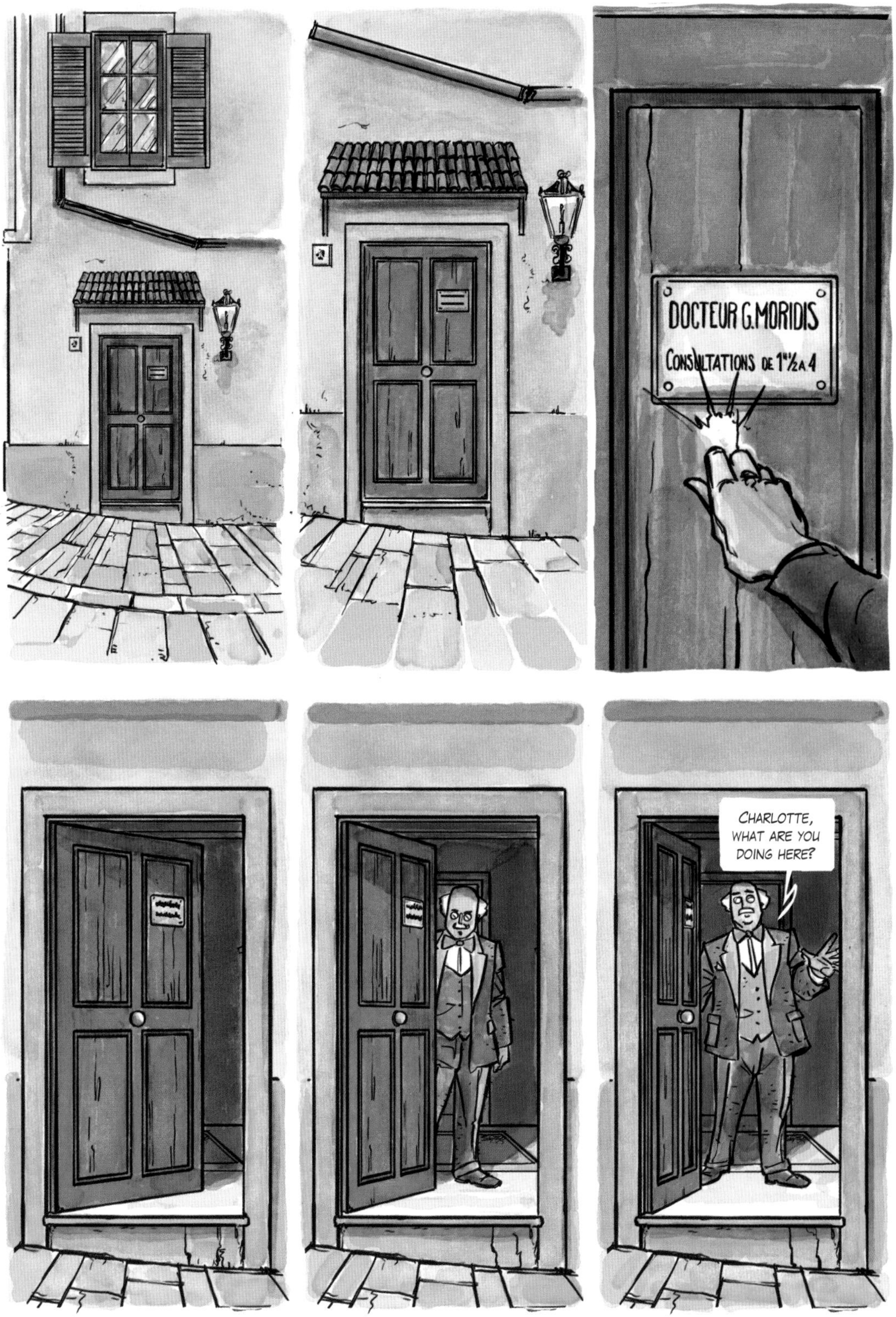
DOCTEUR G.MORIDIS
CONSULTATIONS DE 1H½ A 4
CHARLOTTE, WHAT ARE YOU DOING HERE?

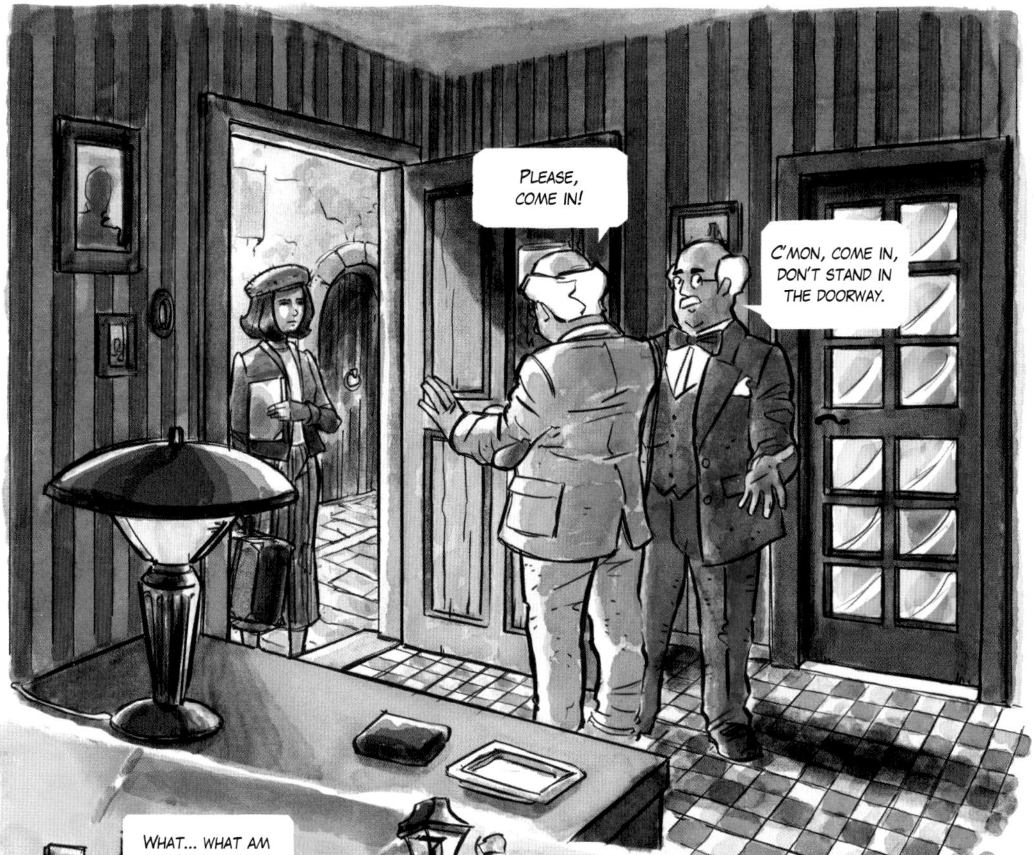
PLEASE, COME IN!
C'MON, COME IN, DON'T STAND IN THE DOORWAY.

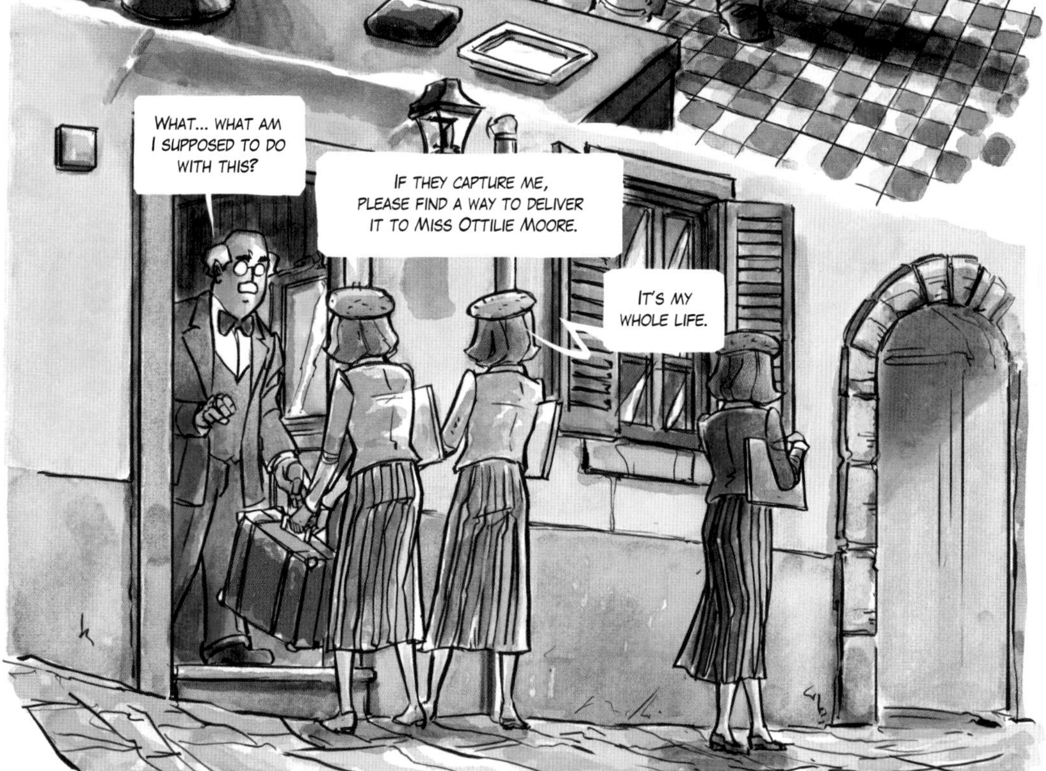
WHAT... WHAT AM I SUPPOSED TO DO WITH THIS?
IF THEY CAPTURE ME, PLEASE FIND A WAY TO DELIVER IT TO MISS OTTILIE MOORE.
IT'S MY WHOLE LIFE.

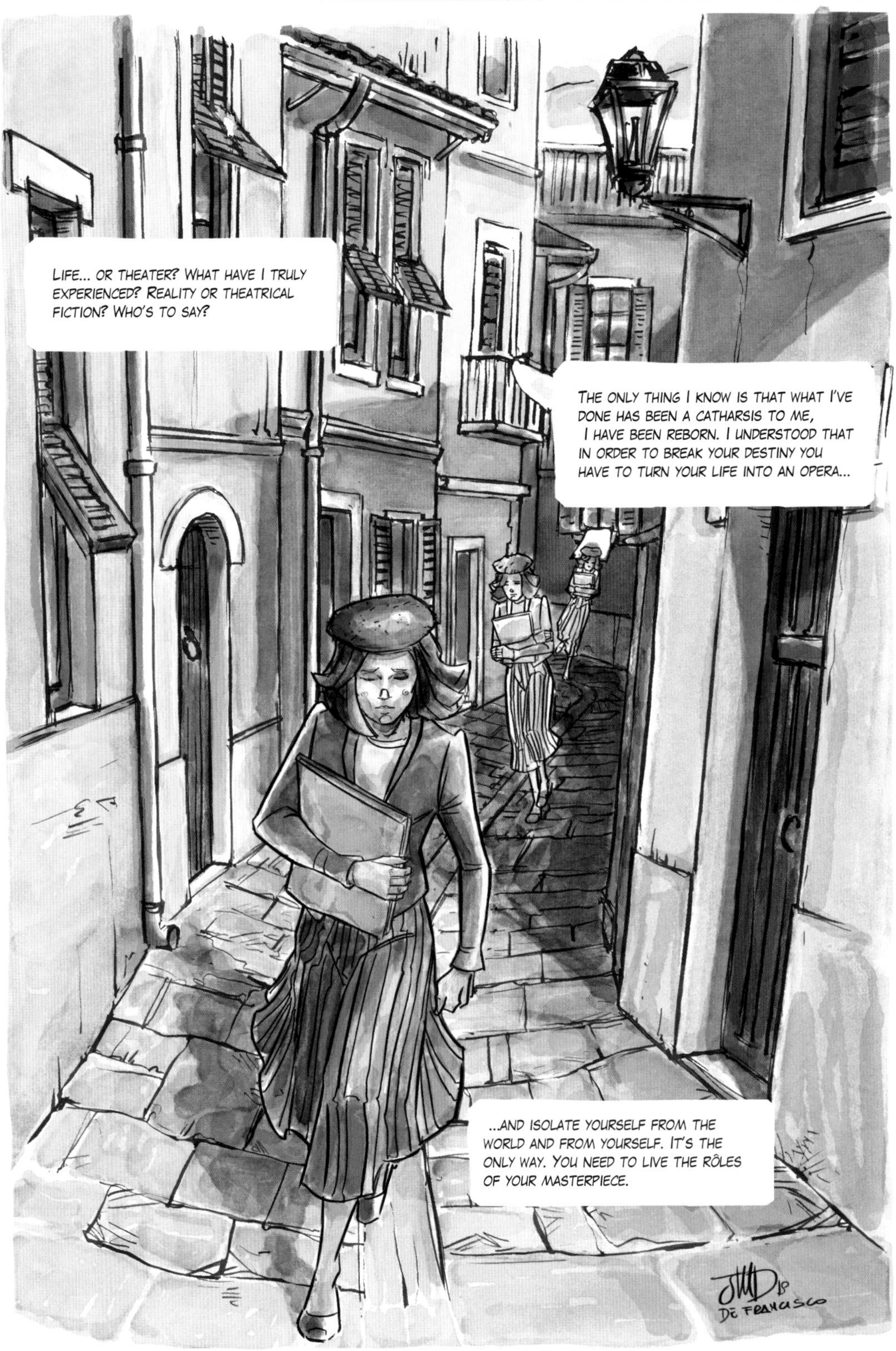
LIFE... OR THEATER? WHAT HAVE I TRULY EXPERIENCED? REALITY OR THEATRICAL FICTION? WHO'S TO SAY?
THE ONLY THING I KNOW IS THAT WHAT I'VE DONE HAS BEEN A CATHARSIS TO ME, I HAVE BEEN REBORN. I UNDERSTOOD THAT IN ORDER TO BREAK YOUR DESTINY YOU HAVE TO TURN YOUR LIFE INTO AN OPERA...
...AND ISOLATE YOURSELF FROM THE WORLD AND FROM YOURSELF. IT'S THE ONLY WAY. YOU NEED TO LIVE THE RÔLES OF YOUR MASTERPIECE.
De Francisco

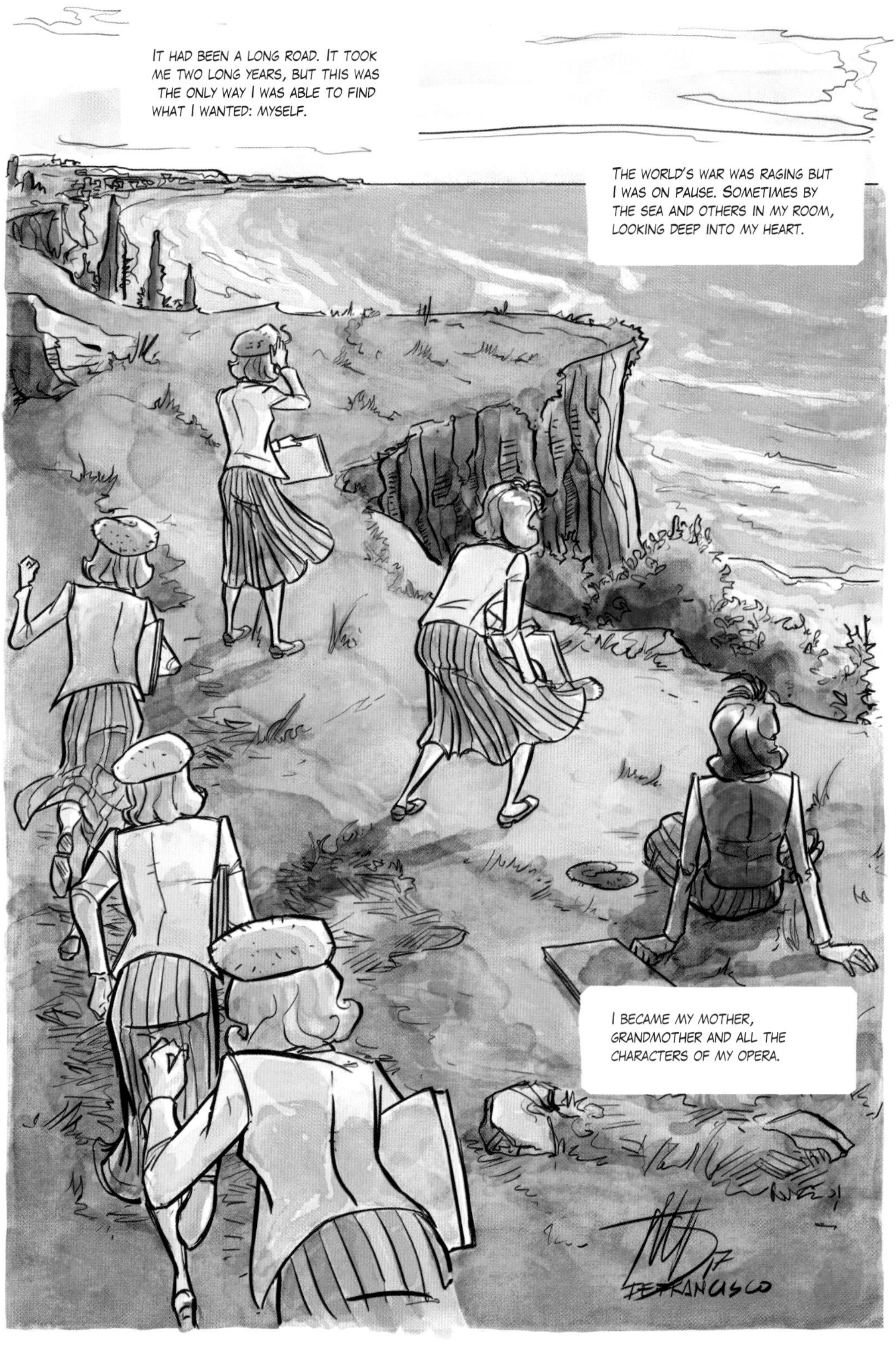
IT HAD BEEN A LONG ROAD. IT TOOK ME TWO LONG YEARS, BUT THIS WAS THE ONLY WAY I WAS ABLE TO FIND WHAT I WANTED: MYSELF.
THE WORLD'S WAR WAS RAGING BUT I WAS ON PAUSE. SOMETIMES BY THE SEA AND OTHERS IN MY ROOM, LOOKING DEEP INTO MY HEART.
I BECAME MY MOTHER, GRANDMOTHER AND ALL THE CHARACTERS OF MY OPERA.
DEFRANCISCO

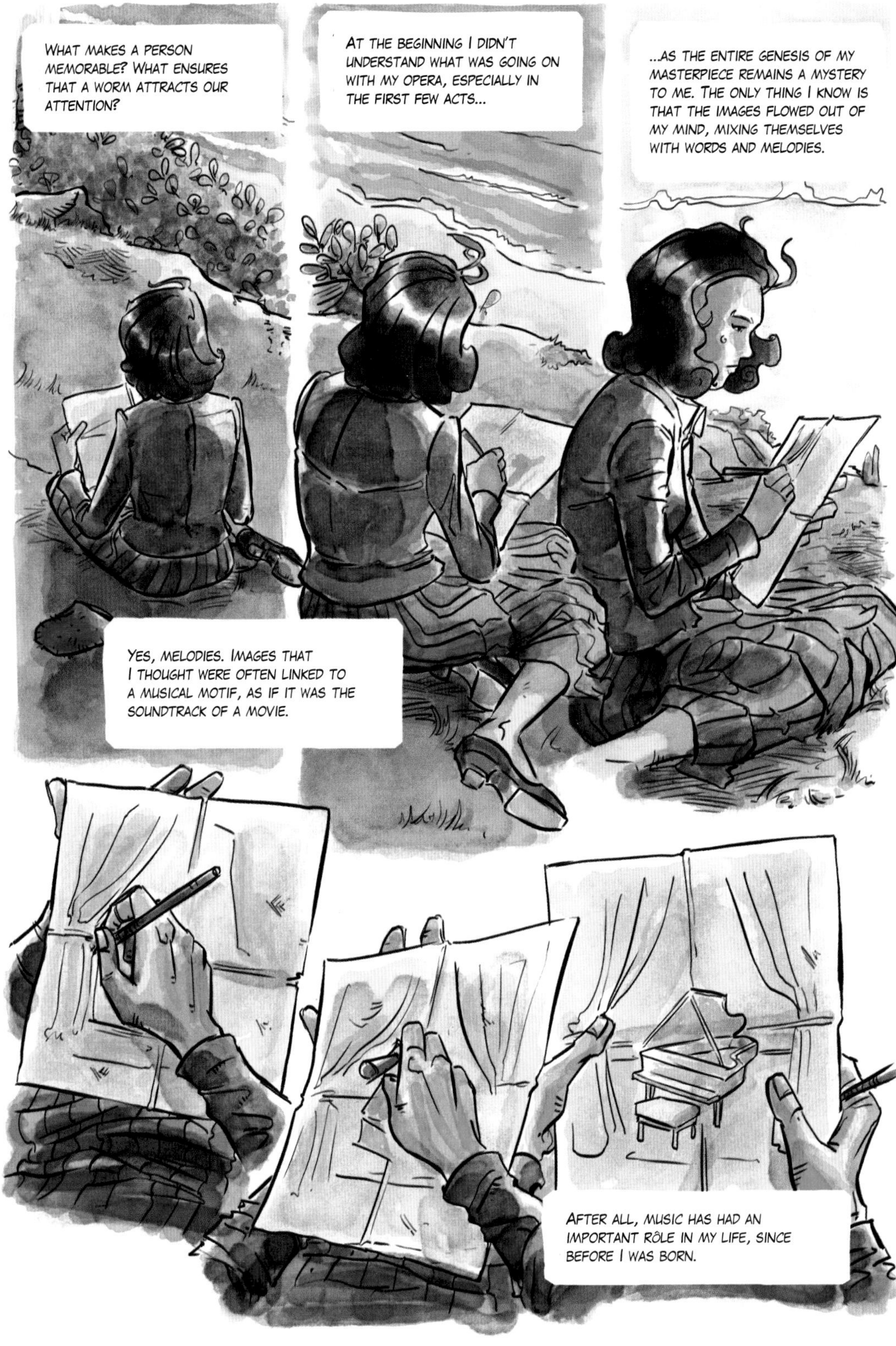
WHAT MAKES A PERSON MEMORABLE? WHAT ENSURES THAT A WORM ATTRACTS OUR ATTENTION?
AT THE BEGINNING I DIDN'T UNDERSTAND WHAT WAS GOING ON WITH MY OPERA, ESPECIALLY IN THE FIRST FEW ACTS...
...AS THE ENTIRE GENESIS OF MY MASTERPIECE REMAINS A MYSTERY TO ME. THE ONLY THING I KNOW IS THAT THE IMAGES FLOWED OUT OF MY MIND, MIXING THEMSELVES WITH WORDS AND MELODIES.
YES, MELODIES. IMAGES THAT I THOUGHT WERE OFTEN LINKED TO A MUSICAL MOTIF, AS IF IT WAS THE SOUNDTRACK OF A MOVIE.
AFTER ALL, MUSIC HAS HAD AN IMPORTANT RÔLE IN MY LIFE, SINCE BEFORE I WAS BORN.

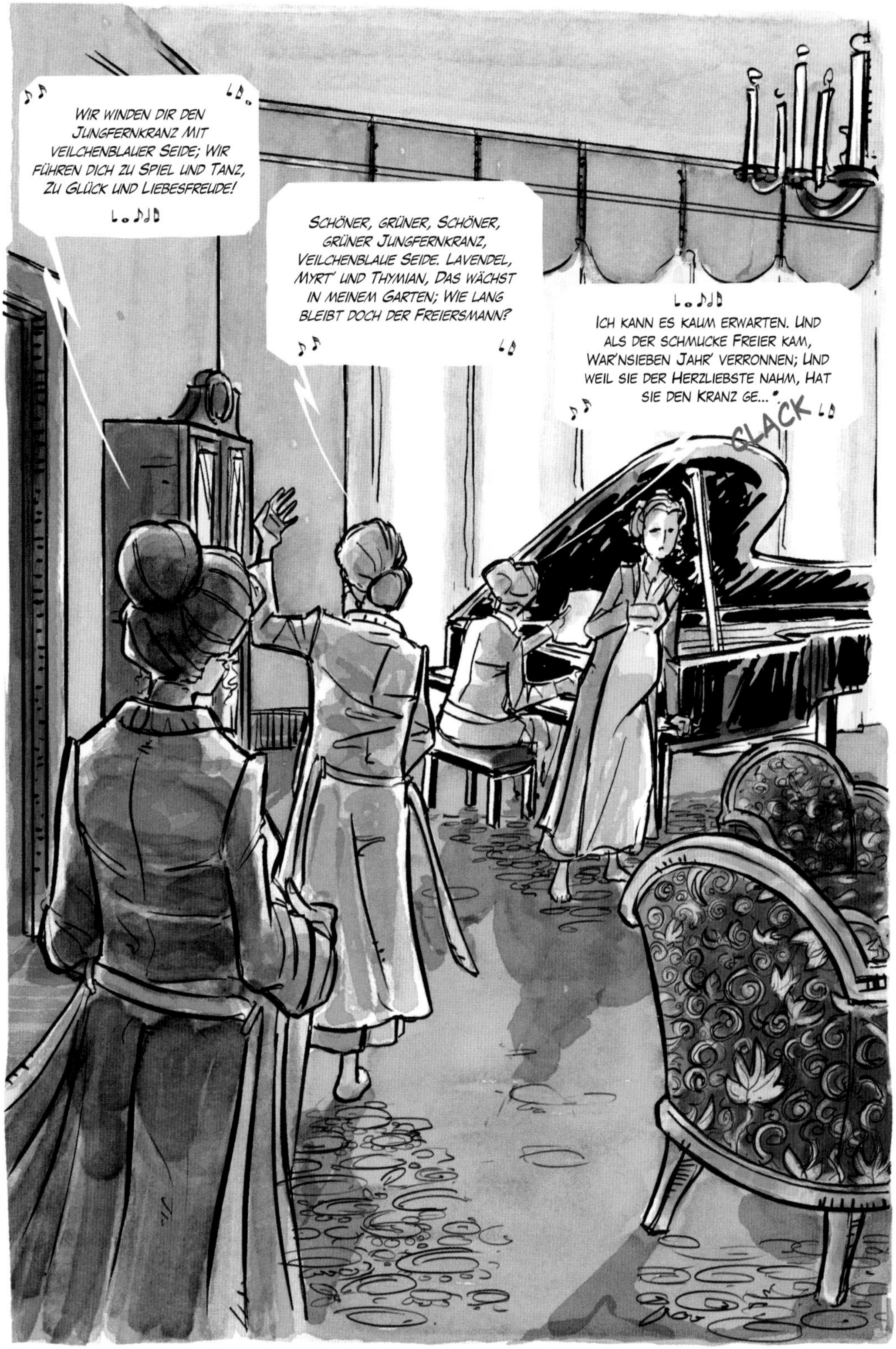
Wir winden dir den Jungfernkranz Mit veilchenblauer Seide; Wir führen dich zu Spiel und Tanz, Zu Glück und Liebesfreude!
Schöner, grüner, Schöner, grüner Jungfernkranz, Veilchenblaue Seide. Lavendel, Myrt' und Thymian, Das wächst in meinem Garten; Wie lang bleibt doch der Freiersmann?
Ich kann es kaum erwarten. Und als der schmucke Freier kam, War'nsieben Jahr' verronnen; Und weil sie der Herzliebste nahm, Hat sie den Kranz ge...*
CLACK

* 'We wind round thee the bridal wreath.' from the third act of *Der Freischütz* [The Marksman] by Carl Maria von Weber {libretto by Freidrich Kind}

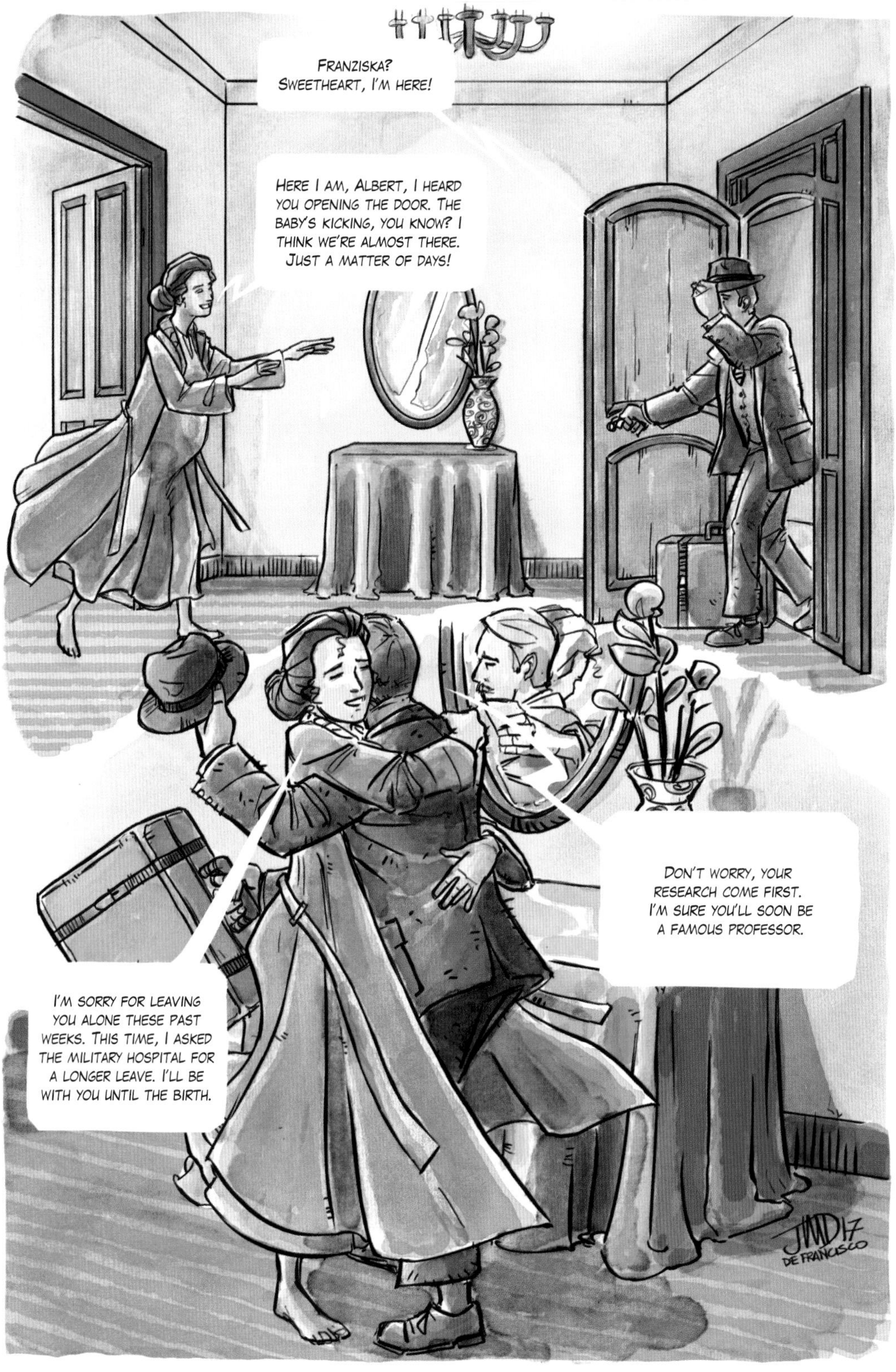
FRANZISKA? SWEETHEART, I'M HERE!
HERE I AM, ALBERT, I HEARD YOU OPENING THE DOOR. THE BABY'S KICKING, YOU KNOW? I THINK WE'RE ALMOST THERE. JUST A MATTER OF DAYS!
I'M SORRY FOR LEAVING YOU ALONE THESE PAST WEEKS. THIS TIME, I ASKED THE MILITARY HOSPITAL FOR A LONGER LEAVE. I'LL BE WITH YOU UNTIL THE BIRTH.
DON'T WORRY, YOUR RESEARCH COME FIRST. I'M SURE YOU'LL SOON BE A FAMOUS PROFESSOR.
JMD17 DE FRANCISCO

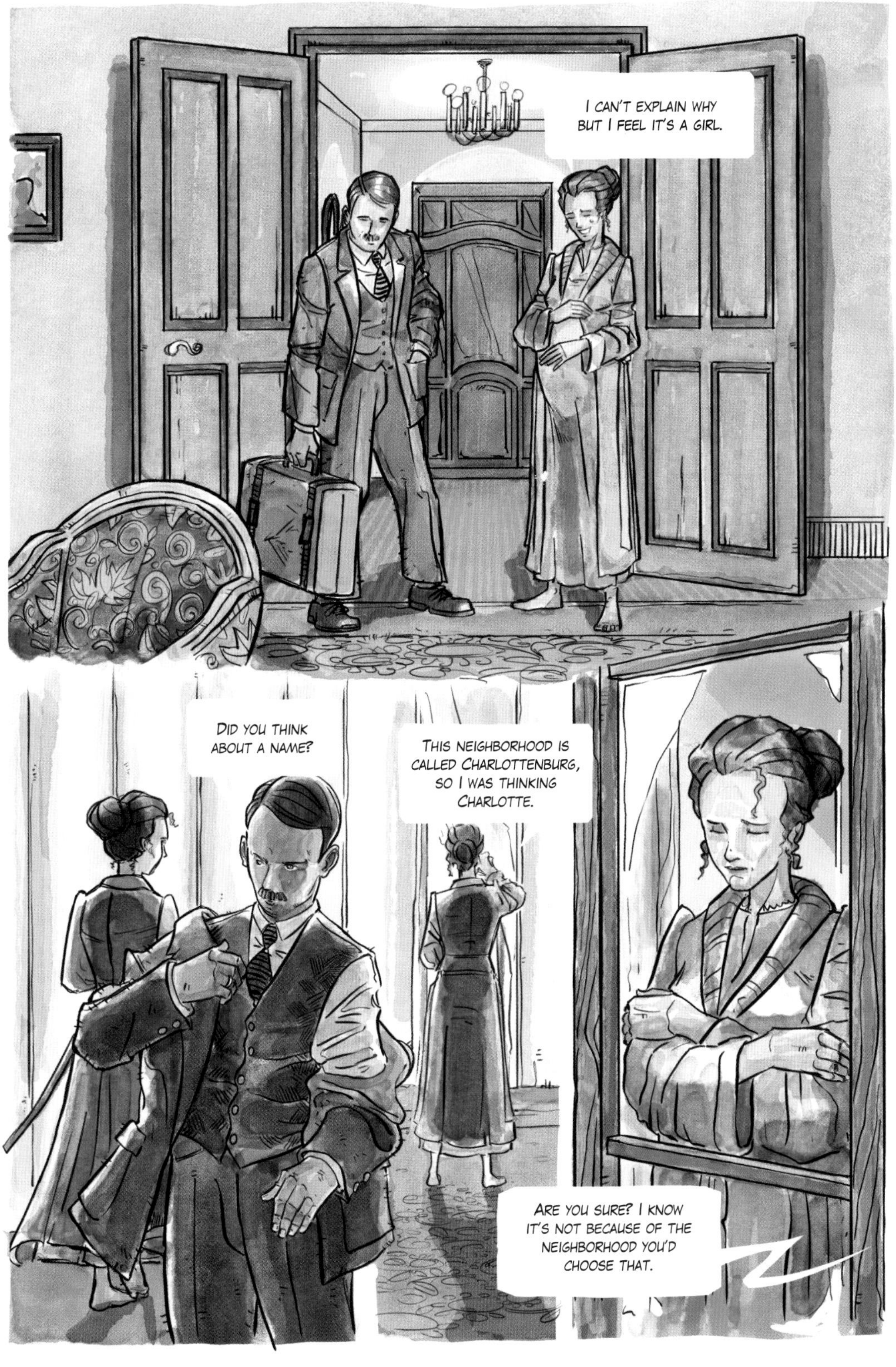
I CAN'T EXPLAIN WHY BUT I FEEL IT'S A GIRL.
DID YOU THINK ABOUT A NAME?
THIS NEIGHBORHOOD IS CALLED CHARLOTTENBURG, SO I WAS THINKING CHARLOTTE.
ARE YOU SURE? I KNOW IT'S NOT BECAUSE OF THE NEIGHBORHOOD YOU'D CHOOSE THAT.

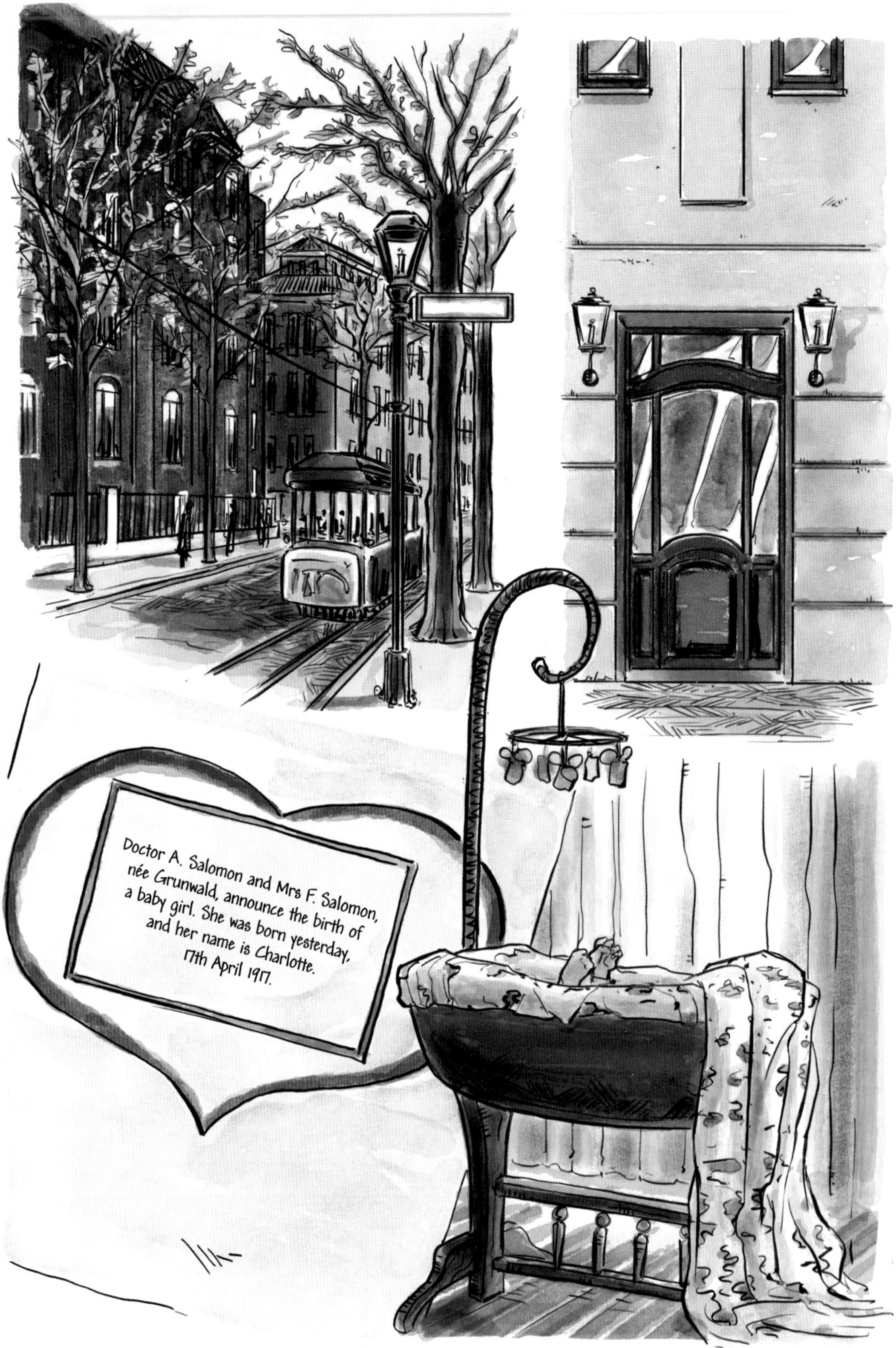
Doctor A. Salomon and Mrs F. Salomon, née Grunwald, announce the birth of a baby girl. She was born yesterday, and her name is Charlotte. 17th April 1917.

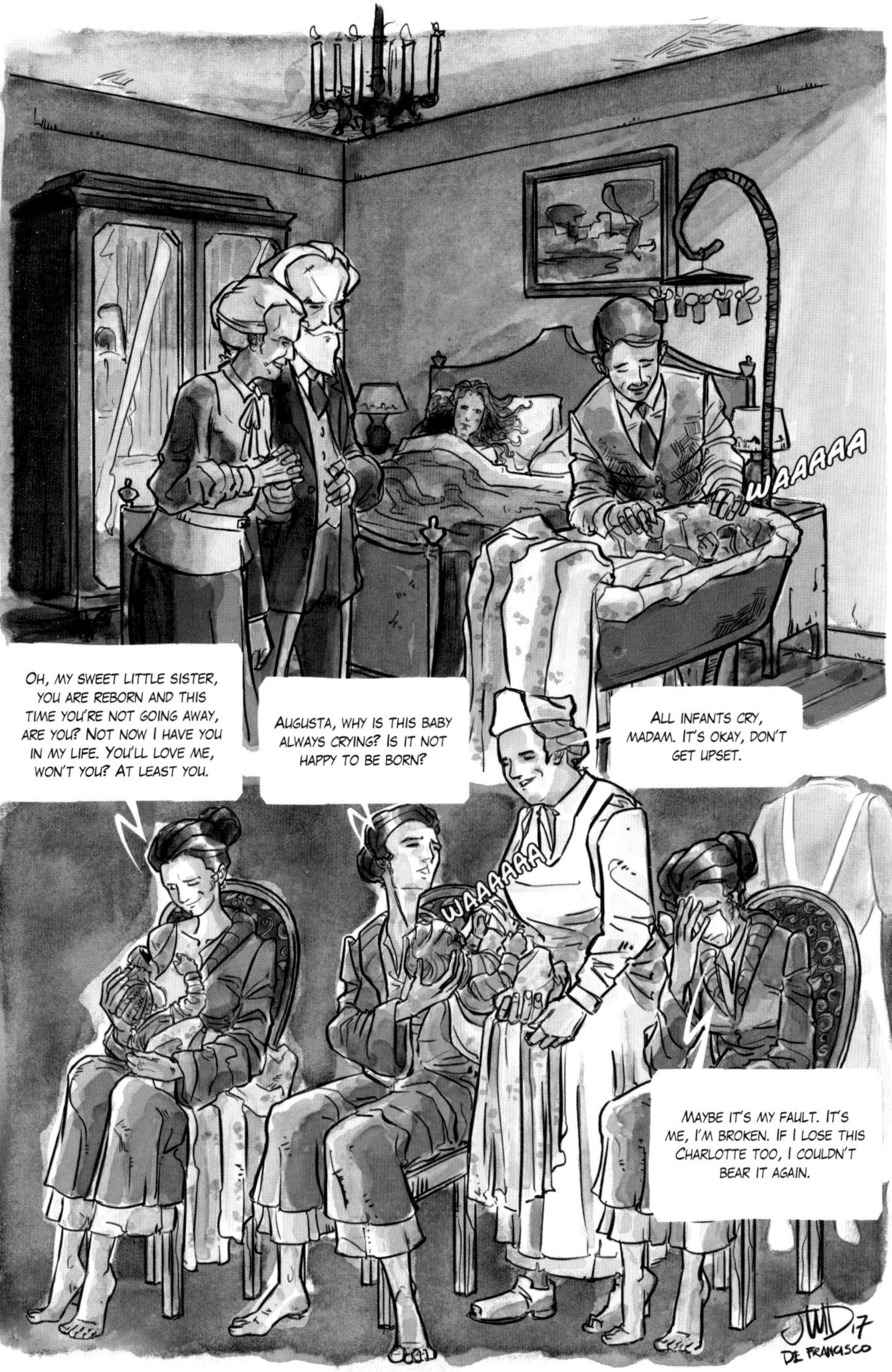
WAAAAAA
Oh, my sweet little sister, you are reborn and this time you're not going away, are you? Not now I have you in my life. You'll love me, won't you? At least you.
Augusta, why is this baby always crying? Is it not happy to be born?
All infants cry, madam. It's okay, don't get upset.
WAAAAAA
WAAAAA
Maybe it's my fault. It's me, I'm broken. If I lose this Charlotte too, I couldn't bear it again.
JMD 17
De Francisco

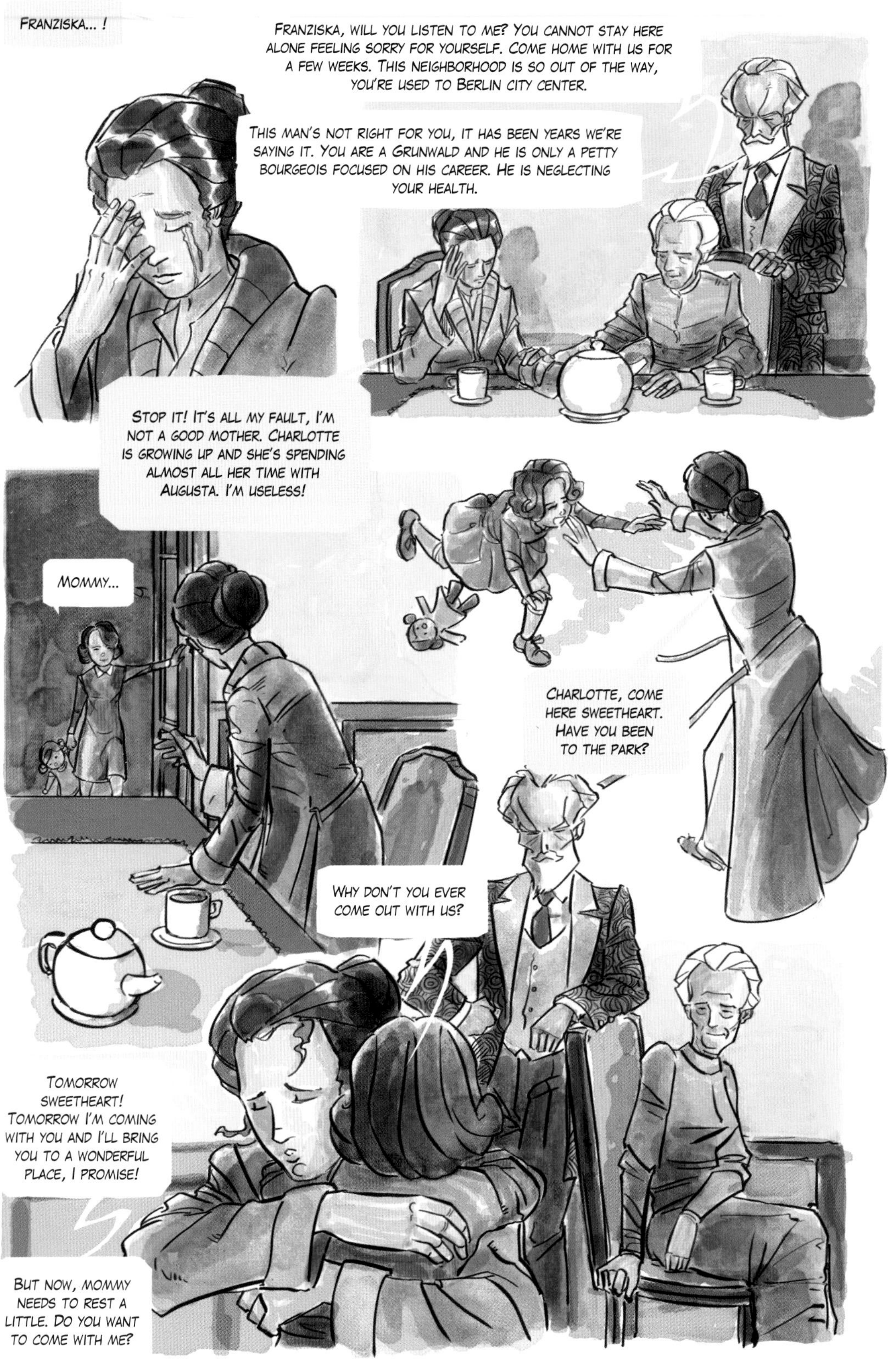
FRANZISKA... !
FRANZISKA, WILL YOU LISTEN TO ME? YOU CANNOT STAY HERE ALONE FEELING SORRY FOR YOURSELF. COME HOME WITH US FOR A FEW WEEKS. THIS NEIGHBORHOOD IS SO OUT OF THE WAY, YOU'RE USED TO BERLIN CITY CENTER.
THIS MAN'S NOT RIGHT FOR YOU, IT HAS BEEN YEARS WE'RE SAYING IT. YOU ARE A GRUNWALD AND HE IS ONLY A PETTY BOURGEOIS FOCUSED ON HIS CAREER. HE IS NEGLECTING YOUR HEALTH.
STOP IT! IT'S ALL MY FAULT, I'M NOT A GOOD MOTHER. CHARLOTTE IS GROWING UP AND SHE'S SPENDING ALMOST ALL HER TIME WITH AUGUSTA. I'M USELESS!
MOMMY...
CHARLOTTE, COME HERE SWEETHEART. HAVE YOU BEEN TO THE PARK?
WHY DON'T YOU EVER COME OUT WITH US?
TOMORROW SWEETHEART! TOMORROW I'M COMING WITH YOU AND I'LL BRING YOU TO A WONDERFUL PLACE, I PROMISE!
BUT NOW, MOMMY NEEDS TO REST A LITTLE. DO YOU WANT TO COME WITH ME?

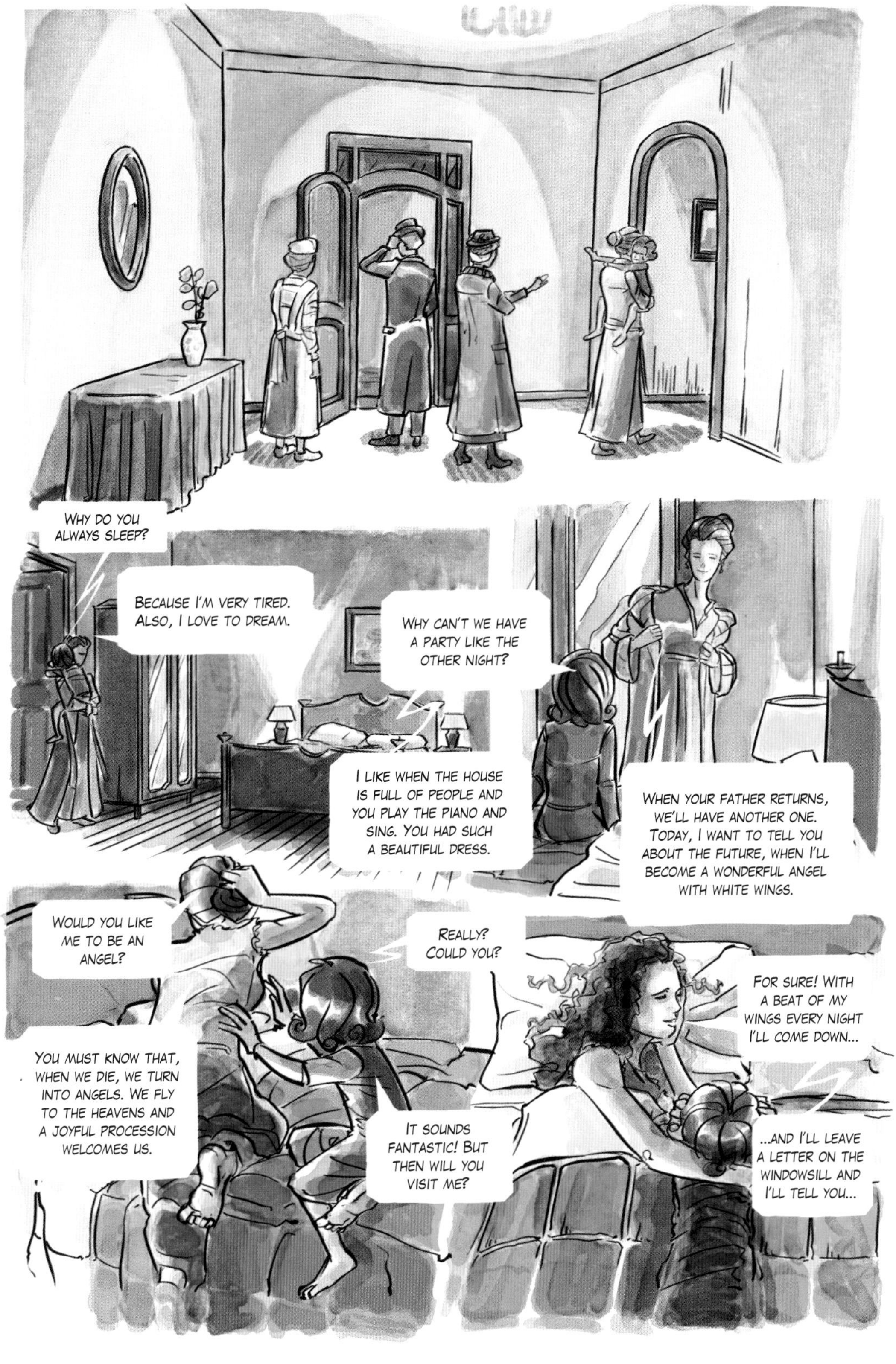

Why do you always sleep?
Because I'm very tired. Also, I love to dream.
Why can't we have a party like the other night?
I like when the house is full of people and you play the piano and sing. You had such a beautiful dress.
When your father returns, we'll have another one. Today, I want to tell you about the future, when I'll become a wonderful angel with white wings.
Would you like me to be an angel?
Really? Could you?
You must know that, when we die, we turn into angels. We fly to the heavens and a joyful procession welcomes us.
It sounds fantastic! But then will you visit me?
For sure! With a beat of my wings every night I'll come down...
...and I'll leave a letter on the windowsill and I'll tell you...

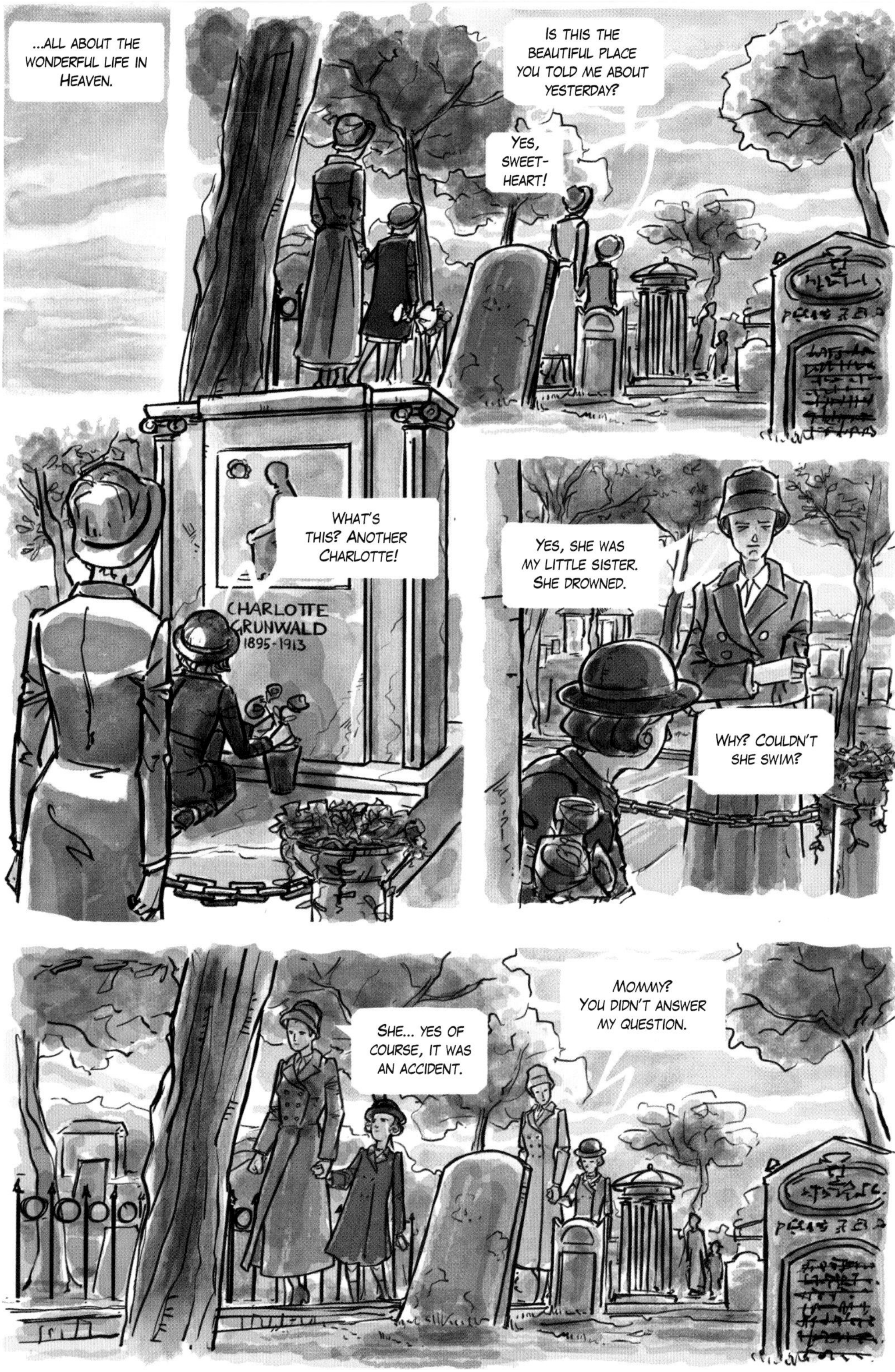
...ALL ABOUT THE WONDERFUL LIFE IN HEAVEN.
IS THIS THE BEAUTIFUL PLACE YOU TOLD ME ABOUT YESTERDAY?
YES, SWEET-HEART!
WHAT'S THIS? ANOTHER CHARLOTTE!
CHARLOTTE GRUNWALD 1895-1913
YES, SHE WAS MY LITTLE SISTER. SHE DROWNED.
WHY? COULDN'T SHE SWIM?
SHE... YES OF COURSE, IT WAS AN ACCIDENT.
MOMMY? YOU DIDN'T ANSWER MY QUESTION.

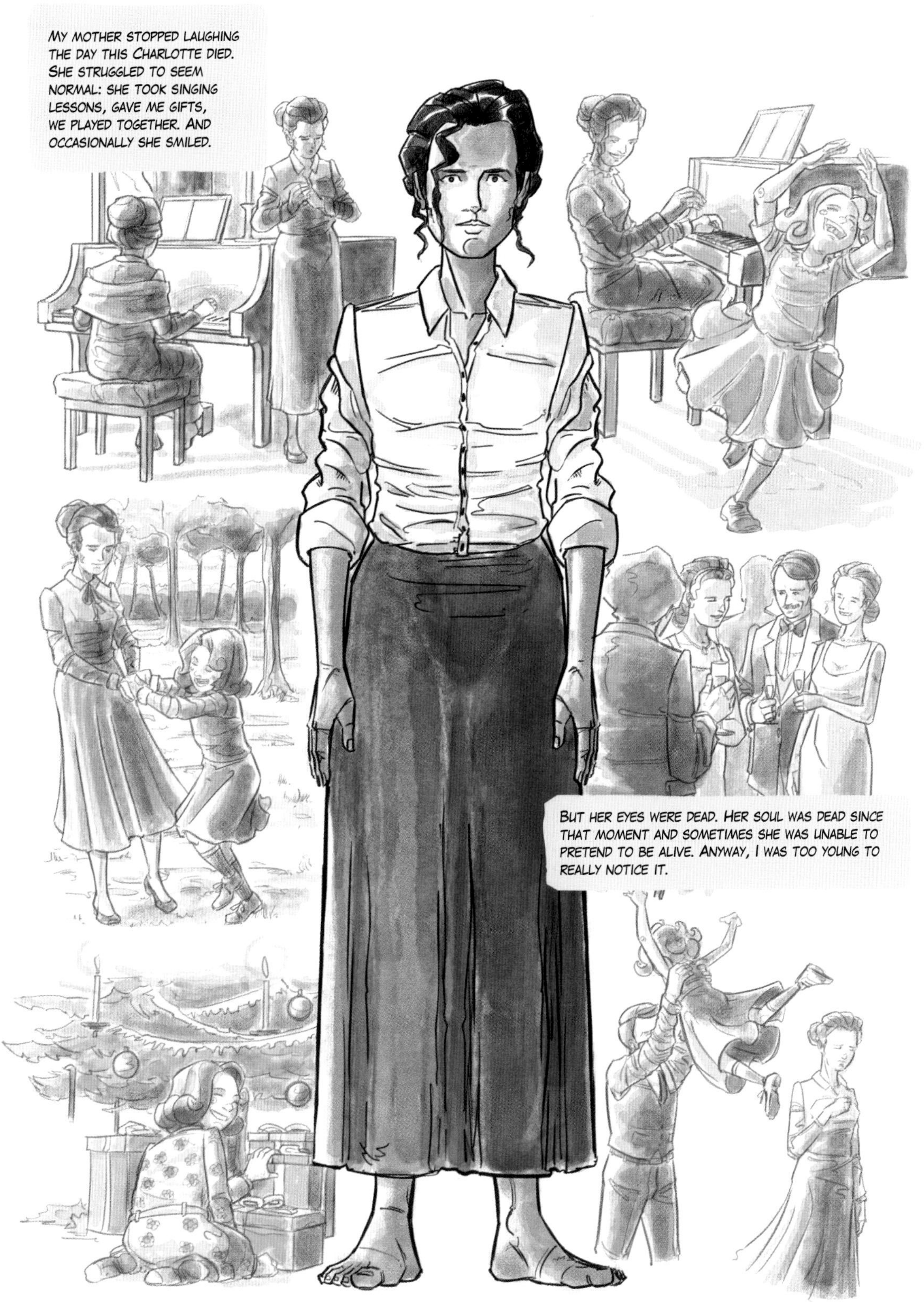
MY MOTHER STOPPED LAUGHING THE DAY THIS CHARLOTTE DIED. SHE STRUGGLED TO SEEM NORMAL: SHE TOOK SINGING LESSONS, GAVE ME GIFTS, WE PLAYED TOGETHER. AND OCCASIONALLY SHE SMILED.
BUT HER EYES WERE DEAD. HER SOUL WAS DEAD SINCE THAT MOMENT AND SOMETIMES SHE WAS UNABLE TO PRETEND TO BE ALIVE. ANYWAY, I WAS TOO YOUNG TO REALLY NOTICE IT.

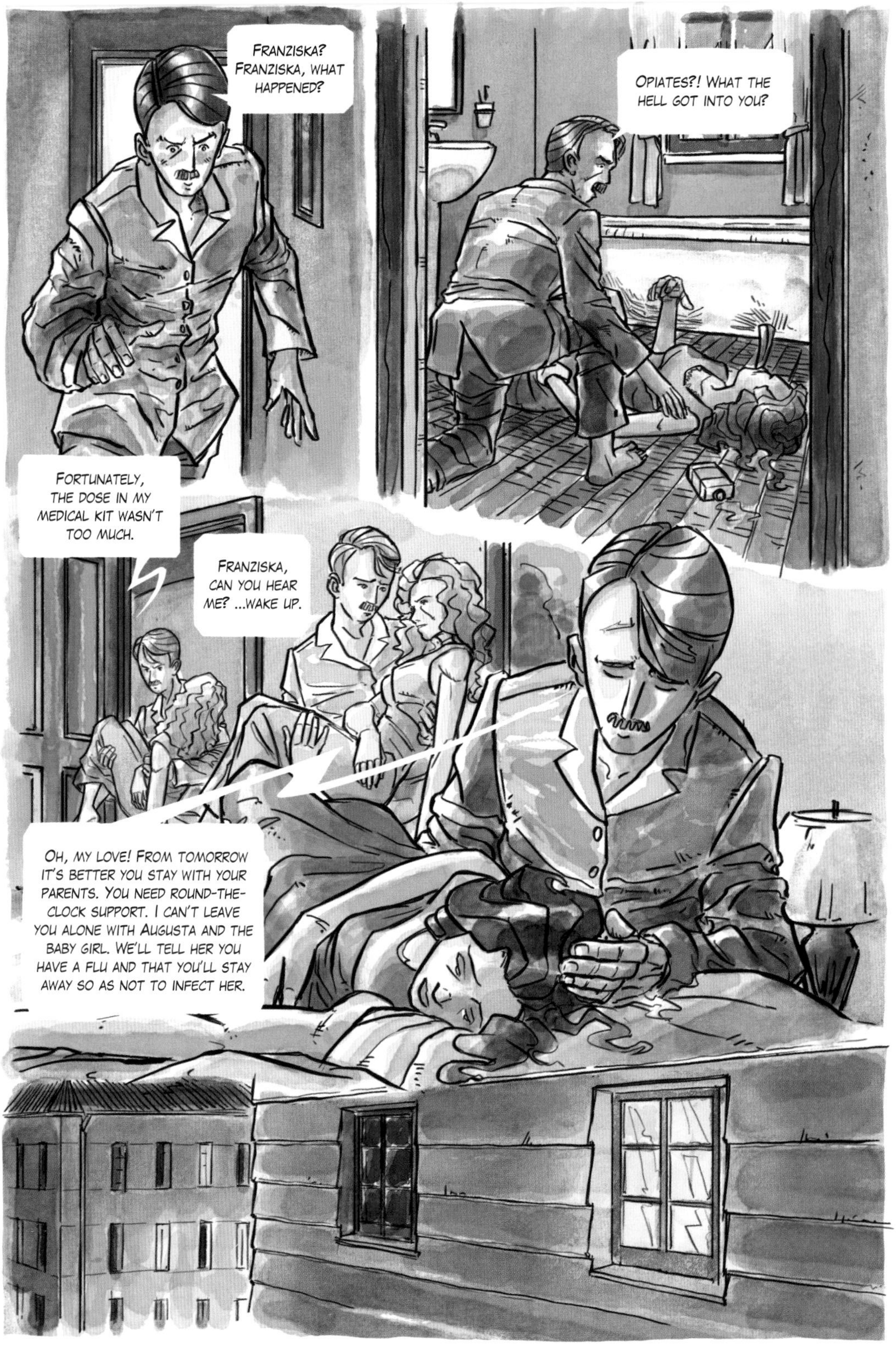
FRANZISKA? FRANZISKA, WHAT HAPPENED?
OPIATES?! WHAT THE HELL GOT INTO YOU?
FORTUNATELY, THE DOSE IN MY MEDICAL KIT WASN'T TOO MUCH.
FRANZISKA, CAN YOU HEAR ME? ...WAKE UP.
OH, MY LOVE! FROM TOMORROW IT'S BETTER YOU STAY WITH YOUR PARENTS. YOU NEED ROUND-THE-CLOCK SUPPORT. I CAN'T LEAVE YOU ALONE WITH AUGUSTA AND THE BABY GIRL. WE'LL TELL HER YOU HAVE A FLU AND THAT YOU'LL STAY AWAY SO AS NOT TO INFECT HER.

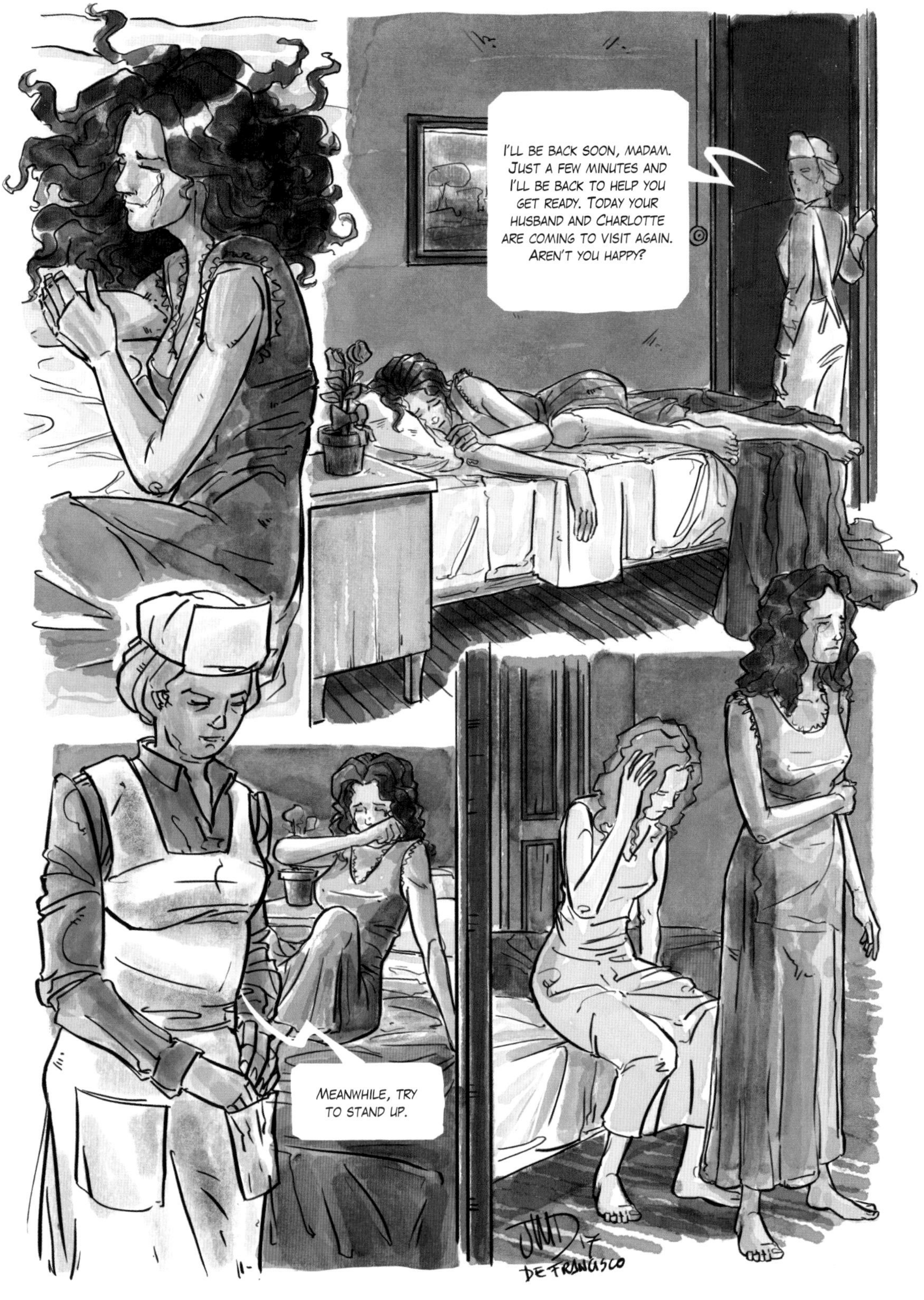
I'LL BE BACK SOON, MADAM. JUST A FEW MINUTES AND I'LL BE BACK TO HELP YOU GET READY. TODAY YOUR HUSBAND AND CHARLOTTE ARE COMING TO VISIT AGAIN. AREN'T YOU HAPPY?
MEANWHILE, TRY TO STAND UP.
DE FRANCISCO

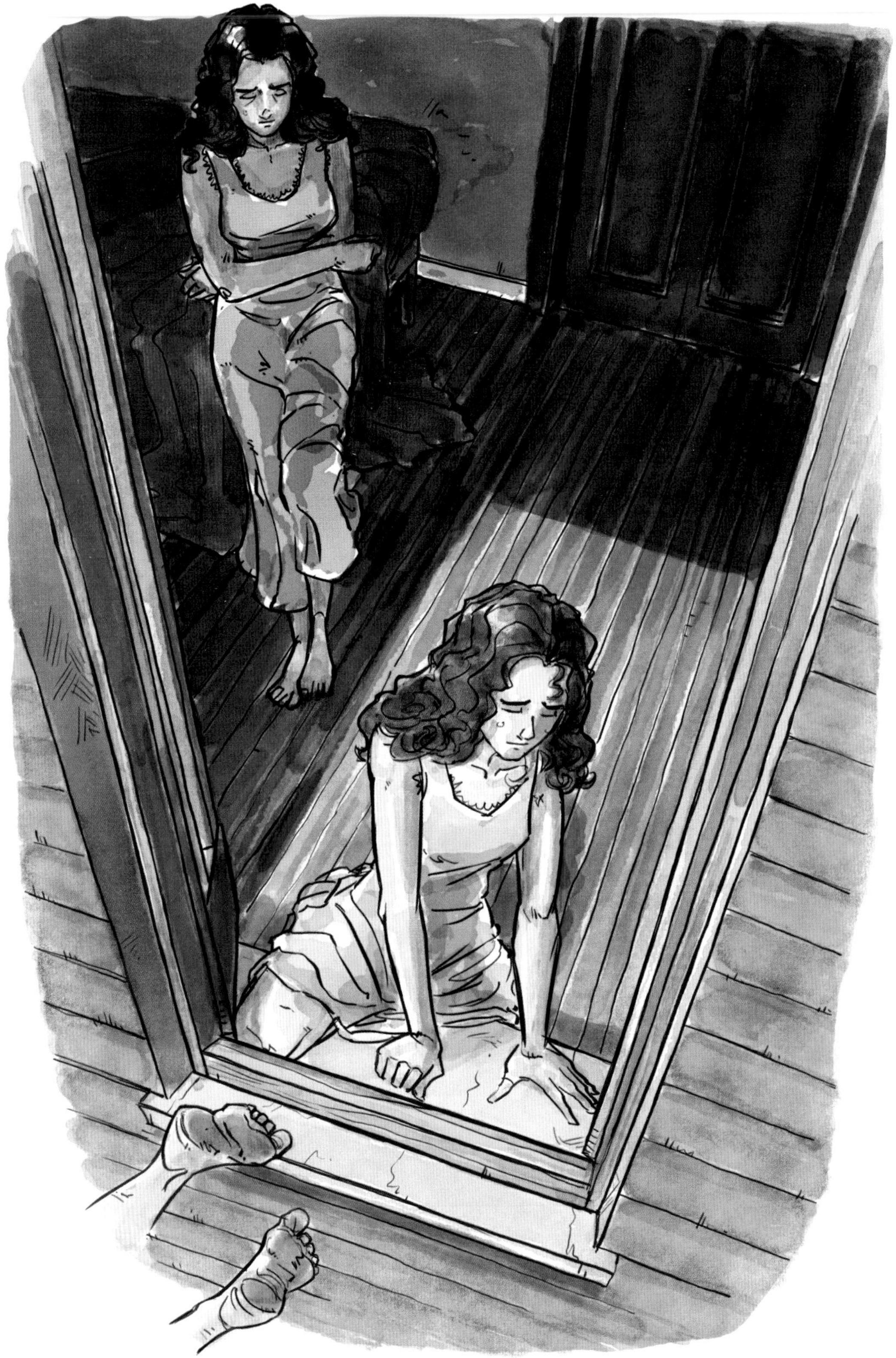

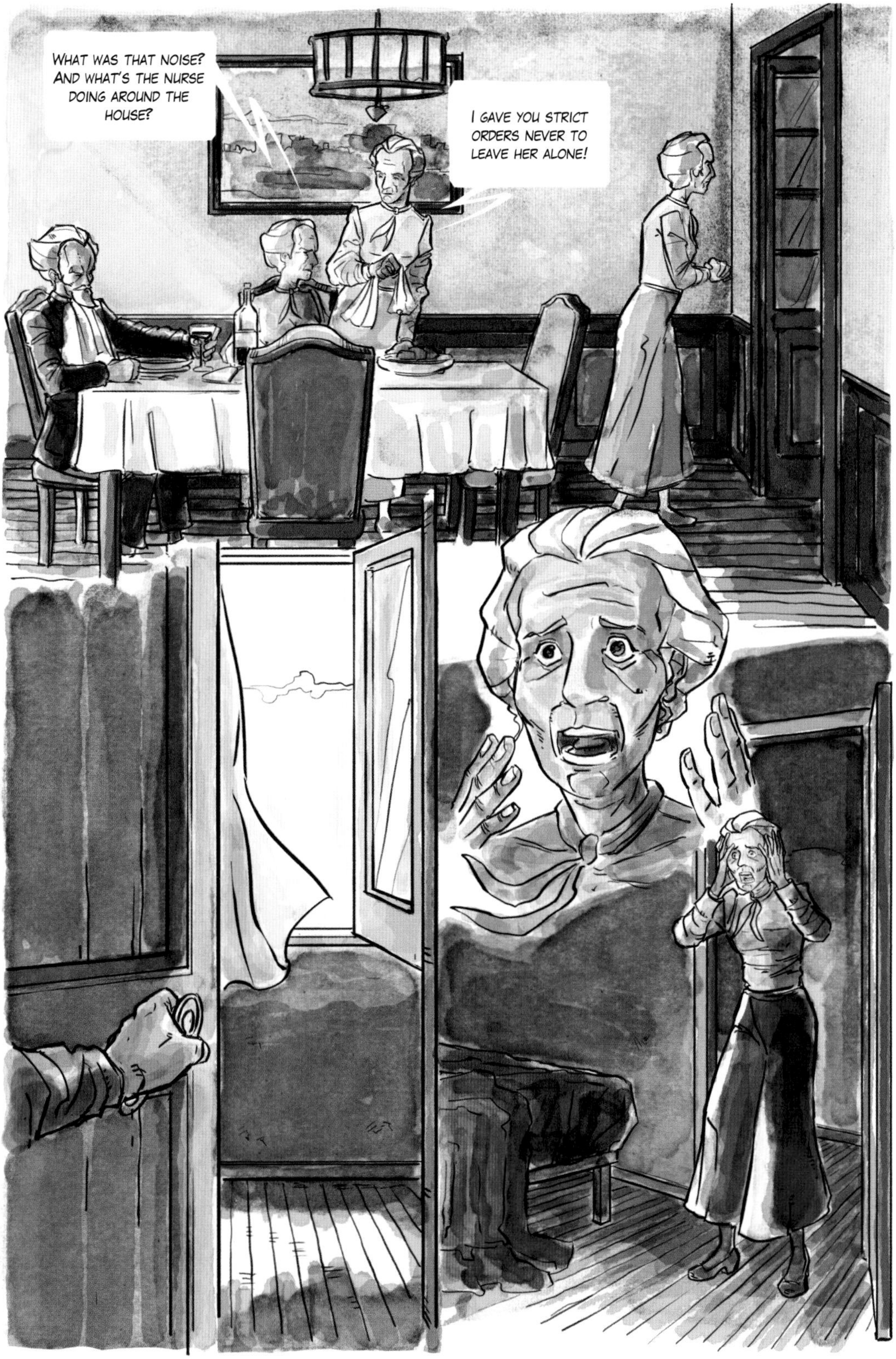
WHAT WAS THAT NOISE? AND WHAT'S THE NURSE DOING AROUND THE HOUSE?
I GAVE YOU STRICT ORDERS NEVER TO LEAVE HER ALONE!

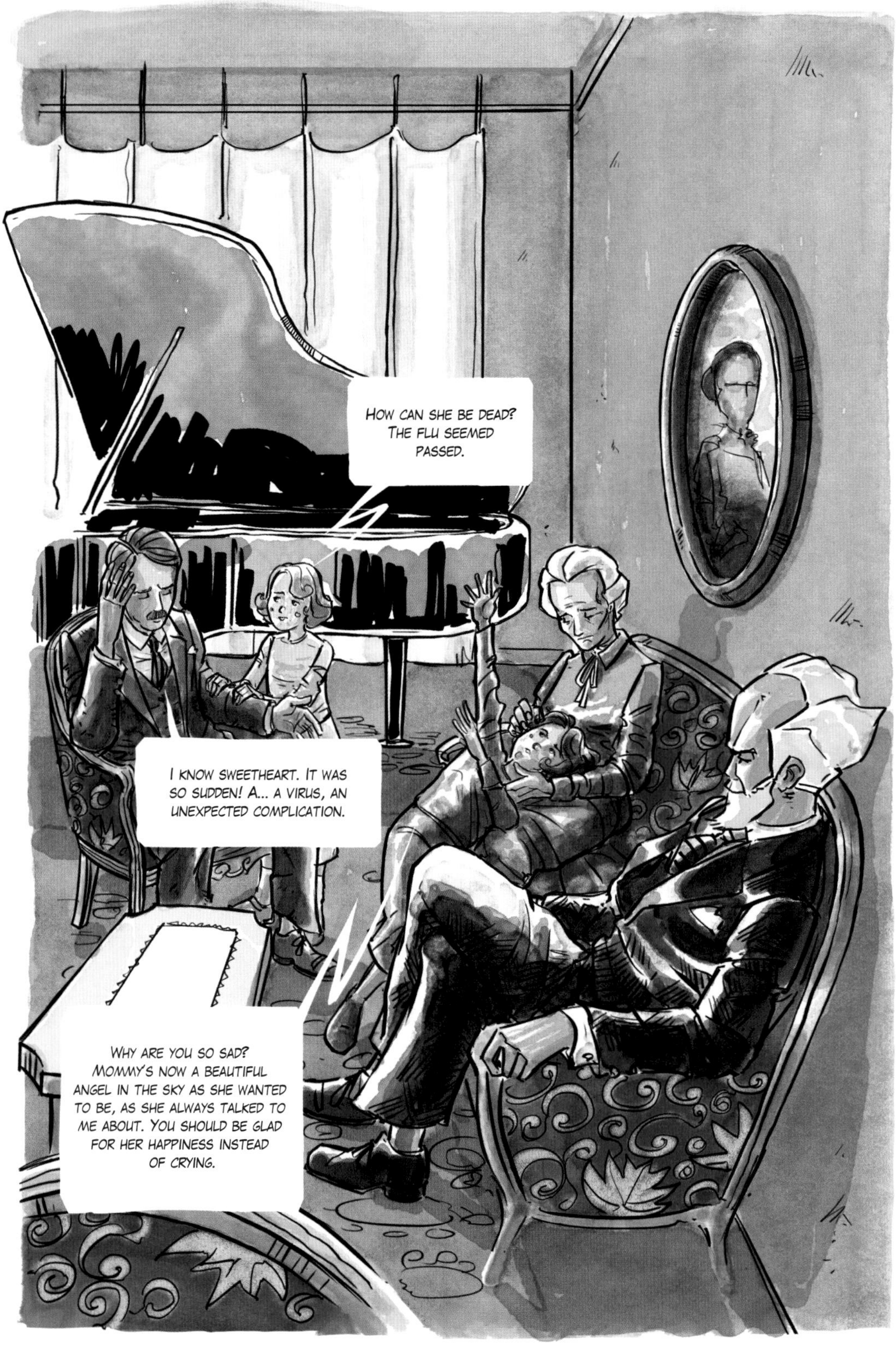
How can she be dead? The flu seemed passed.
I know sweetheart. It was so sudden! A... a virus, an unexpected complication.
Why are you so sad? Mommy's now a beautiful angel in the sky as she wanted to be, as she always talked to me about. You should be glad for her happiness instead of crying.

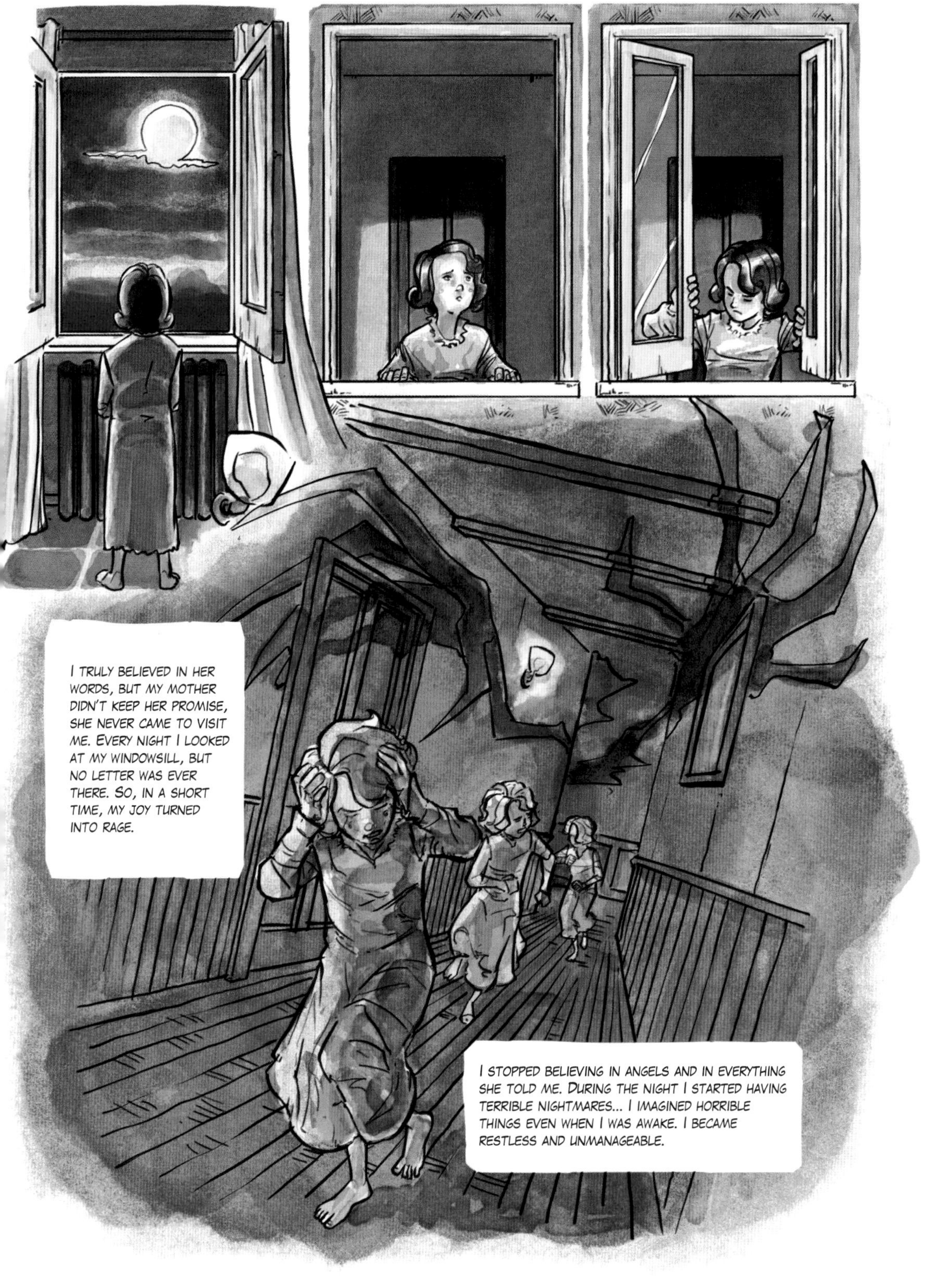
I TRULY BELIEVED IN HER WORDS, BUT MY MOTHER DIDN'T KEEP HER PROMISE, SHE NEVER CAME TO VISIT ME. EVERY NIGHT I LOOKED AT MY WINDOWSILL, BUT NO LETTER WAS EVER THERE. SO, IN A SHORT TIME, MY JOY TURNED INTO RAGE.
I STOPPED BELIEVING IN ANGELS AND IN EVERYTHING SHE TOLD ME. DURING THE NIGHT I STARTED HAVING TERRIBLE NIGHTMARES... I IMAGINED HORRIBLE THINGS EVEN WHEN I WAS AWAKE. I BECAME RESTLESS AND UNMANAGEABLE.

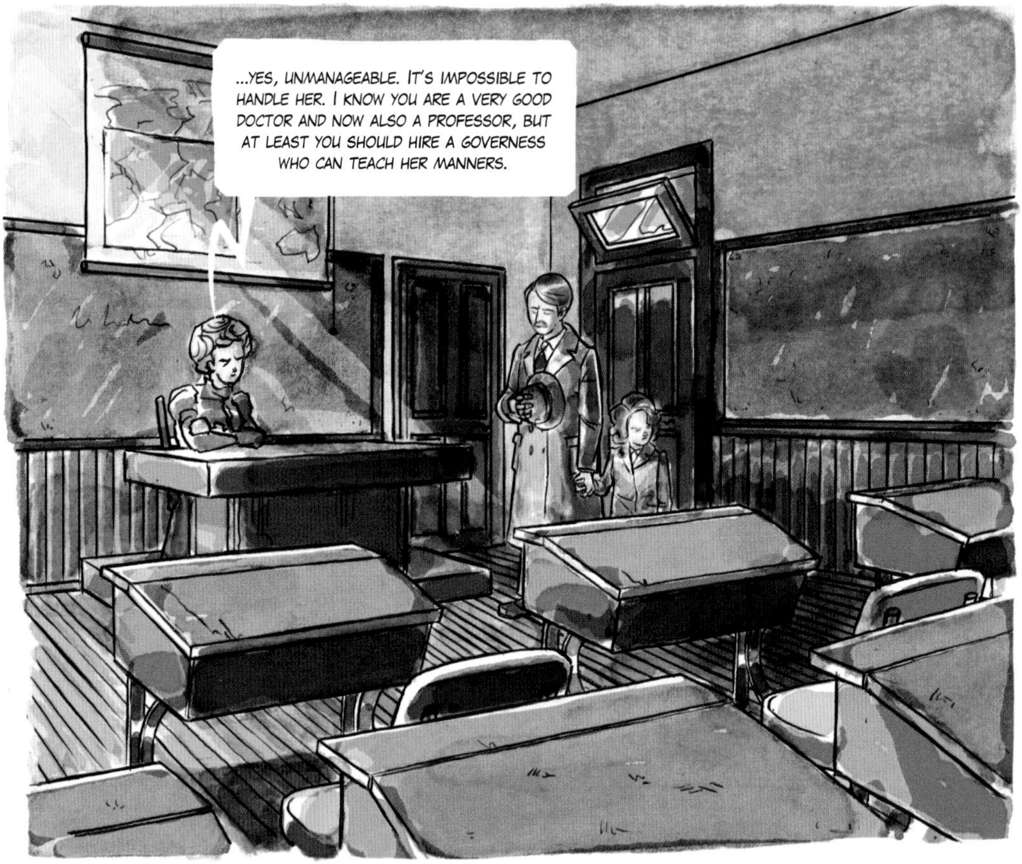
...YES, UNMANAGEABLE. IT'S IMPOSSIBLE TO HANDLE HER. I KNOW YOU ARE A VERY GOOD DOCTOR AND NOW ALSO A PROFESSOR, BUT AT LEAST YOU SHOULD HIRE A GOVERNESS WHO CAN TEACH HER MANNERS.

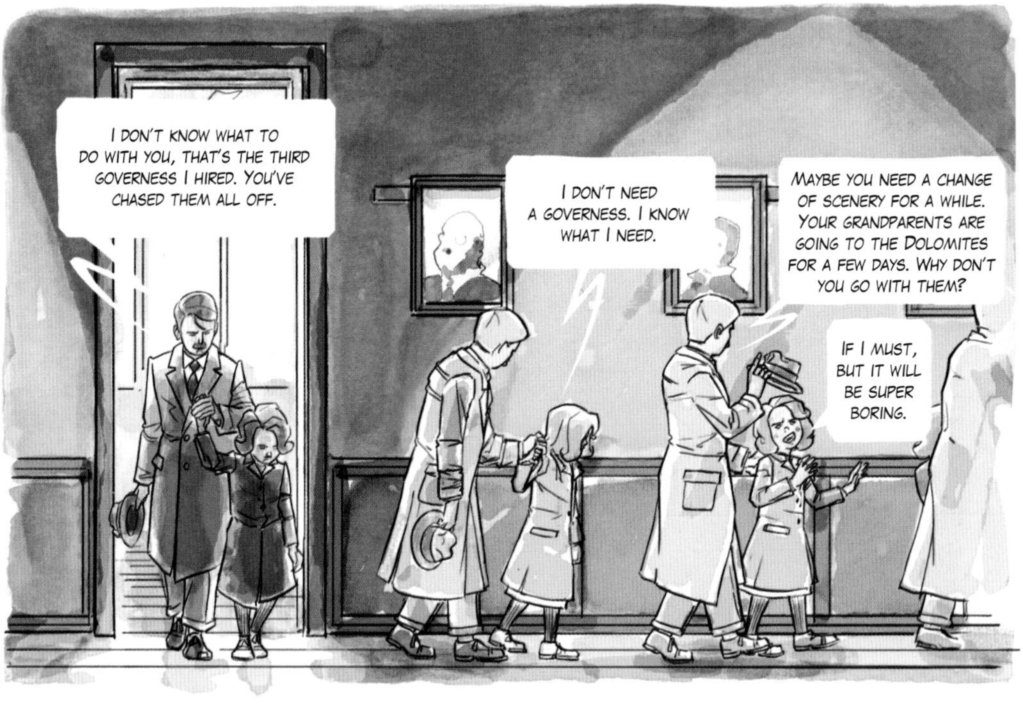
I DON'T KNOW WHAT TO DO WITH YOU, THAT'S THE THIRD GOVERNESS I HIRED. YOU'VE CHASED THEM ALL OFF.
I DON'T NEED A GOVERNESS. I KNOW WHAT I NEED.
MAYBE YOU NEED A CHANGE OF SCENERY FOR A WHILE. YOUR GRANDPARENTS ARE GOING TO THE DOLOMITES FOR A FEW DAYS. WHY DON'T YOU GO WITH THEM?
IF I MUST, BUT IT WILL BE SUPER BORING.

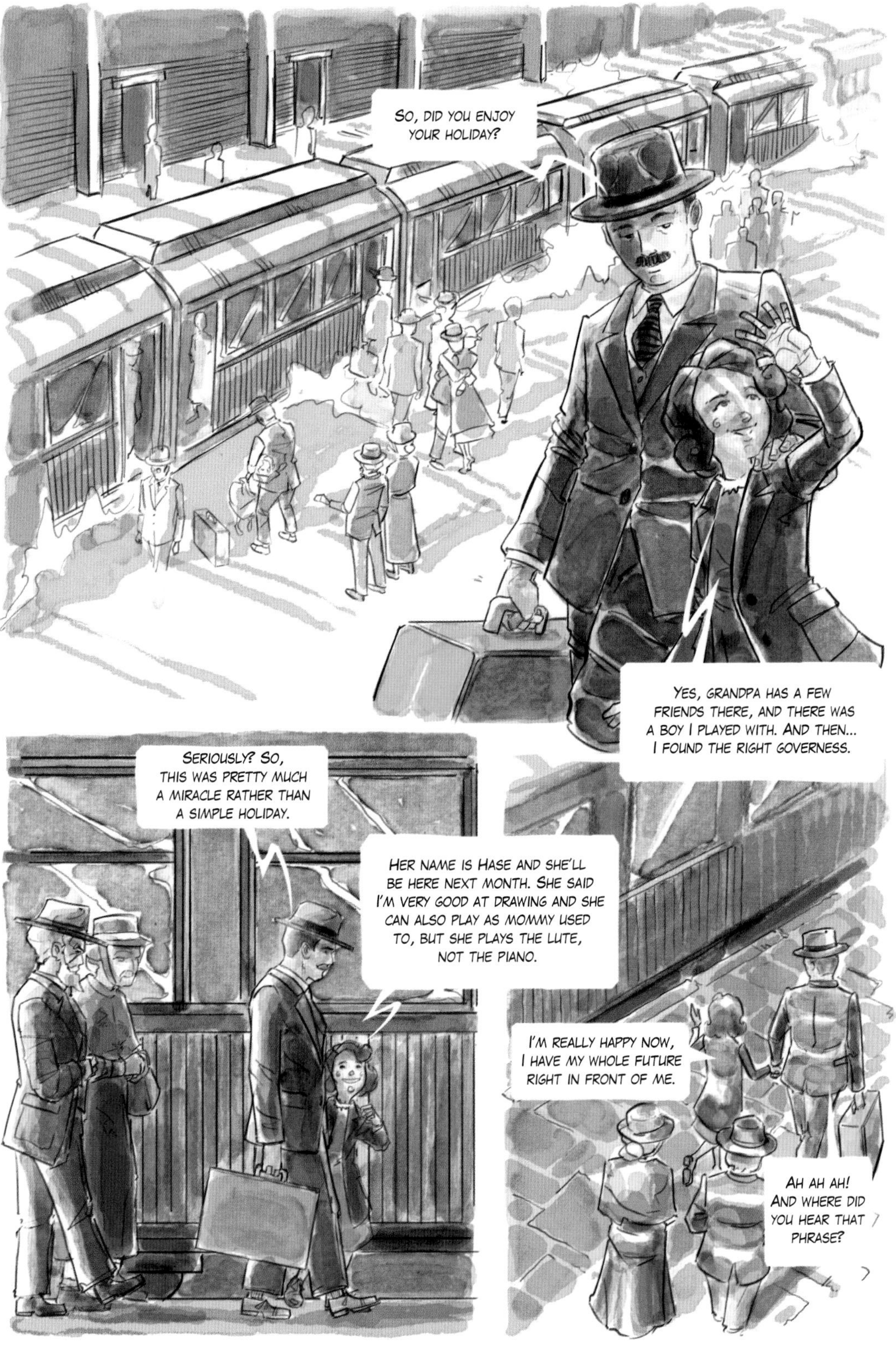
So, did you enjoy your holiday?
Yes, Grandpa has a few friends there, and there was a boy I played with. And then... I found the right governess.
Seriously? So, this was pretty much a miracle rather than a simple holiday.
Her name is Hase and she'll be here next month. She said I'm very good at drawing and she can also play as mommy used to, but she plays the lute, not the piano.
I'm really happy now, I have my whole future right in front of me.
Ah ah ah! And where did you hear that phrase?

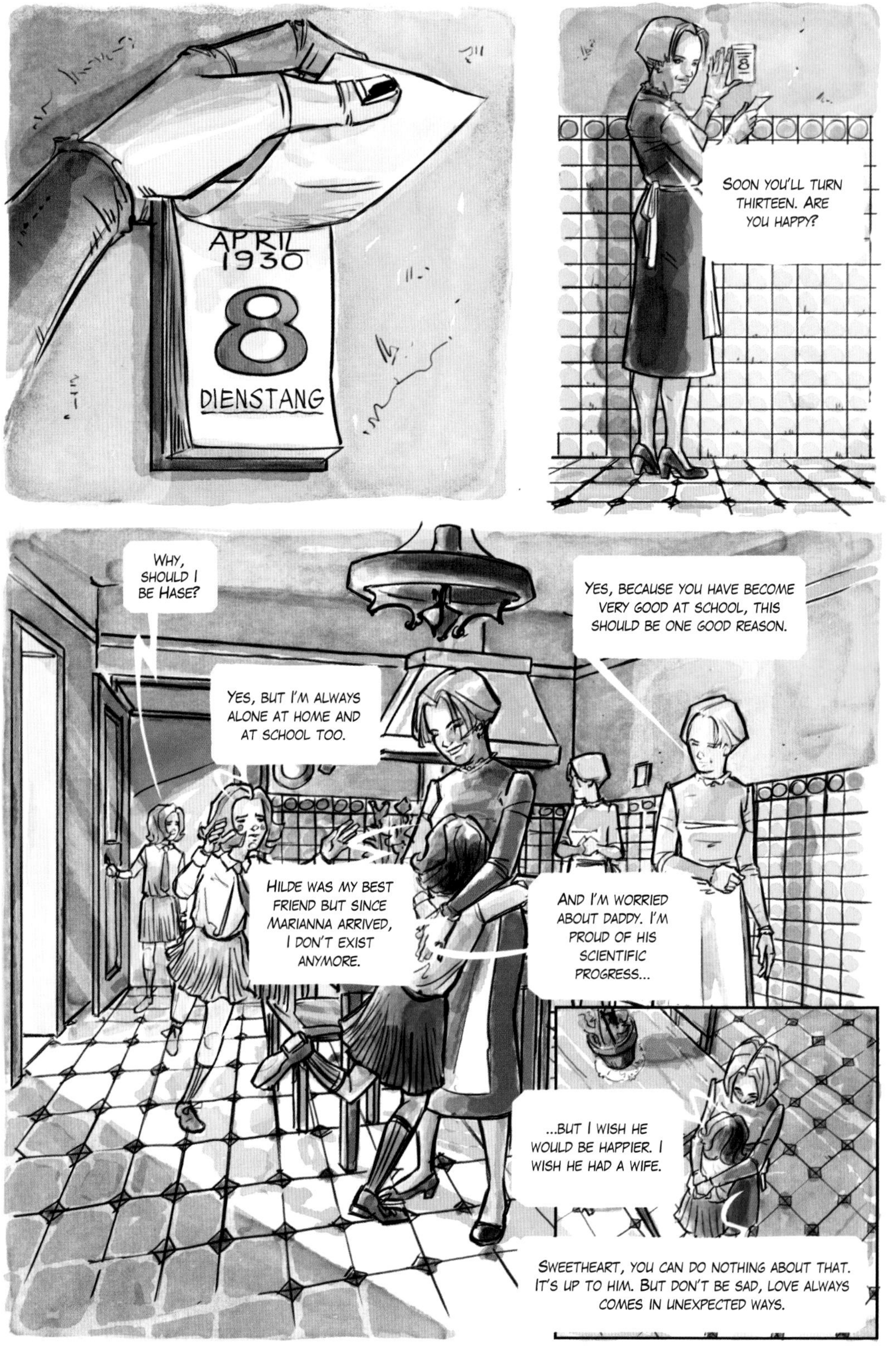
APRIL 1930
8
DIENSTANG
SOON YOU'LL TURN THIRTEEN. ARE YOU HAPPY?
WHY, SHOULD I BE HASE?
YES, BECAUSE YOU HAVE BECOME VERY GOOD AT SCHOOL, THIS SHOULD BE ONE GOOD REASON.
YES, BUT I'M ALWAYS ALONE AT HOME AND AT SCHOOL TOO.
HILDE WAS MY BEST FRIEND BUT SINCE MARIANNA ARRIVED, I DON'T EXIST ANYMORE.
AND I'M WORRIED ABOUT DADDY. I'M PROUD OF HIS SCIENTIFIC PROGRESS...
...BUT I WISH HE WOULD BE HAPPIER. I WISH HE HAD A WIFE.
SWEETHEART, YOU CAN DO NOTHING ABOUT THAT. IT'S UP TO HIM. BUT DON'T BE SAD, LOVE ALWAYS COMES IN UNEXPECTED WAYS.

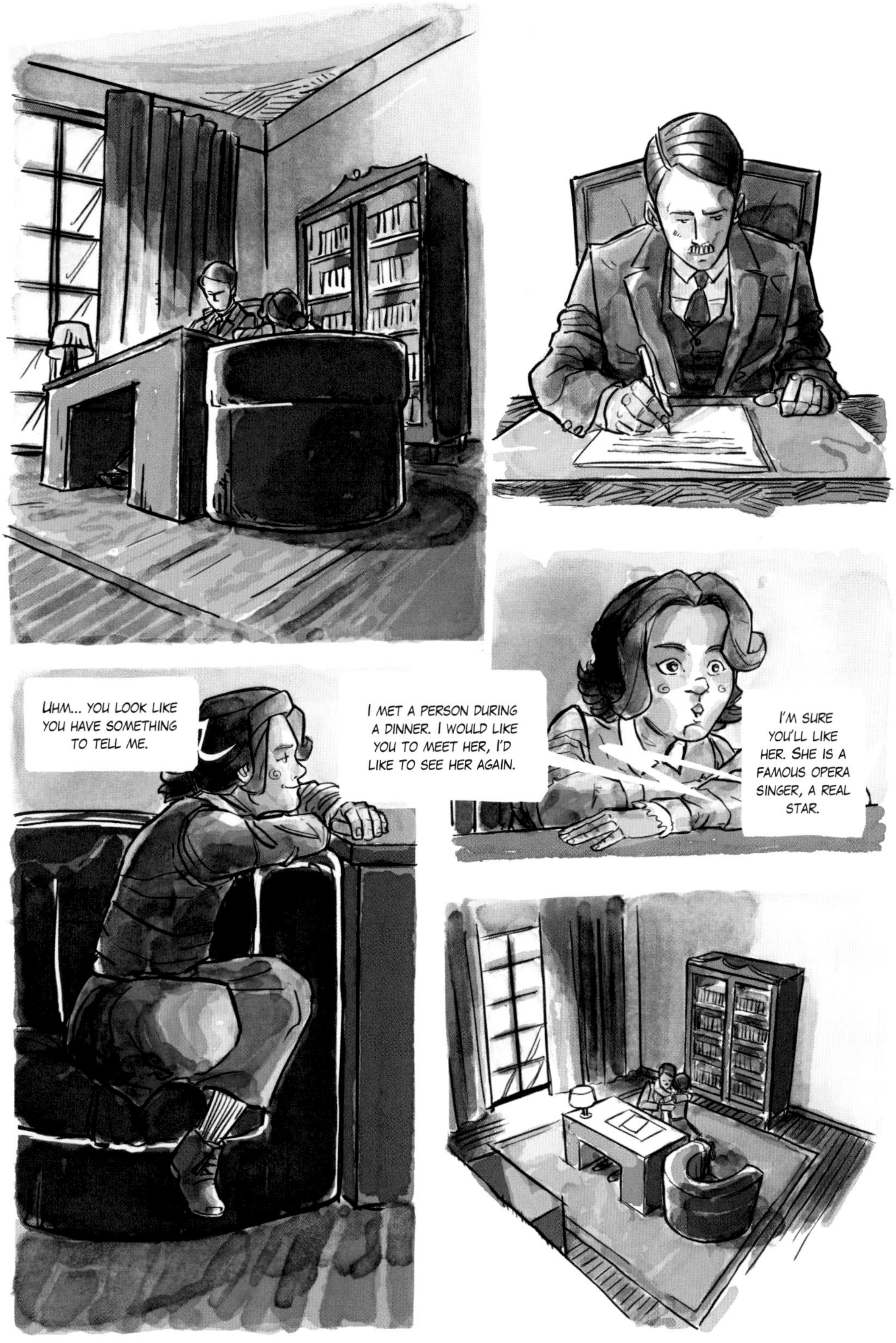
UHM... YOU LOOK LIKE YOU HAVE SOMETHING TO TELL ME.
I MET A PERSON DURING A DINNER. I WOULD LIKE YOU TO MEET HER, I'D LIKE TO SEE HER AGAIN.
I'M SURE YOU'LL LIKE HER. SHE IS A FAMOUS OPERA SINGER, A REAL STAR.

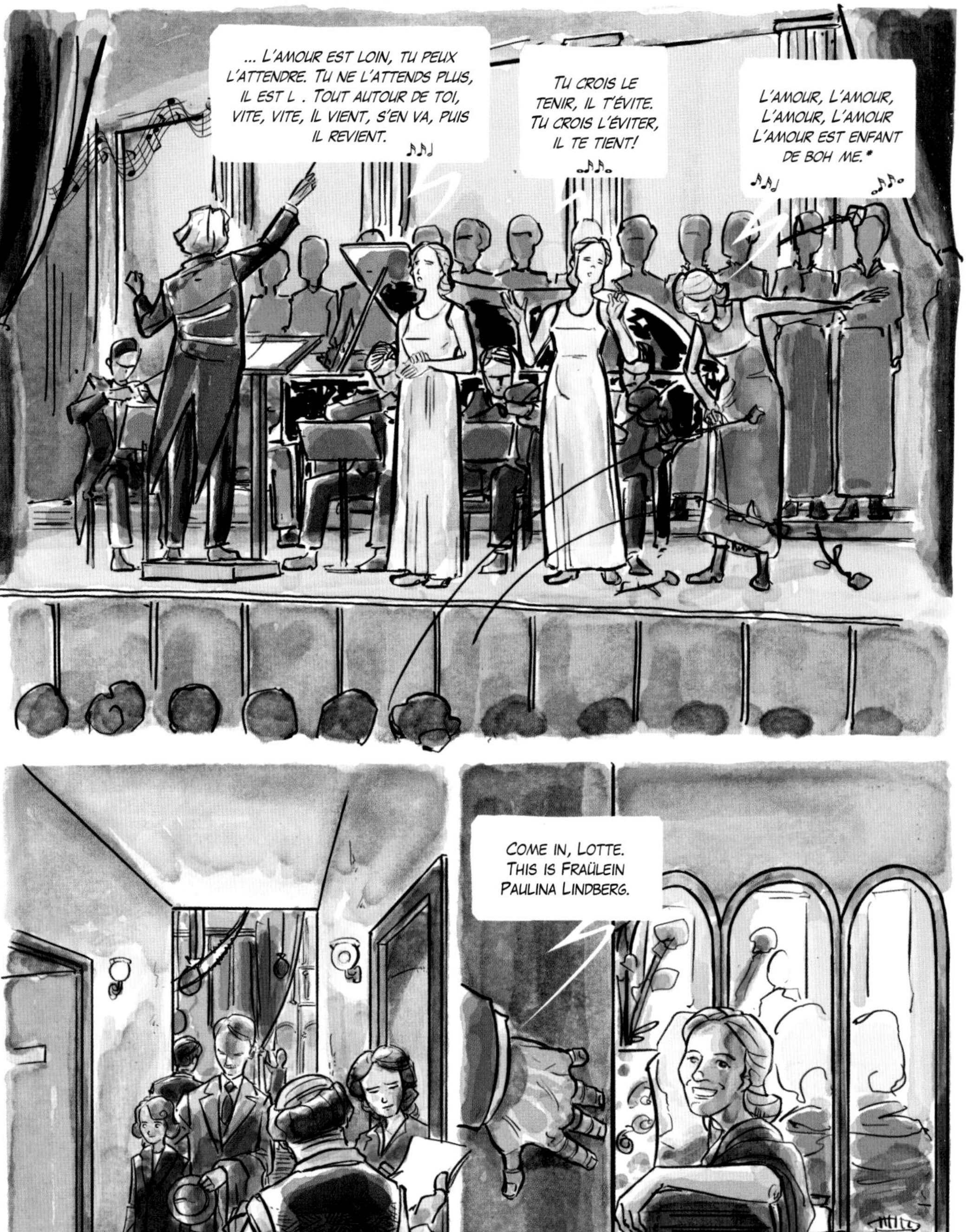
... L'AMOUR EST LOIN, TU PEUX L'ATTENDRE. TU NE L'ATTENDS PLUS, IL EST L . TOUT AUTOUR DE TOI, VITE, VITE, IL VIENT, S'EN VA, PUIS IL REVIENT.
TU CROIS LE TENIR, IL T'ÉVITE. TU CROIS L'ÉVITER, IL TE TIENT!
L'AMOUR, L'AMOUR, L'AMOUR, L'AMOUR L'AMOUR EST ENFANT DE BOH ME.*
COME IN, LOTTE. THIS IS FRAÜLEIN PAULINA LINDBERG.

*PART OF THE ARIA 'HABANERA' FROM GEORGES BIZET'S 1875 OPERA CARMEN

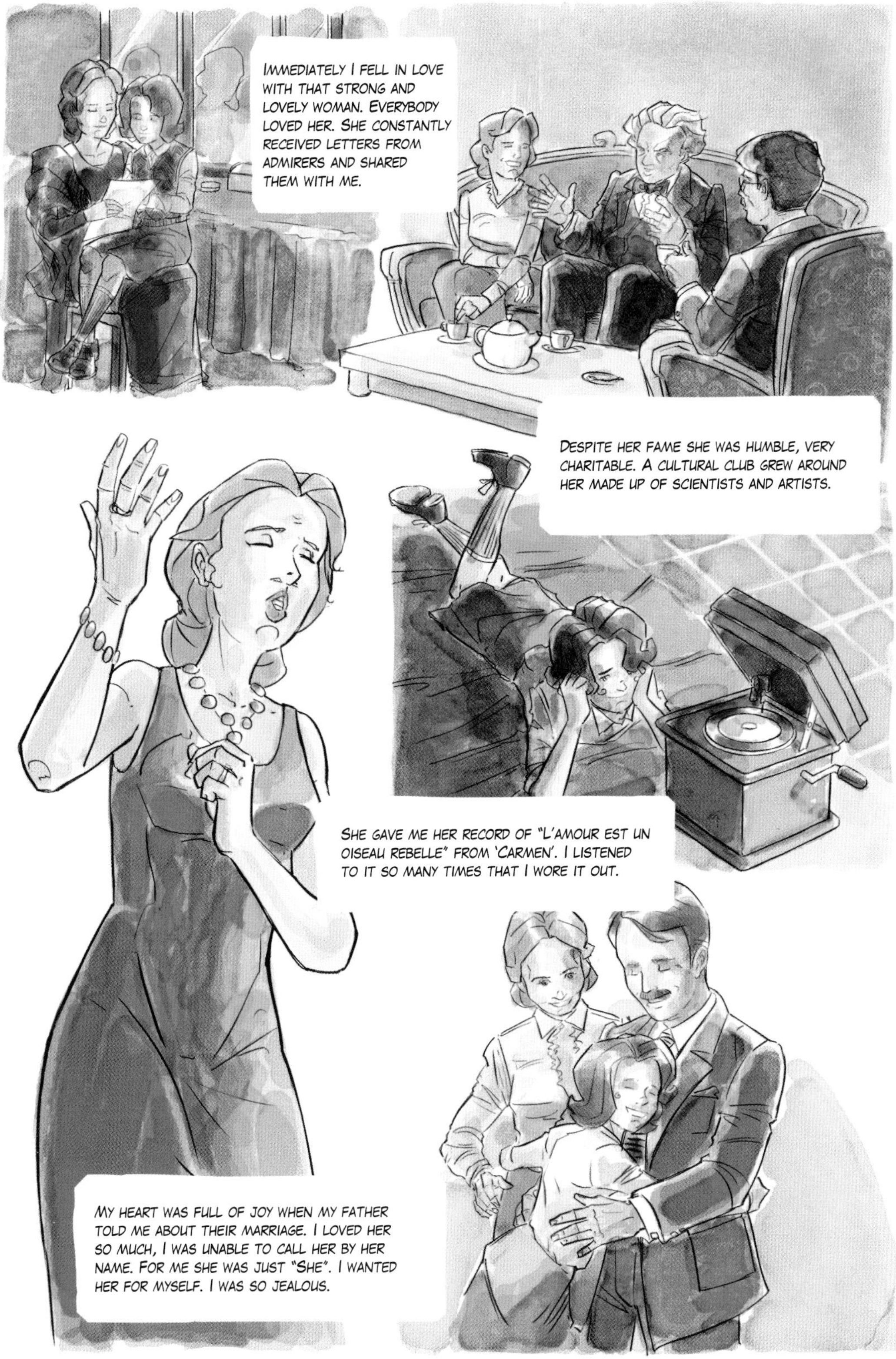
IMMEDIATELY I FELL IN LOVE WITH THAT STRONG AND LOVELY WOMAN. EVERYBODY LOVED HER. SHE CONSTANTLY RECEIVED LETTERS FROM ADMIRERS AND SHARED THEM WITH ME.
DESPITE HER FAME SHE WAS HUMBLE, VERY CHARITABLE. A CULTURAL CLUB GREW AROUND HER MADE UP OF SCIENTISTS AND ARTISTS.
SHE GAVE ME HER RECORD OF "L'AMOUR EST UN OISEAU REBELLE" FROM 'CARMEN'. I LISTENED TO IT SO MANY TIMES THAT I WORE IT OUT.
MY HEART WAS FULL OF JOY WHEN MY FATHER TOLD ME ABOUT THEIR MARRIAGE. I LOVED HER SO MUCH, I WAS UNABLE TO CALL HER BY HER NAME. FOR ME SHE WAS JUST "SHE". I WANTED HER FOR MYSELF. I WAS SO JEALOUS.

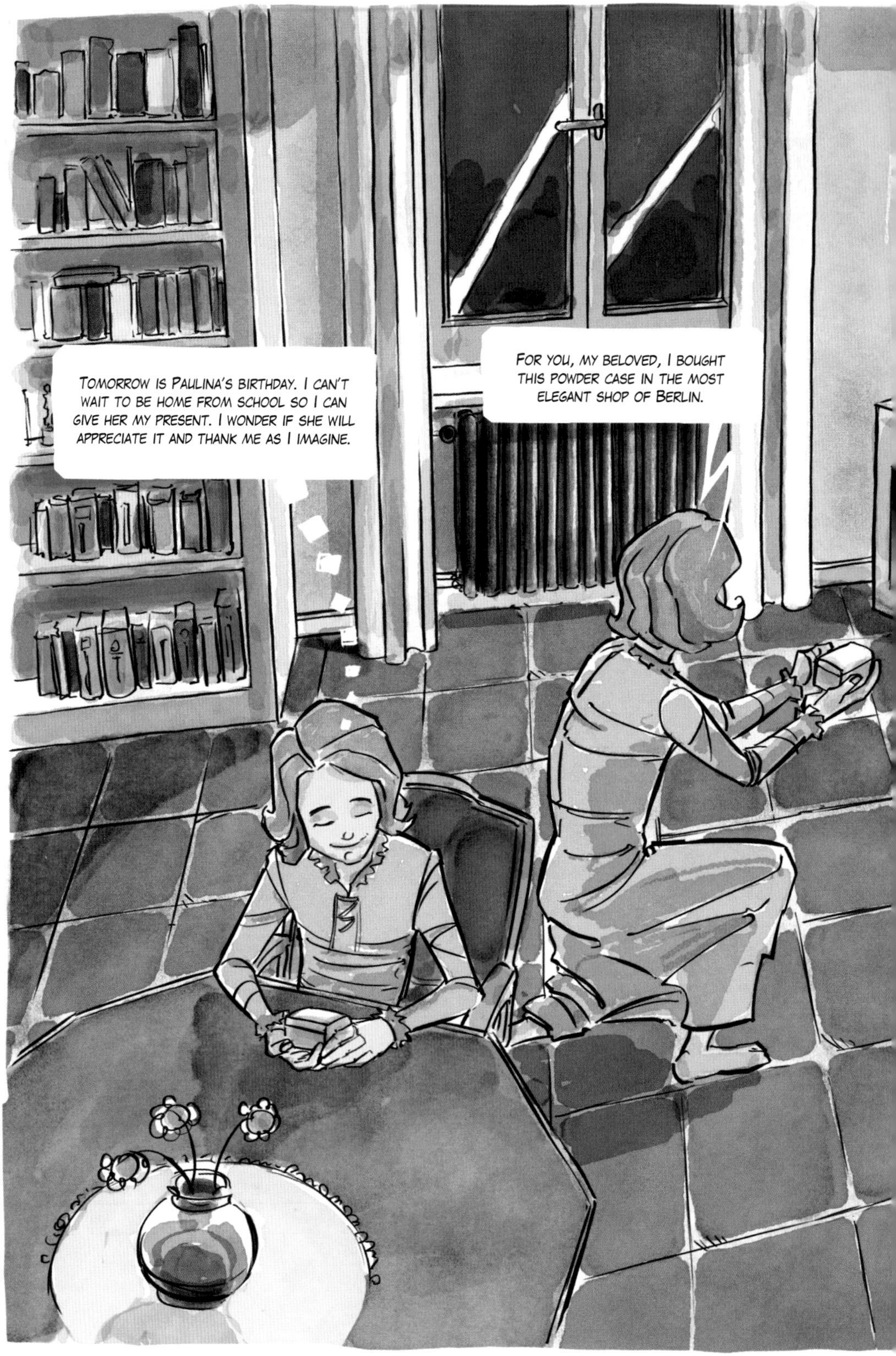
Tomorrow is Paulina's birthday. I can't wait to be home from school so I can give her my present. I wonder if she will appreciate it and thank me as I imagine.
For you, my beloved, I bought this powder case in the most elegant shop of Berlin.

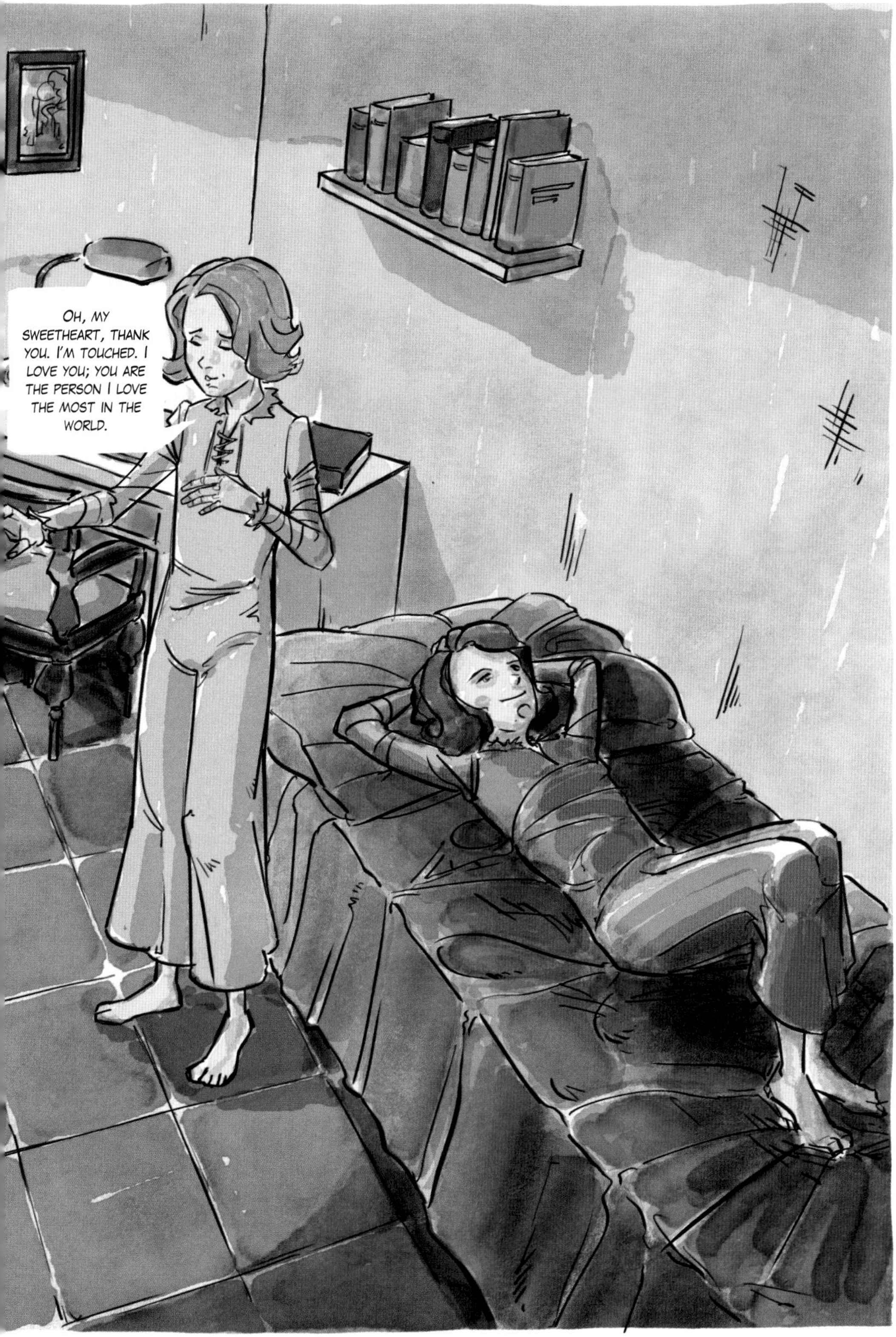
OH, MY SWEETHEART, THANK YOU. I'M TOUCHED. I LOVE YOU; YOU ARE THE PERSON I LOVE THE MOST IN THE WORLD.

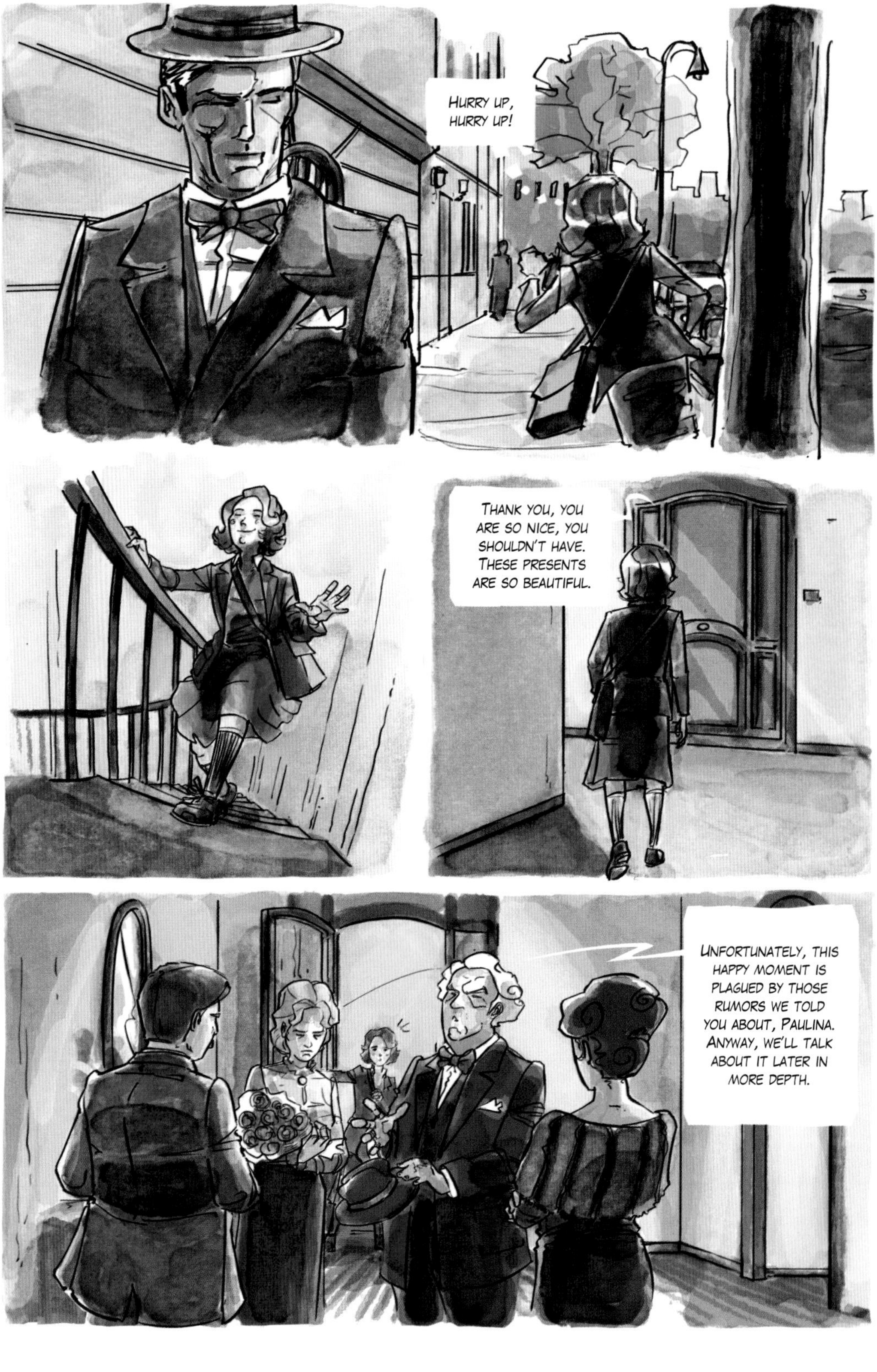
HURRY UP, HURRY UP!
THANK YOU, YOU ARE SO NICE, YOU SHOULDN'T HAVE. THESE PRESENTS ARE SO BEAUTIFUL.
UNFORTUNATELY, THIS HAPPY MOMENT IS PLAGUED BY THOSE RUMORS WE TOLD YOU ABOUT, PAULINA. ANYWAY, WE'LL TALK ABOUT IT LATER IN MORE DEPTH.

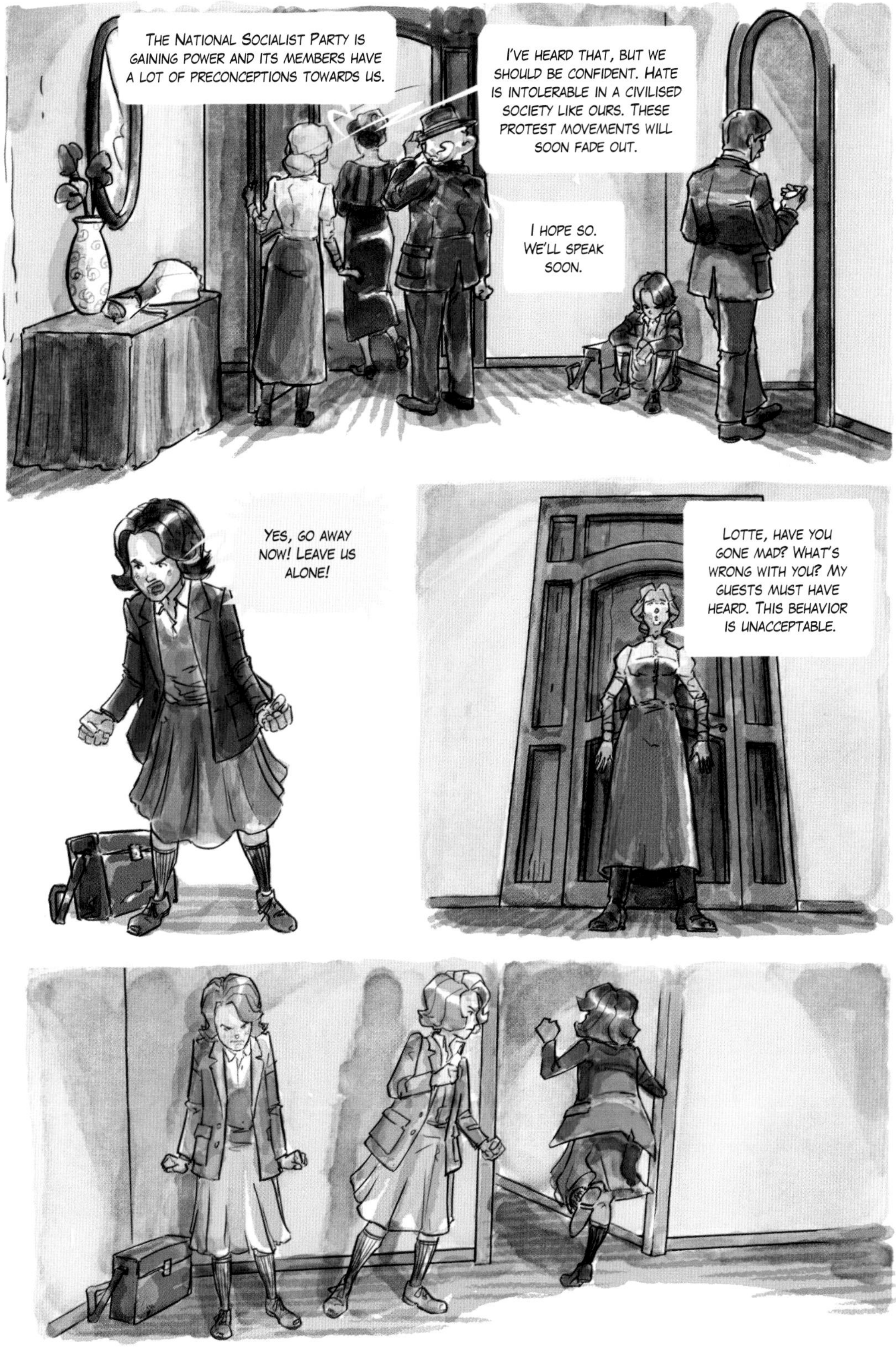
THE NATIONAL SOCIALIST PARTY IS GAINING POWER AND ITS MEMBERS HAVE A LOT OF PRECONCEPTIONS TOWARDS US.
I'VE HEARD THAT, BUT WE SHOULD BE CONFIDENT. HATE IS INTOLERABLE IN A CIVILISED SOCIETY LIKE OURS. THESE PROTEST MOVEMENTS WILL SOON FADE OUT.
I HOPE SO. WE'LL SPEAK SOON.
YES, GO AWAY NOW! LEAVE US ALONE!
LOTTE, HAVE YOU GONE MAD? WHAT'S WRONG WITH YOU? MY GUESTS MUST HAVE HEARD. THIS BEHAVIOR IS UNACCEPTABLE.

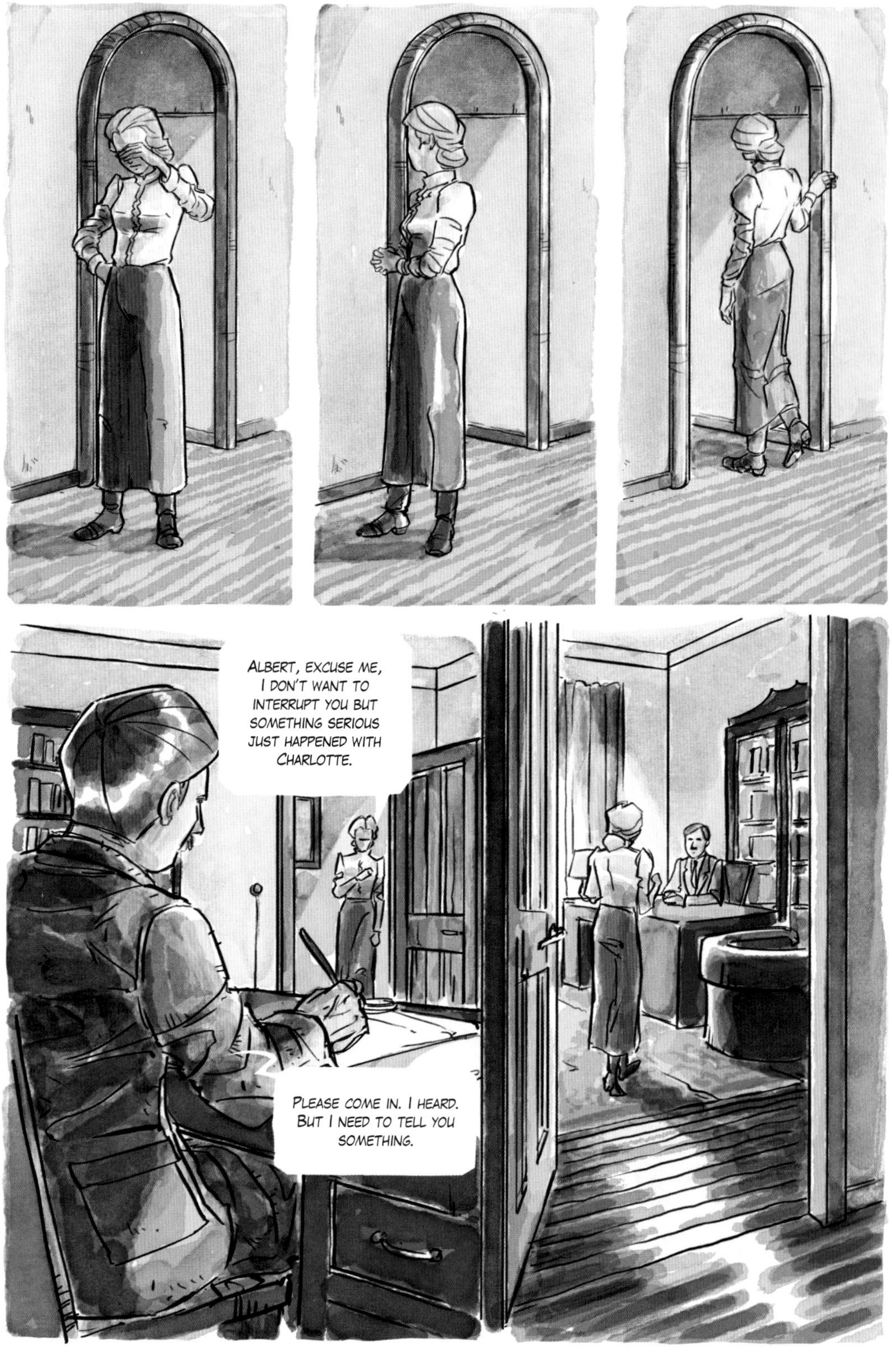

ALBERT, EXCUSE ME, I DON'T WANT TO INTERRUPT YOU BUT SOMETHING SERIOUS JUST HAPPENED WITH CHARLOTTE.
PLEASE COME IN. I HEARD. BUT I NEED TO TELL YOU SOMETHING.

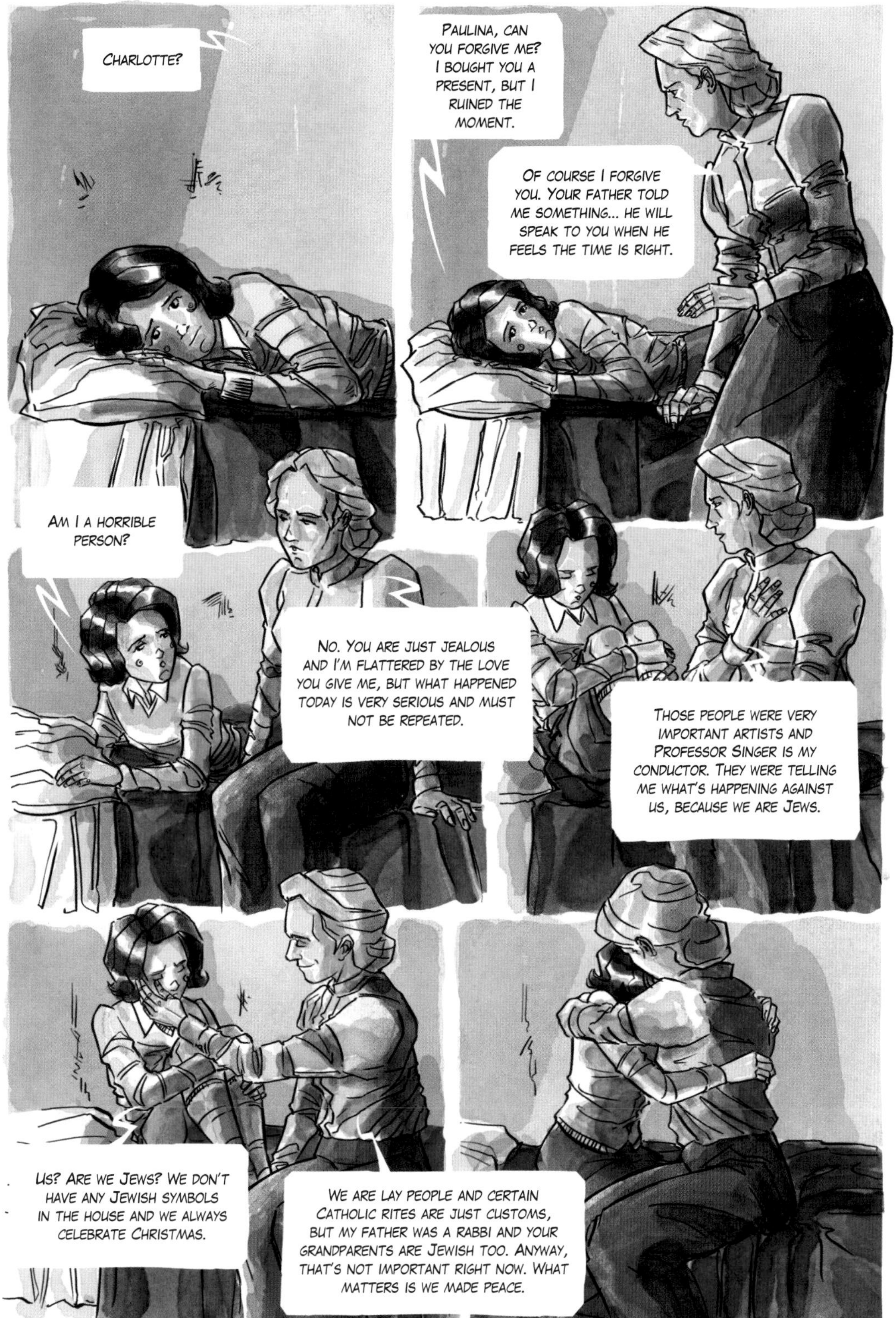

CHARLOTTE?
PAULINA, CAN YOU FORGIVE ME? I BOUGHT YOU A PRESENT, BUT I RUINED THE MOMENT.
OF COURSE I FORGIVE YOU. YOUR FATHER TOLD ME SOMETHING... HE WILL SPEAK TO YOU WHEN HE FEELS THE TIME IS RIGHT.
AM I A HORRIBLE PERSON?
NO. YOU ARE JUST JEALOUS AND I'M FLATTERED BY THE LOVE YOU GIVE ME, BUT WHAT HAPPENED TODAY IS VERY SERIOUS AND MUST NOT BE REPEATED.
THOSE PEOPLE WERE VERY IMPORTANT ARTISTS AND PROFESSOR SINGER IS MY CONDUCTOR. THEY WERE TELLING ME WHAT'S HAPPENING AGAINST US, BECAUSE WE ARE JEWS.
US? ARE WE JEWS? WE DON'T HAVE ANY JEWISH SYMBOLS IN THE HOUSE AND WE ALWAYS CELEBRATE CHRISTMAS.
WE ARE LAY PEOPLE AND CERTAIN CATHOLIC RITES ARE JUST CUSTOMS, BUT MY FATHER WAS A RABBI AND YOUR GRANDPARENTS ARE JEWISH TOO. ANYWAY, THAT'S NOT IMPORTANT RIGHT NOW. WHAT MATTERS IS WE MADE PEACE.

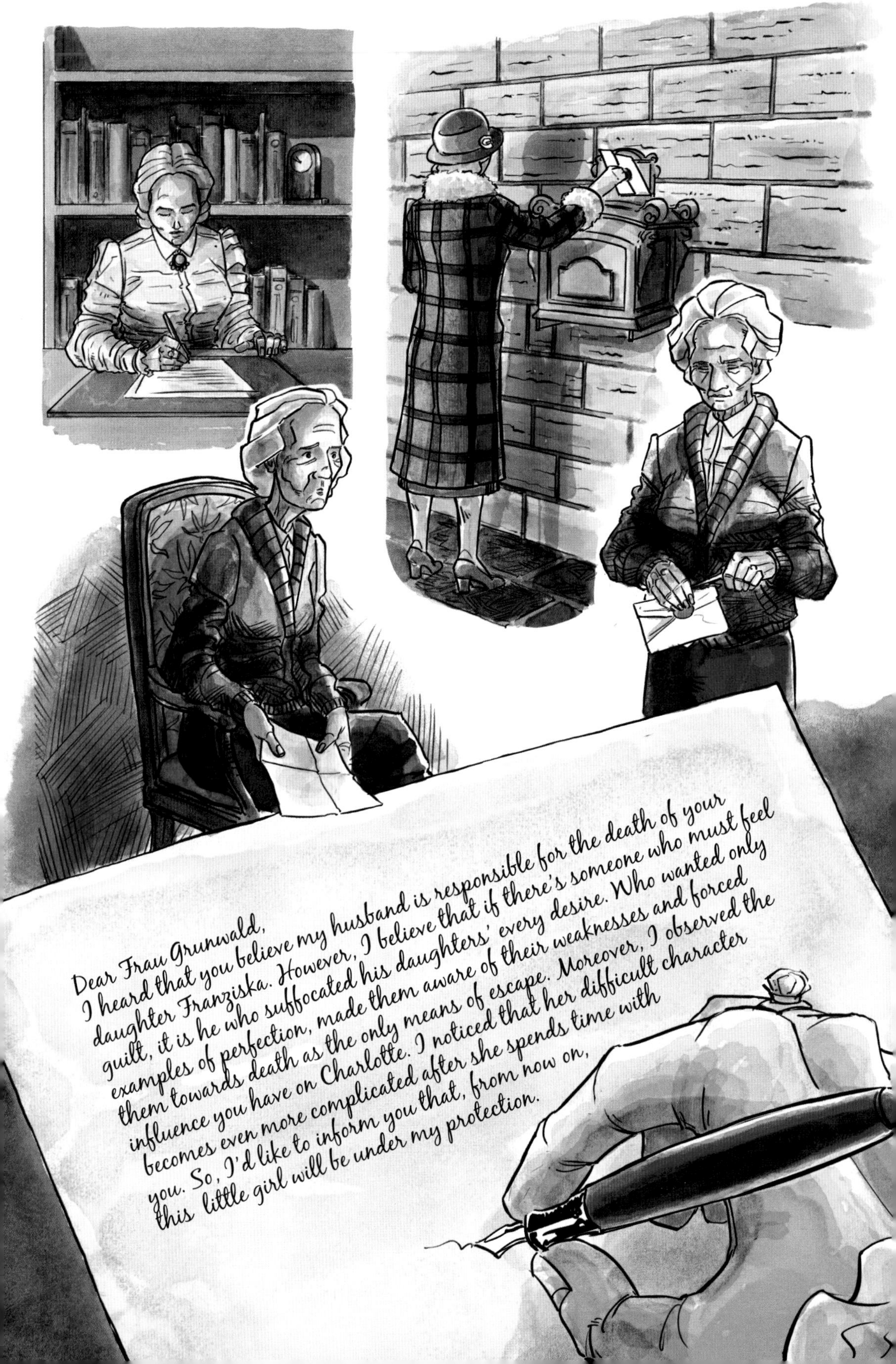
Dear Frau Grunwald,
I heard that you believe my husband is responsible for the death of your daughter Franziska. However, I believe that if there's someone who must feel guilt, it is he who suffocated his daughters' every desire. Who wanted only examples of perfection, made them aware of their weaknesses and forced them towards death as the only means of escape. Moreover, I observed the influence you have on Charlotte. I noticed that her difficult character becomes even more complicated after she spends time with you. So, I'd like to inform you that, from now on, this little girl will be under my protection.

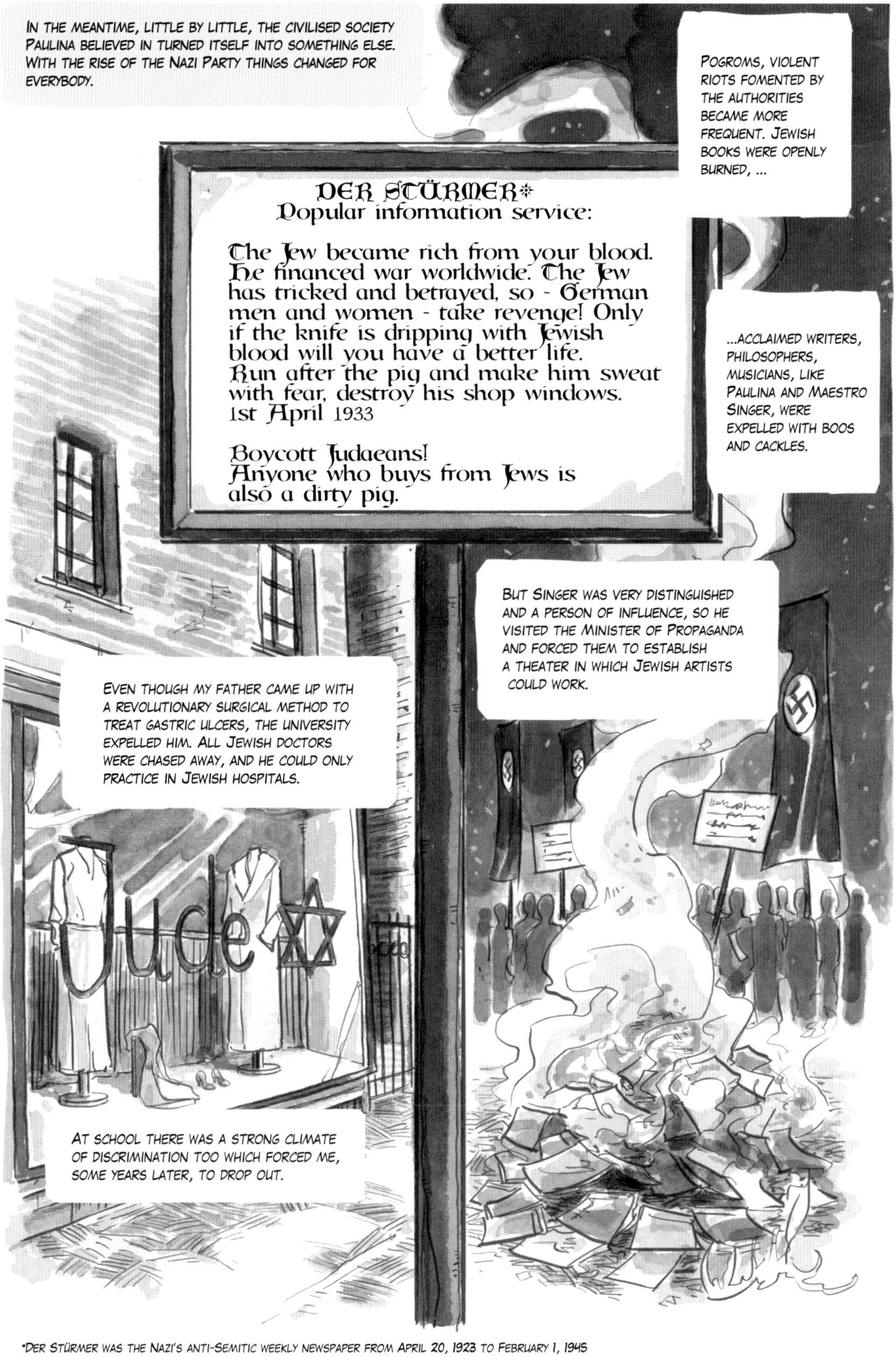
In the meantime, little by little, the civilised society Paulina believed in turned itself into something else. With the rise of the Nazi Party things changed for everybody.
Pogroms, violent riots fomented by the authorities became more frequent. Jewish books were openly burned, ...
DER STÜRMER*
Popular information service:
The Jew became rich from your blood. He financed war worldwide. The Jew has tricked and betrayed, so - German men and women - take revenge! Only if the knife is dripping with Jewish blood will you have a better life. Run after the pig and make him sweat with fear, destroy his shop windows.
1st April 1933
Boycott Judaeans!
Anyone who buys from Jews is also a dirty pig.
...acclaimed writers, philosophers, musicians, like Paulina and Maestro Singer, were expelled with boos and cackles.
But Singer was very distinguished and a person of influence, so he visited the Minister of Propaganda and forced them to establish a theater in which Jewish artists could work.
Even though my father came up with a revolutionary surgical method to treat gastric ulcers, the university expelled him. All Jewish doctors were chased away, and he could only practice in Jewish hospitals.
Jude
At school there was a strong climate of discrimination too which forced me, some years later, to drop out.

*Der Stürmer was the Nazi's anti-Semitic weekly newspaper from April 20, 1923 to February 1, 1945

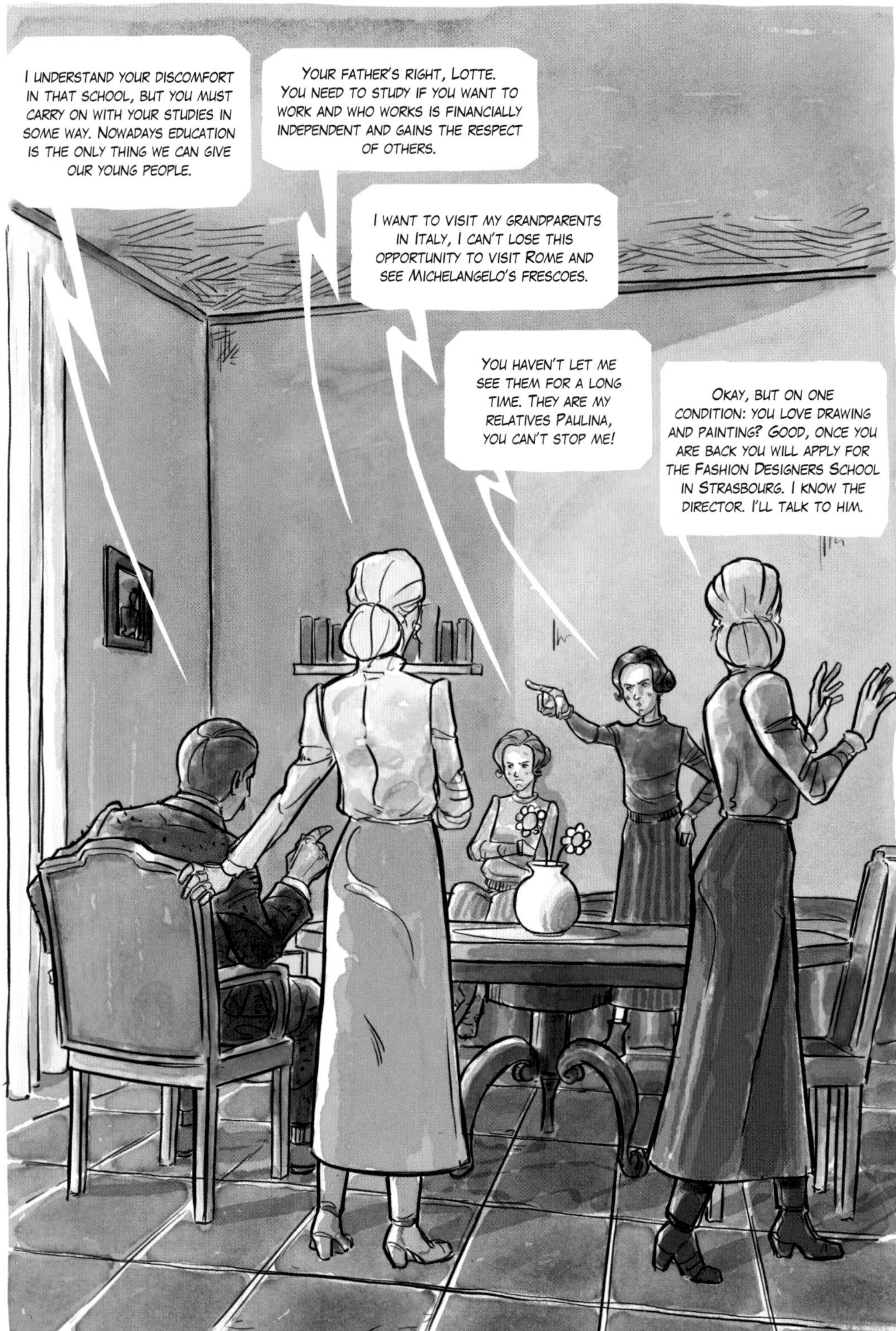
I UNDERSTAND YOUR DISCOMFORT IN THAT SCHOOL, BUT YOU MUST CARRY ON WITH YOUR STUDIES IN SOME WAY. NOWADAYS EDUCATION IS THE ONLY THING WE CAN GIVE OUR YOUNG PEOPLE.
YOUR FATHER'S RIGHT, LOTTE. YOU NEED TO STUDY IF YOU WANT TO WORK AND WHO WORKS IS FINANCIALLY INDEPENDENT AND GAINS THE RESPECT OF OTHERS.
I WANT TO VISIT MY GRANDPARENTS IN ITALY, I CAN'T LOSE THIS OPPORTUNITY TO VISIT ROME AND SEE MICHELANGELO'S FRESCOES.
YOU HAVEN'T LET ME SEE THEM FOR A LONG TIME. THEY ARE MY RELATIVES PAULINA, YOU CAN'T STOP ME!
OKAY, BUT ON ONE CONDITION: YOU LOVE DRAWING AND PAINTING? GOOD, ONCE YOU ARE BACK YOU WILL APPLY FOR THE FASHION DESIGNERS SCHOOL IN STRASBOURG. I KNOW THE DIRECTOR. I'LL TALK TO HIM.

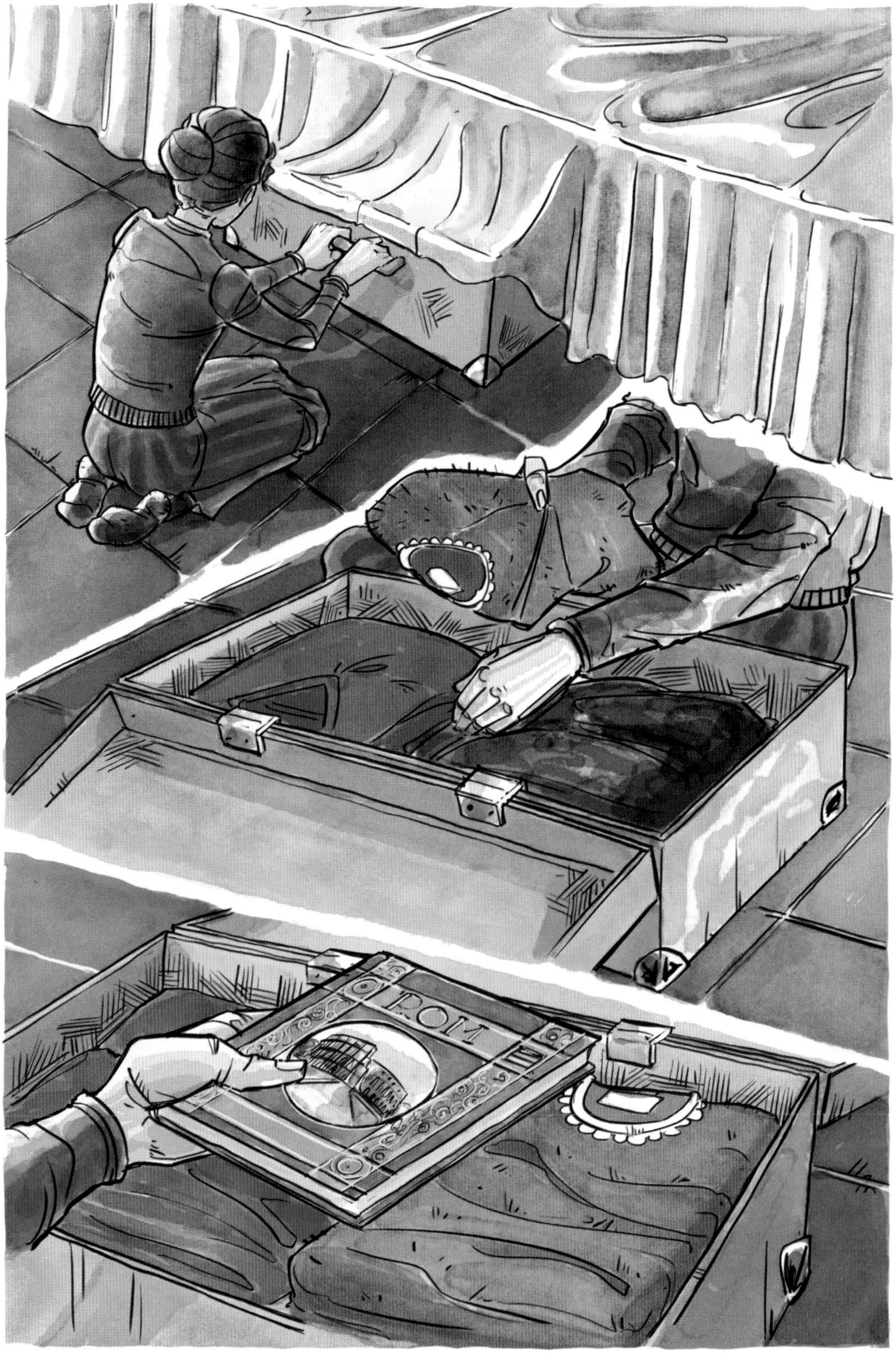
ROM

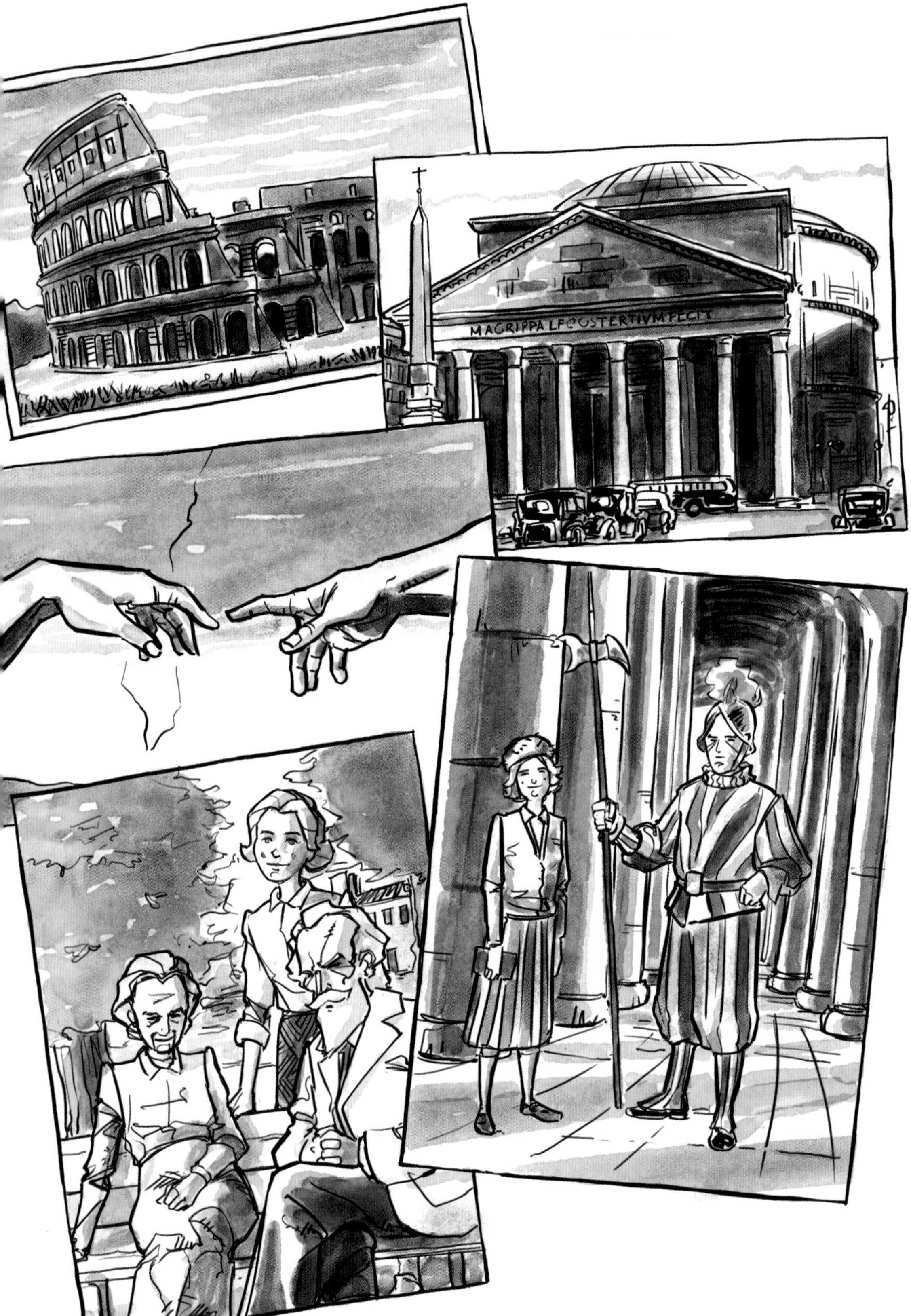
MAGRIPPA LFCOSTERTIVM FECIT

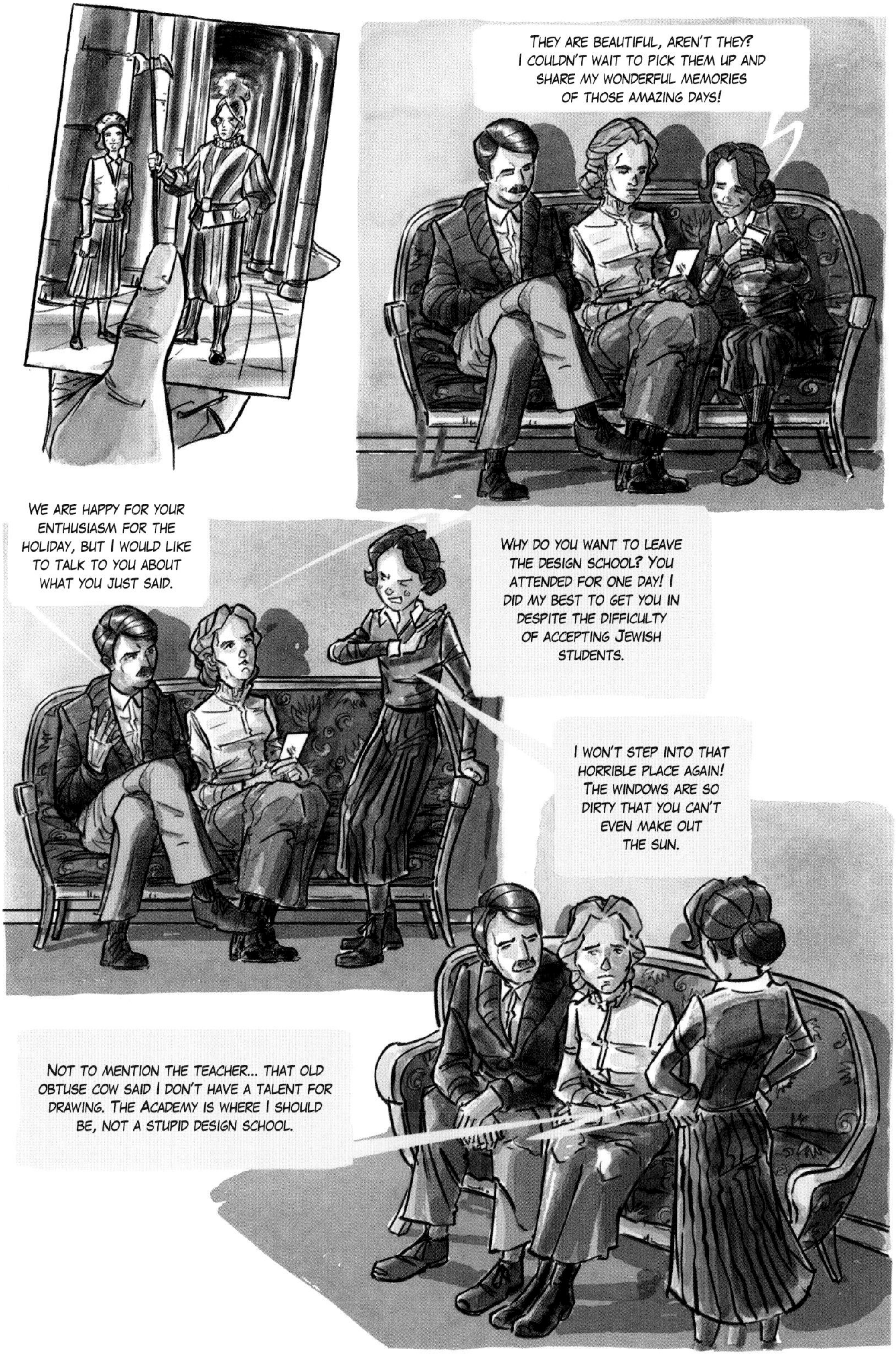
THEY ARE BEAUTIFUL, AREN'T THEY? I COULDN'T WAIT TO PICK THEM UP AND SHARE MY WONDERFUL MEMORIES OF THOSE AMAZING DAYS!
WE ARE HAPPY FOR YOUR ENTHUSIASM FOR THE HOLIDAY, BUT I WOULD LIKE TO TALK TO YOU ABOUT WHAT YOU JUST SAID.
WHY DO YOU WANT TO LEAVE THE DESIGN SCHOOL? YOU ATTENDED FOR ONE DAY! I DID MY BEST TO GET YOU IN DESPITE THE DIFFICULTY OF ACCEPTING JEWISH STUDENTS.
I WON'T STEP INTO THAT HORRIBLE PLACE AGAIN! THE WINDOWS ARE SO DIRTY THAT YOU CAN'T EVEN MAKE OUT THE SUN.
NOT TO MENTION THE TEACHER... THAT OLD OBTUSE COW SAID I DON'T HAVE A TALENT FOR DRAWING. THE ACADEMY IS WHERE I SHOULD BE, NOT A STUPID DESIGN SCHOOL.

I was fascinated by the Academy's motto: "Nur der wagt, der kann gewinnen. Nur der wagt, der kann beginnen"*

So I took the risk and spoke to the director. He said it was very difficult to accept young Jews at that moment, but he gave me the chance to try the admission exam anyway. The professors would be the ones to decide.

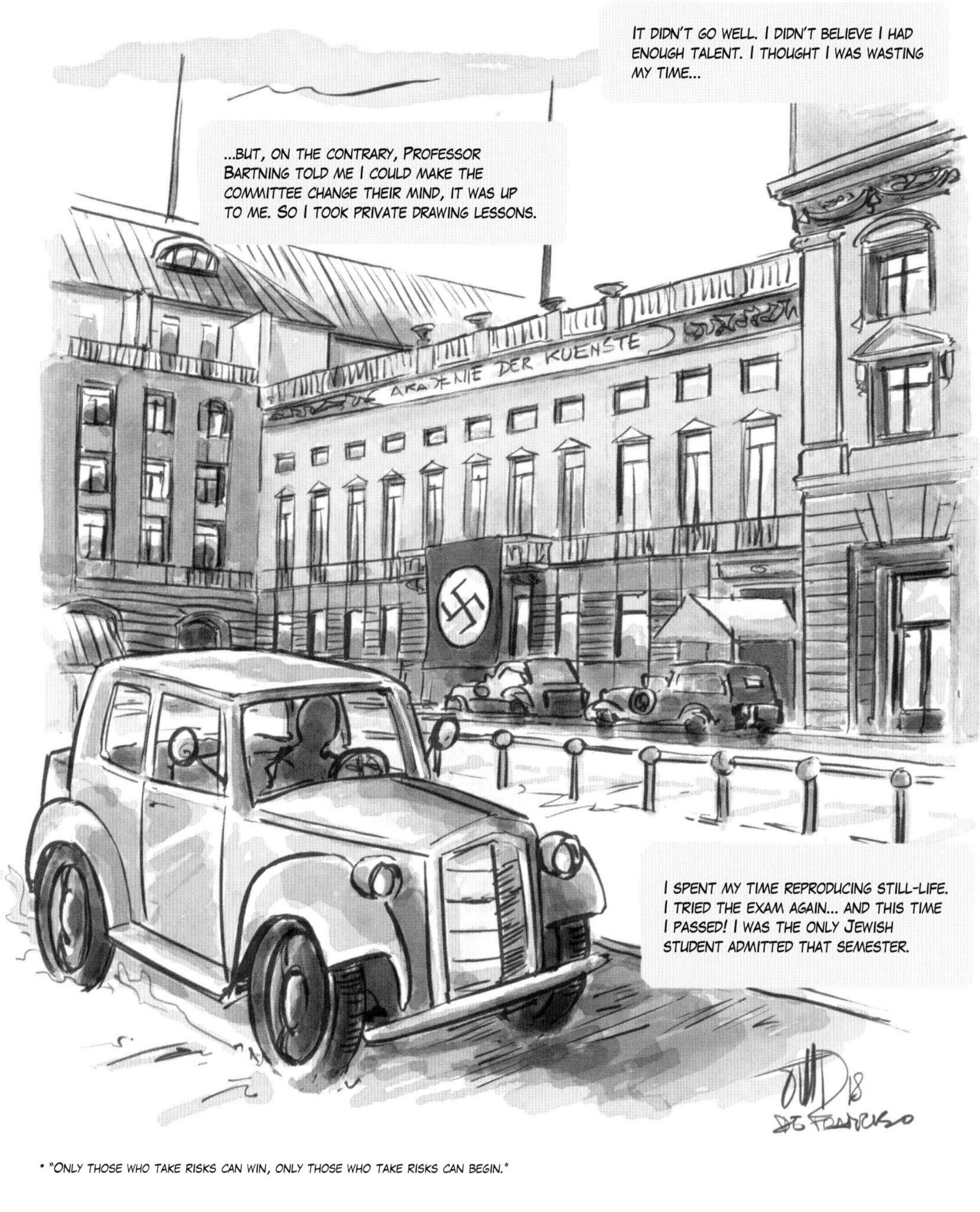
It didn't go well. I didn't believe I had enough talent. I thought I was wasting my time...
...but, on the contrary, Professor Bartning told me I could make the committee change their mind, it was up to me. So I took private drawing lessons.
AKADEMIE DER KUENSTE
I spent my time reproducing still-life. I tried the exam again... and this time I passed! I was the only Jewish student admitted that semester.

* "Only those who take risks can win, only those who take risks can begin."

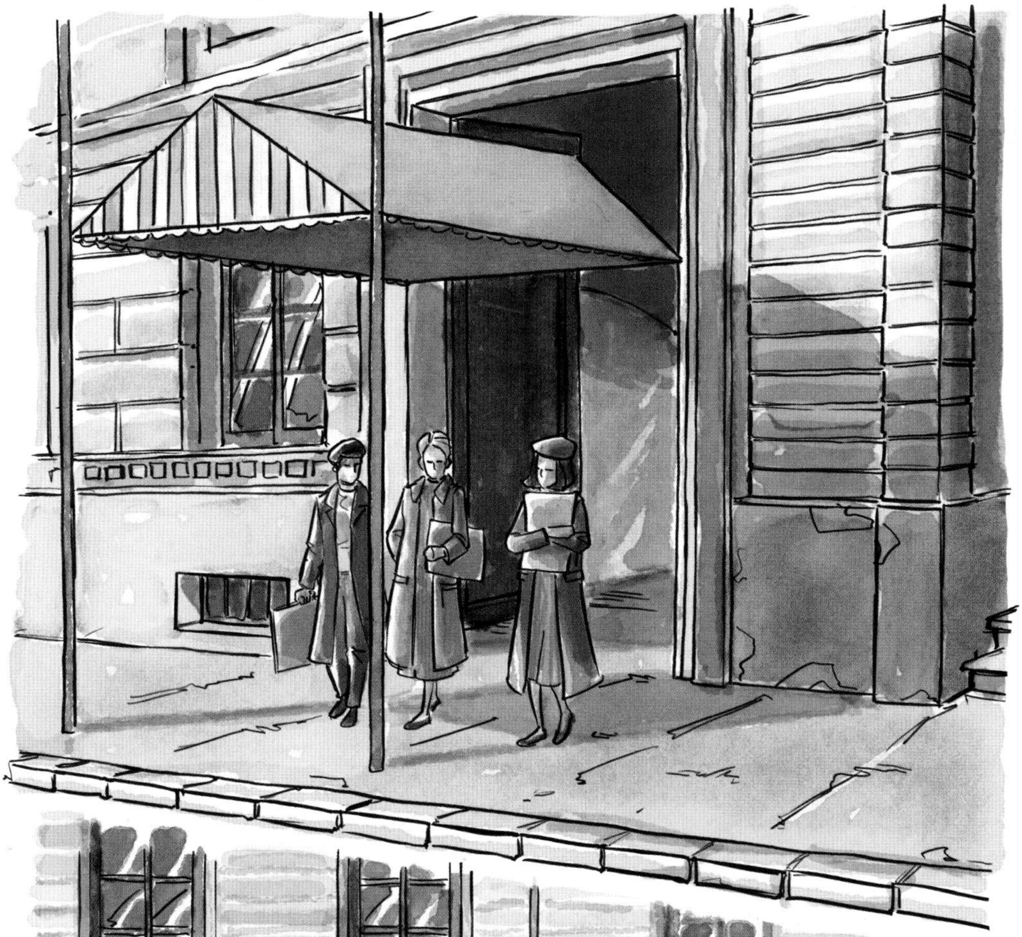

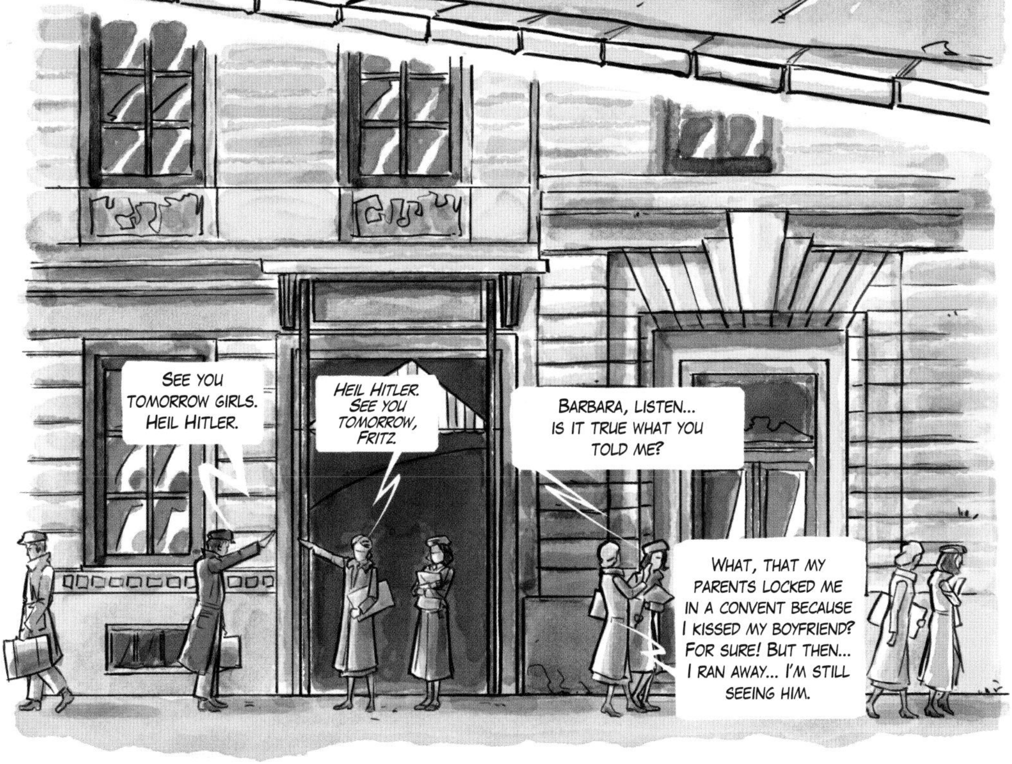

SEE YOU TOMORROW GIRLS. HEIL HITLER.
HEIL HITLER. SEE YOU TOMORROW, FRITZ.
BARBARA, LISTEN... IS IT TRUE WHAT YOU TOLD ME?
WHAT, THAT MY PARENTS LOCKED ME IN A CONVENT BECAUSE I KISSED MY BOYFRIEND? FOR SURE! BUT THEN... I RAN AWAY... I'M STILL SEEING HIM.

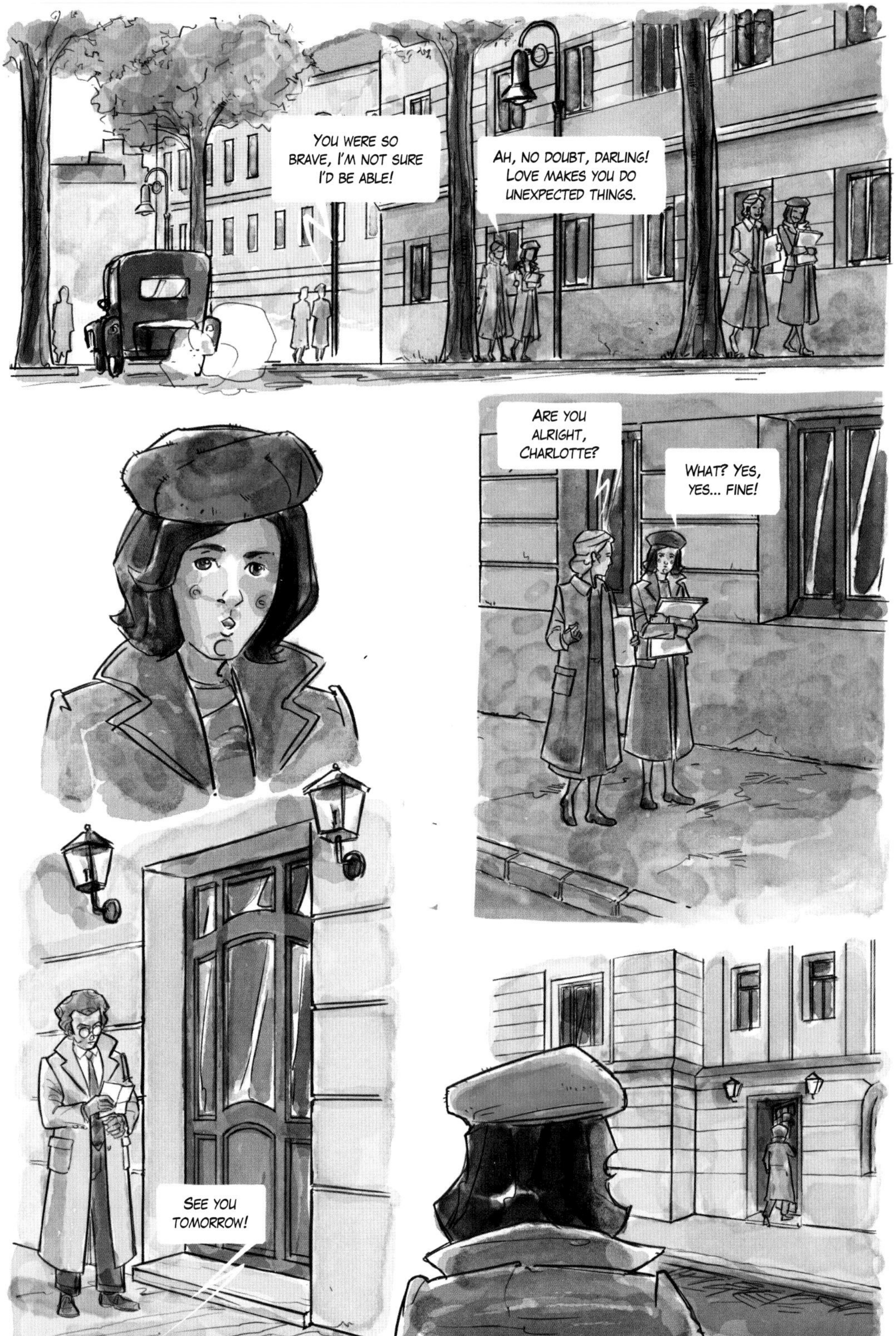
YOU WERE SO BRAVE, I'M NOT SURE I'D BE ABLE!
AH, NO DOUBT, DARLING! LOVE MAKES YOU DO UNEXPECTED THINGS.
ARE YOU ALRIGHT, CHARLOTTE?
WHAT? YES, YES... FINE!
SEE YOU TOMORROW!

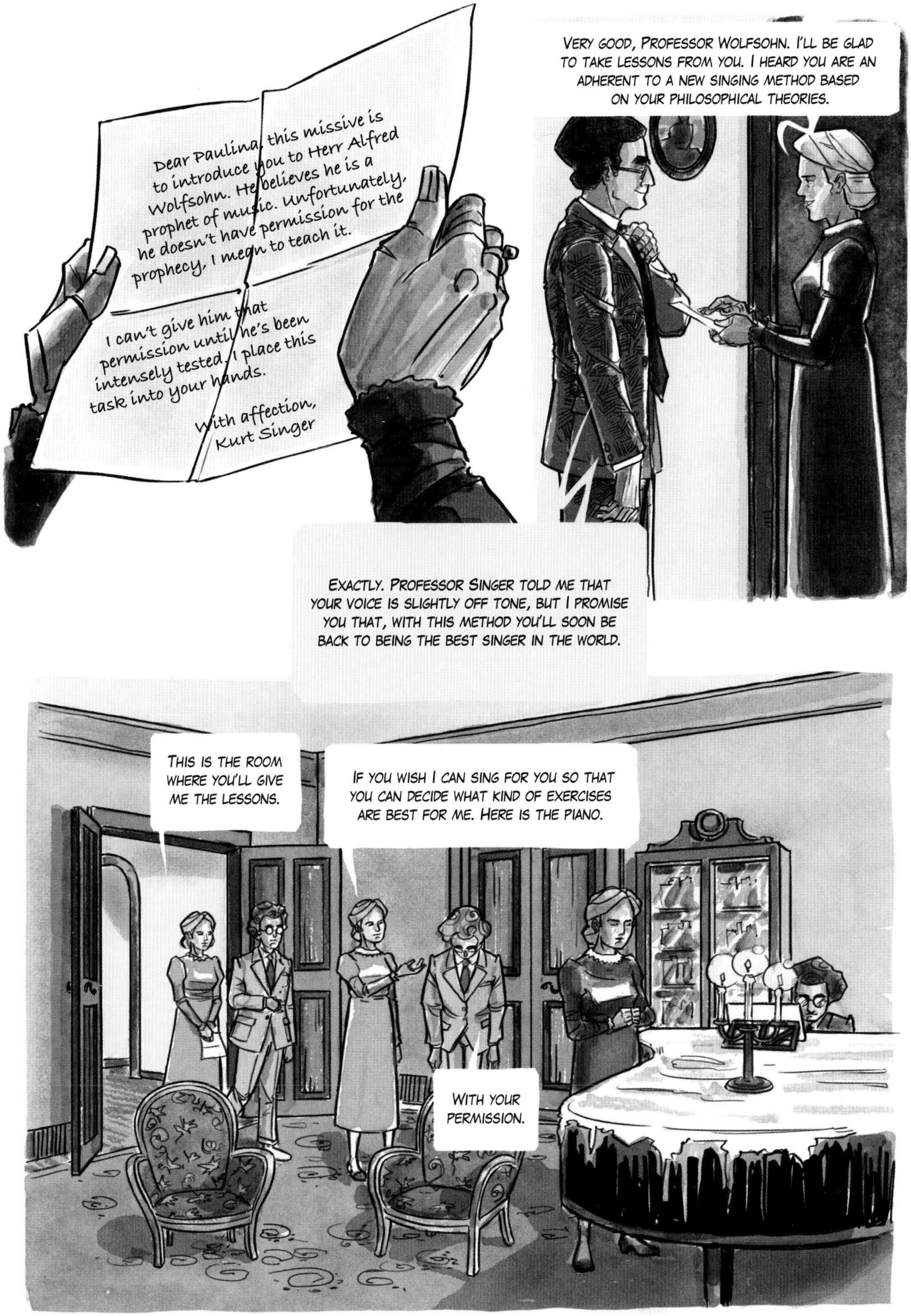
Dear Paulina, this missive is to introduce you to Herr Alfred Wolfsohn. He believes he is a prophet of music. Unfortunately, he doesn't have permission for the prophecy, I mean to teach it.
I can't give him that permission until he's been intensely tested. I place this task into your hands.
With affection,
Kurt Singer
VERY GOOD, PROFESSOR WOLFSOHN. I'LL BE GLAD TO TAKE LESSONS FROM YOU. I HEARD YOU ARE AN ADHERENT TO A NEW SINGING METHOD BASED ON YOUR PHILOSOPHICAL THEORIES.
EXACTLY. PROFESSOR SINGER TOLD ME THAT YOUR VOICE IS SLIGHTLY OFF TONE, BUT I PROMISE YOU THAT, WITH THIS METHOD YOU'LL SOON BE BACK TO BEING THE BEST SINGER IN THE WORLD.
THIS IS THE ROOM WHERE YOU'LL GIVE ME THE LESSONS.
IF YOU WISH I CAN SING FOR YOU SO THAT YOU CAN DECIDE WHAT KIND OF EXERCISES ARE BEST FOR ME. HERE IS THE PIANO.
WITH YOUR PERMISSION.

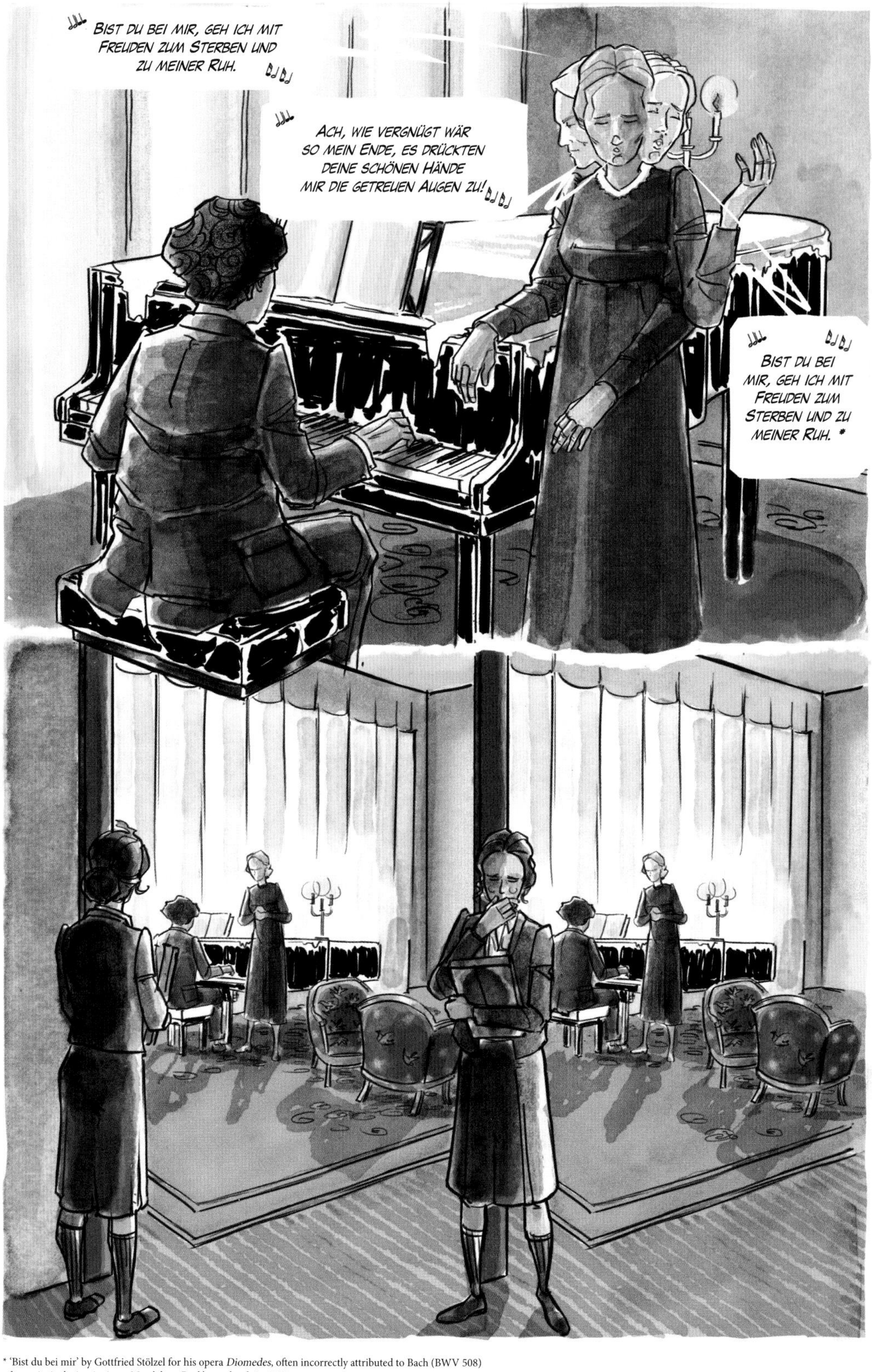
Bist du bei mir, geh ich mit Freuden zum Sterben und zu meiner Ruh.
Ach, wie vergnügt wär so mein Ende, es drückten deine schönen Hände mir die getreuen Augen zu!
Bist du bei mir, geh ich mit Freuden zum Sterben und zu meiner Ruh. *

* 'Bist du bei mir' by Gottfried Stölzel for his opera *Diomedes*, often incorrectly attributed to Bach (BWV 508) due to its inclusion in Anna Magdalena Bach's notebook in 1725.

YOU CAN STOP NOW! YOU SEE, PAULINA, I'M WRITING A BOOK BASED ON MY THEORIES. YOU WILL DOUBT MANY OF THEM, I KNOW THAT ALREADY, BUT THE FINAL RESULT WILL BE TO GO BACK TO YOUR NATURAL VOICE. TAKE FOR INSTANCE A CHILD...

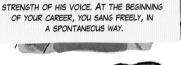

...WHO CRIES BECAUSE HE IS HUNGRY. MOST SINGERS WOULD ENVY THE POWER AND THE STRENGTH OF HIS VOICE. AT THE BEGINNING OF YOUR CAREER, YOU SANG FREELY, IN A SPONTANEOUS WAY.

NOW YOU HAVE YOUR DAILY ROUTINE, MADE OF TROUBLES AND WORRIES, AND YOU SING ONLY FOR THE AUDIENCE. I WANT TO GIVE YOU BACK THAT HUNGER I WAS TALKING ABOUT.

ART CAN'T EXIST AS AN END IN ITSELF, IT MUST FLOW FROM LIFE. THAT IS THE WAY A GENIUS IS BORN. BASICALLY, MY METHOD CONSISTS OF THIS: WHEN THE MEASURE OF LIFE IS FULL THEN LIFE BEGINS.

SINGING IS STRICTLY RELATED TO YOUR LIFE, MORE THAN ANYTHING ELSE. YOU CAN INSTIL THE SOUND WITH AN EXPRESSION THAT SHOWS THE MOST INTIMATE FEELINGS THAT ARE ABLE TO SHAKE THE SOUL.

YOU HAVE A WONDERFUL GIFT AND MY JOB WILL BE A GREAT SUCCESS. BUT NOW LET'S STOP. IT'S YOUR FIRST DAY AND THAT'S ENOUGH THEORY OR I'LL END UP SCARING YOU.

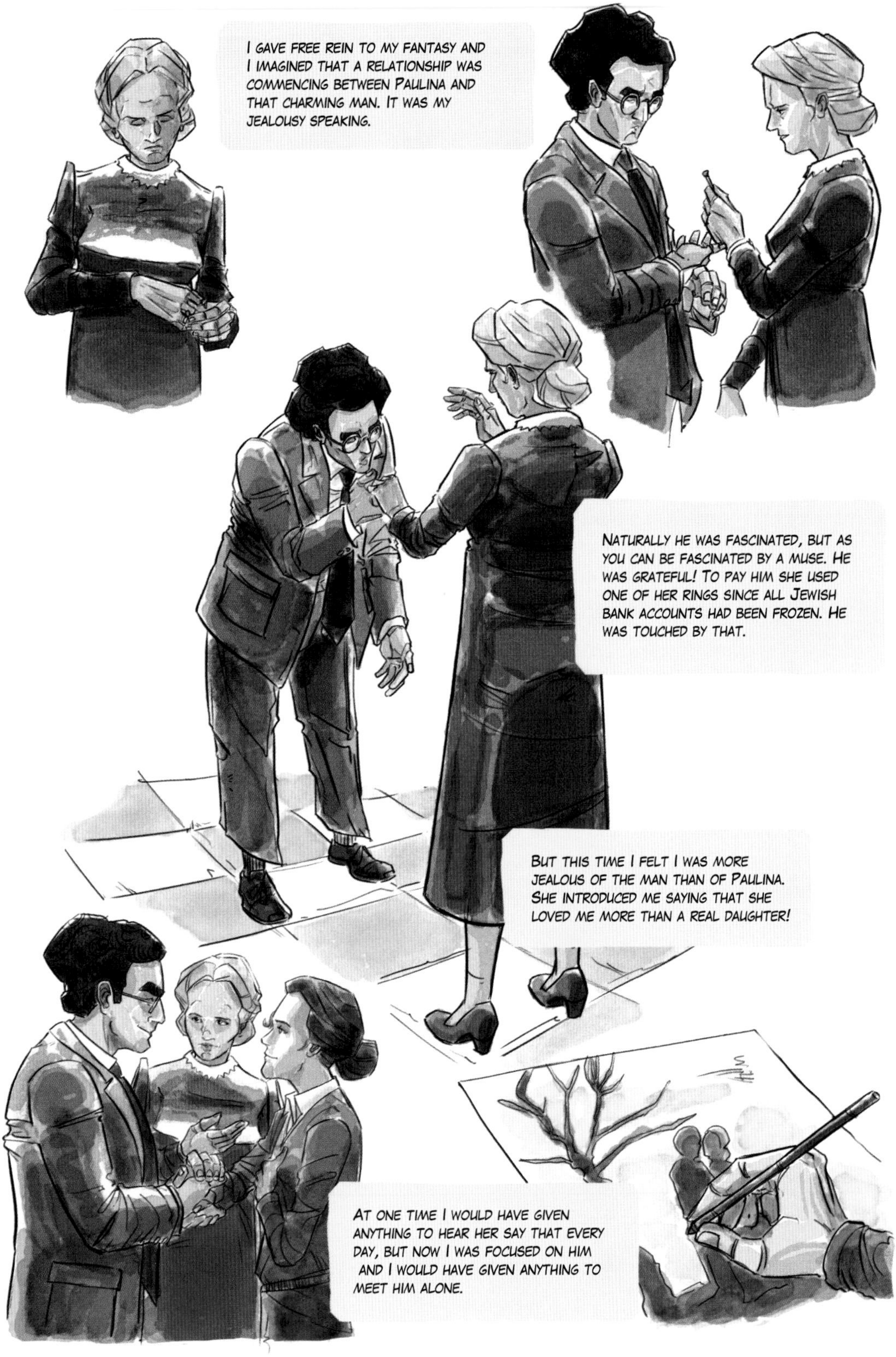
I GAVE FREE REIN TO MY FANTASY AND I IMAGINED THAT A RELATIONSHIP WAS COMMENCING BETWEEN PAULINA AND THAT CHARMING MAN. IT WAS MY JEALOUSY SPEAKING.
NATURALLY HE WAS FASCINATED, BUT AS YOU CAN BE FASCINATED BY A MUSE. HE WAS GRATEFUL! TO PAY HIM SHE USED ONE OF HER RINGS SINCE ALL JEWISH BANK ACCOUNTS HAD BEEN FROZEN. HE WAS TOUCHED BY THAT.
BUT THIS TIME I FELT I WAS MORE JEALOUS OF THE MAN THAN OF PAULINA. SHE INTRODUCED ME SAYING THAT SHE LOVED ME MORE THAN A REAL DAUGHTER!
AT ONE TIME I WOULD HAVE GIVEN ANYTHING TO HEAR HER SAY THAT EVERY DAY, BUT NOW I WAS FOCUSED ON HIM AND I WOULD HAVE GIVEN ANYTHING TO MEET HIM ALONE.

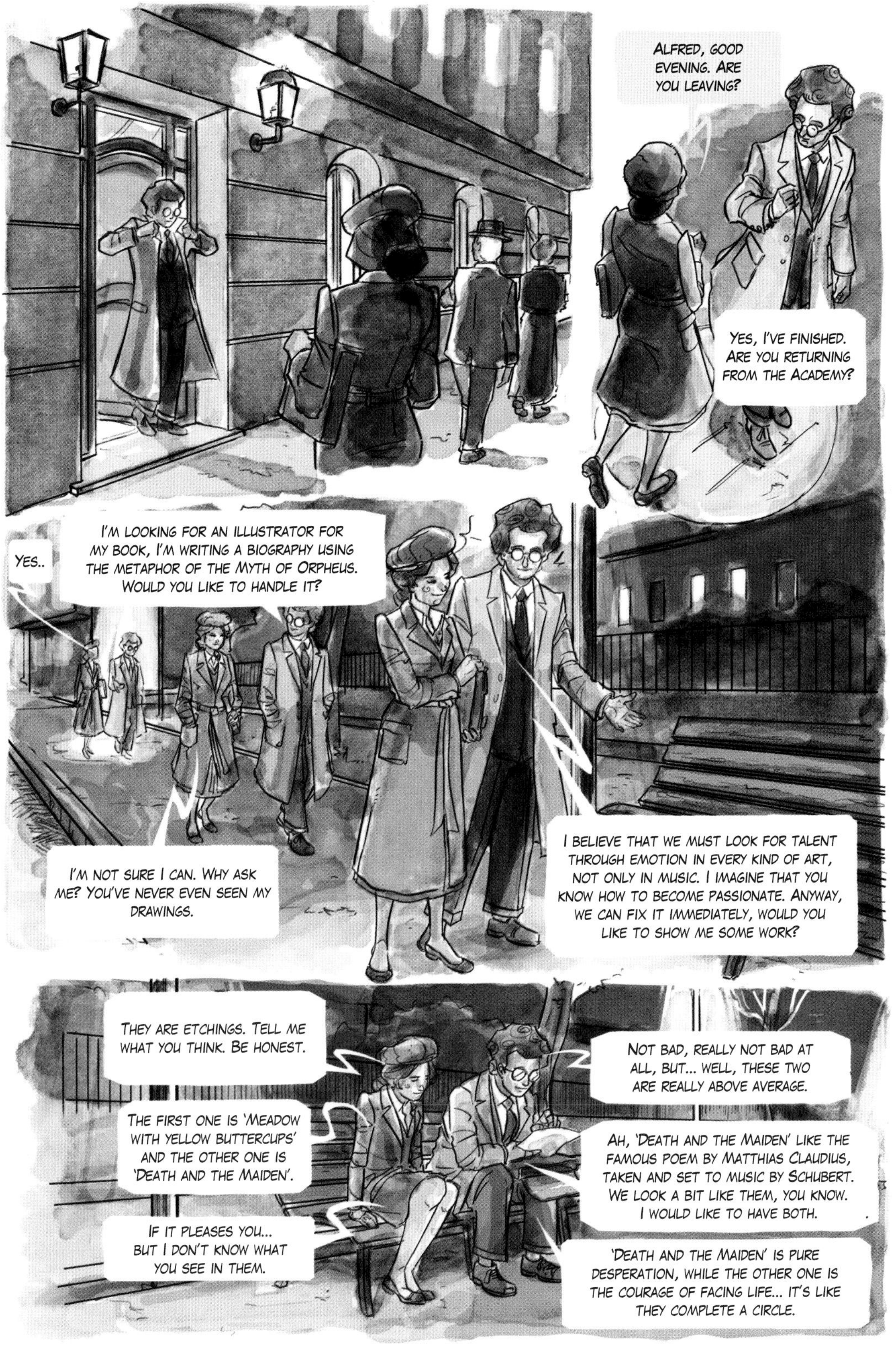
ALFRED, GOOD EVENING. ARE YOU LEAVING?
YES, I'VE FINISHED. ARE YOU RETURNING FROM THE ACADEMY?
YES..
I'M LOOKING FOR AN ILLUSTRATOR FOR MY BOOK, I'M WRITING A BIOGRAPHY USING THE METAPHOR OF THE MYTH OF ORPHEUS. WOULD YOU LIKE TO HANDLE IT?
I'M NOT SURE I CAN. WHY ASK ME? YOU'VE NEVER EVEN SEEN MY DRAWINGS.
I BELIEVE THAT WE MUST LOOK FOR TALENT THROUGH EMOTION IN EVERY KIND OF ART, NOT ONLY IN MUSIC. I IMAGINE THAT YOU KNOW HOW TO BECOME PASSIONATE. ANYWAY, WE CAN FIX IT IMMEDIATELY, WOULD YOU LIKE TO SHOW ME SOME WORK?
THEY ARE ETCHINGS. TELL ME WHAT YOU THINK. BE HONEST.
NOT BAD, REALLY NOT BAD AT ALL, BUT... WELL, THESE TWO ARE REALLY ABOVE AVERAGE.
THE FIRST ONE IS 'MEADOW WITH YELLOW BUTTERCUPS' AND THE OTHER ONE IS 'DEATH AND THE MAIDEN'.
AH, 'DEATH AND THE MAIDEN' LIKE THE FAMOUS POEM BY MATTHIAS CLAUDIUS, TAKEN AND SET TO MUSIC BY SCHUBERT. WE LOOK A BIT LIKE THEM, YOU KNOW. I WOULD LIKE TO HAVE BOTH.
IF IT PLEASES YOU... BUT I DON'T KNOW WHAT YOU SEE IN THEM.
'DEATH AND THE MAIDEN' IS PURE DESPERATION, WHILE THE OTHER ONE IS THE COURAGE OF FACING LIFE... IT'S LIKE THEY COMPLETE A CIRCLE.

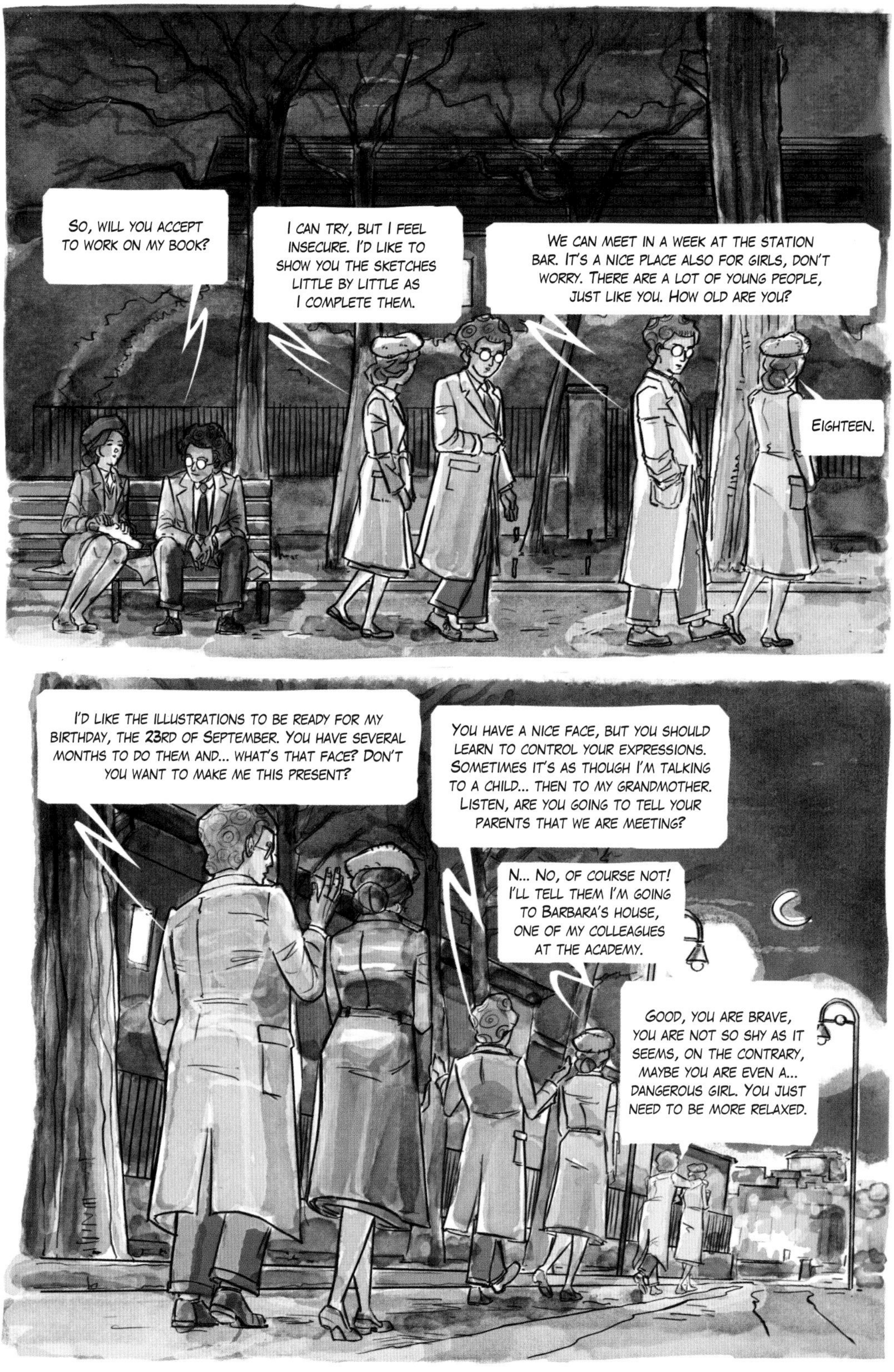
So, will you accept to work on my book?
I can try, but I feel insecure. I'd like to show you the sketches little by little as I complete them.
We can meet in a week at the station bar. It's a nice place also for girls, don't worry. There are a lot of young people, just like you. How old are you?
Eighteen.
I'd like the illustrations to be ready for my birthday, the 23rd of September. You have several months to do them and... what's that face? Don't you want to make me this present?
You have a nice face, but you should learn to control your expressions. Sometimes it's as though I'm talking to a child... then to my grandmother. Listen, are you going to tell your parents that we are meeting?
N... No, of course not! I'll tell them I'm going to Barbara's house, one of my colleagues at the academy.
Good, you are brave, you are not so shy as it seems, on the contrary, maybe you are even a... dangerous girl. You just need to be more relaxed.

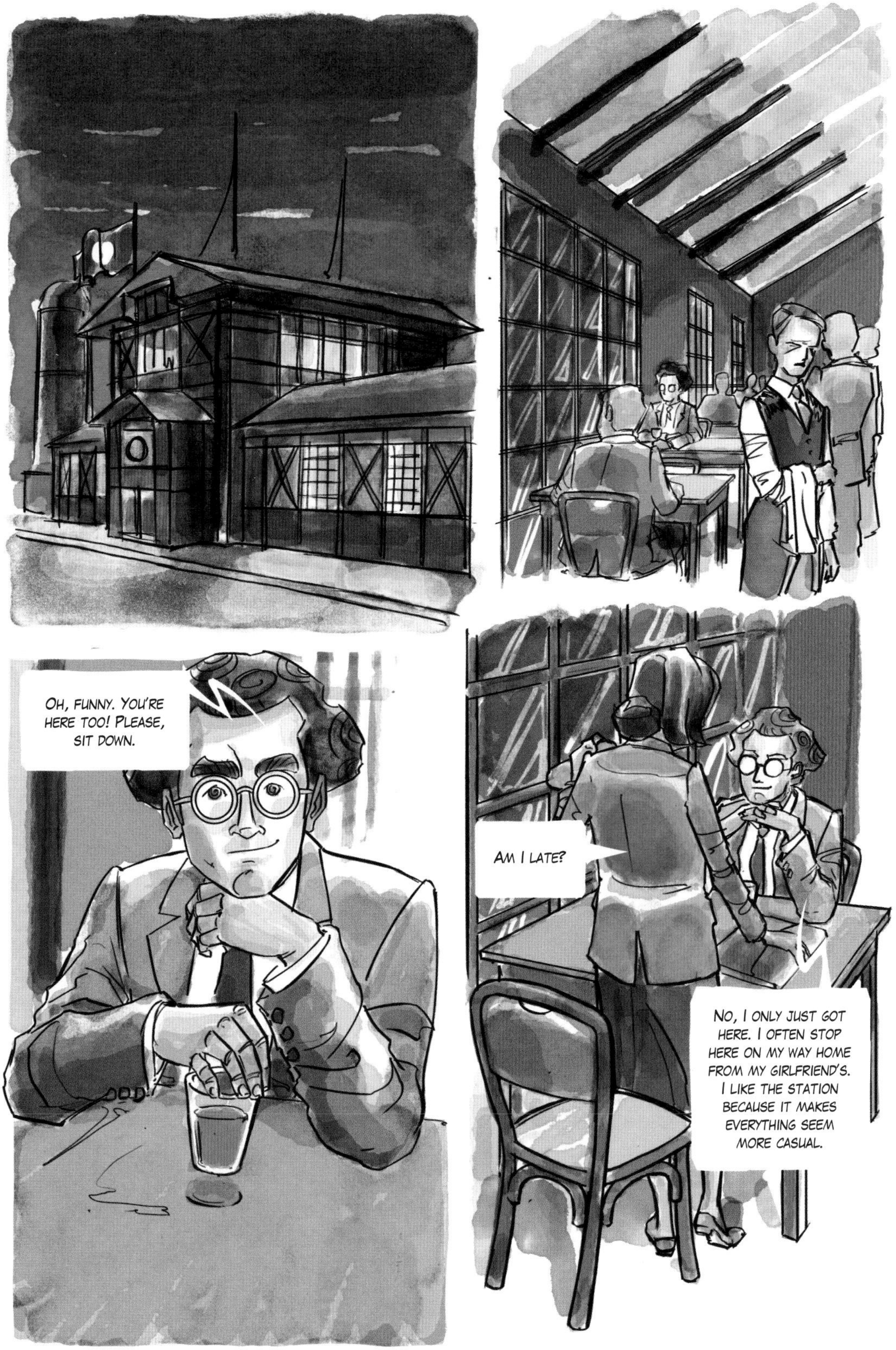
OH, FUNNY. YOU'RE HERE TOO! PLEASE, SIT DOWN.
AM I LATE?
NO, I ONLY JUST GOT HERE. I OFTEN STOP HERE ON MY WAY HOME FROM MY GIRLFRIEND'S. I LIKE THE STATION BECAUSE IT MAKES EVERYTHING SEEM MORE CASUAL.

ARE YOU DISAPPOINTED BECAUSE I HAVE A GIRLFRIEND? YOU ARE FALLING IN LOVE WITH ME, I KNOW IT. SINCE THE LAST TIME WE MET YOU HAVEN'T WORKED ON YOUR EMOTIONS, I CAN READ EVERYTHING ON YOUR FACE. C'MON, GIVE ME YOUR HANDS, I NEED PHYSICAL CONTACT.
I WANT TO TELL YOU SOMETHING ABOUT ME. DURING THE WAR I ALMOST DIED! I SURVIVED BECAUSE I WAS ABLE TO HIDE UNDER ONE OF MY DEAD COMPANIONS.
I WAS SHELL-SHOCKED, I COULDN'T REMEMBER ANYTHING, AND I WAS UNABLE TO TALK. THEN, AFTER A DEEP SELF-ANALYSIS, I RE-EMERGED FROM MY HELL.
SINCE THE MOMENT I CAME BACK FROM DEATH, LIKE ORPHEUS I UNDERSTOOD THAT NOTHING IN OUR LIFE MUST BE OVERLOOKED. EVERY OCCASION MUST BE FULLY EXPERIENCED, WITHOUT REGRET OR HESITATION.
NOW TELL ME, HOW IS MY BIRTHDAY PRESENT COMING ALONG?

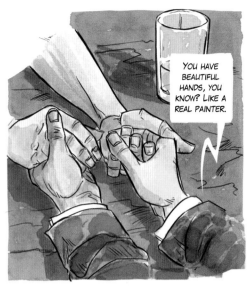

YOU HAVE BEAUTIFUL HANDS, YOU KNOW? LIKE A REAL PAINTER.

C'MON, LET ME SEE... REALLY NOT TOO BAD! I'LL TAKE THEM AND REVIEW THEM CALMLY. BUT NOW LET'S GO, I WANT TO DO AN EXPERIMENT. I FEEL THAT YOU ARE THE PROPER SUBJECT FOR MY THEORIES.

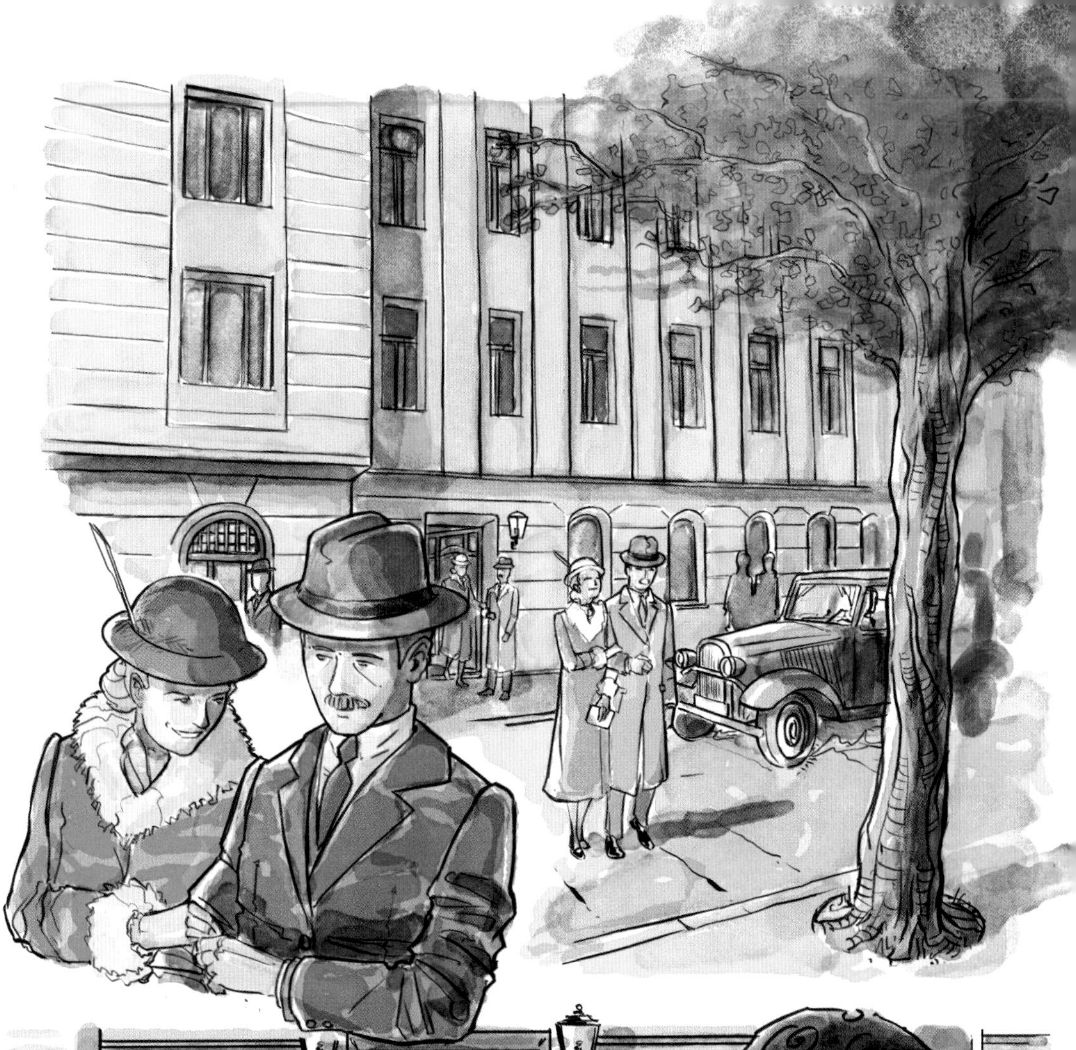

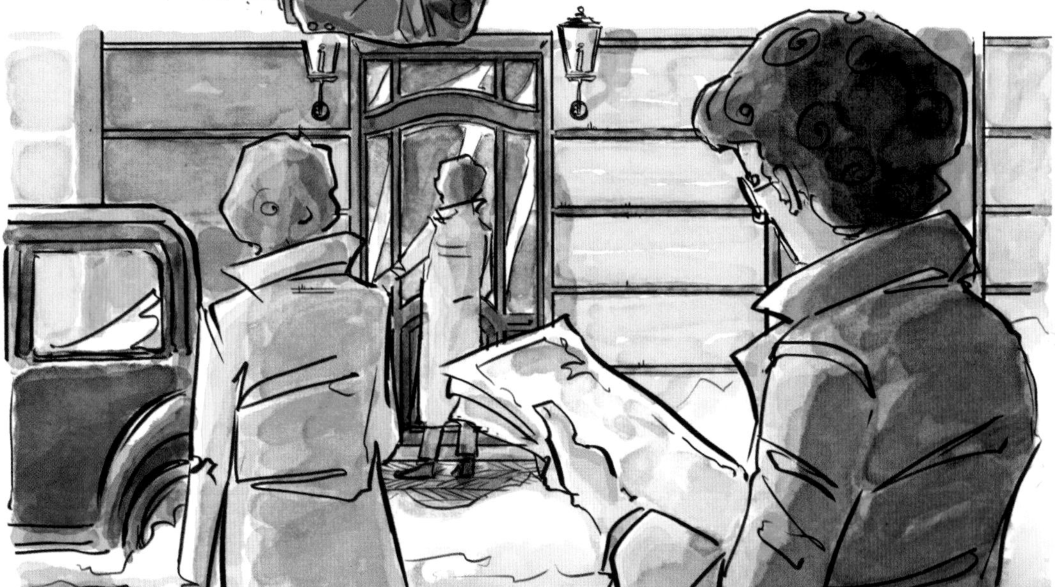

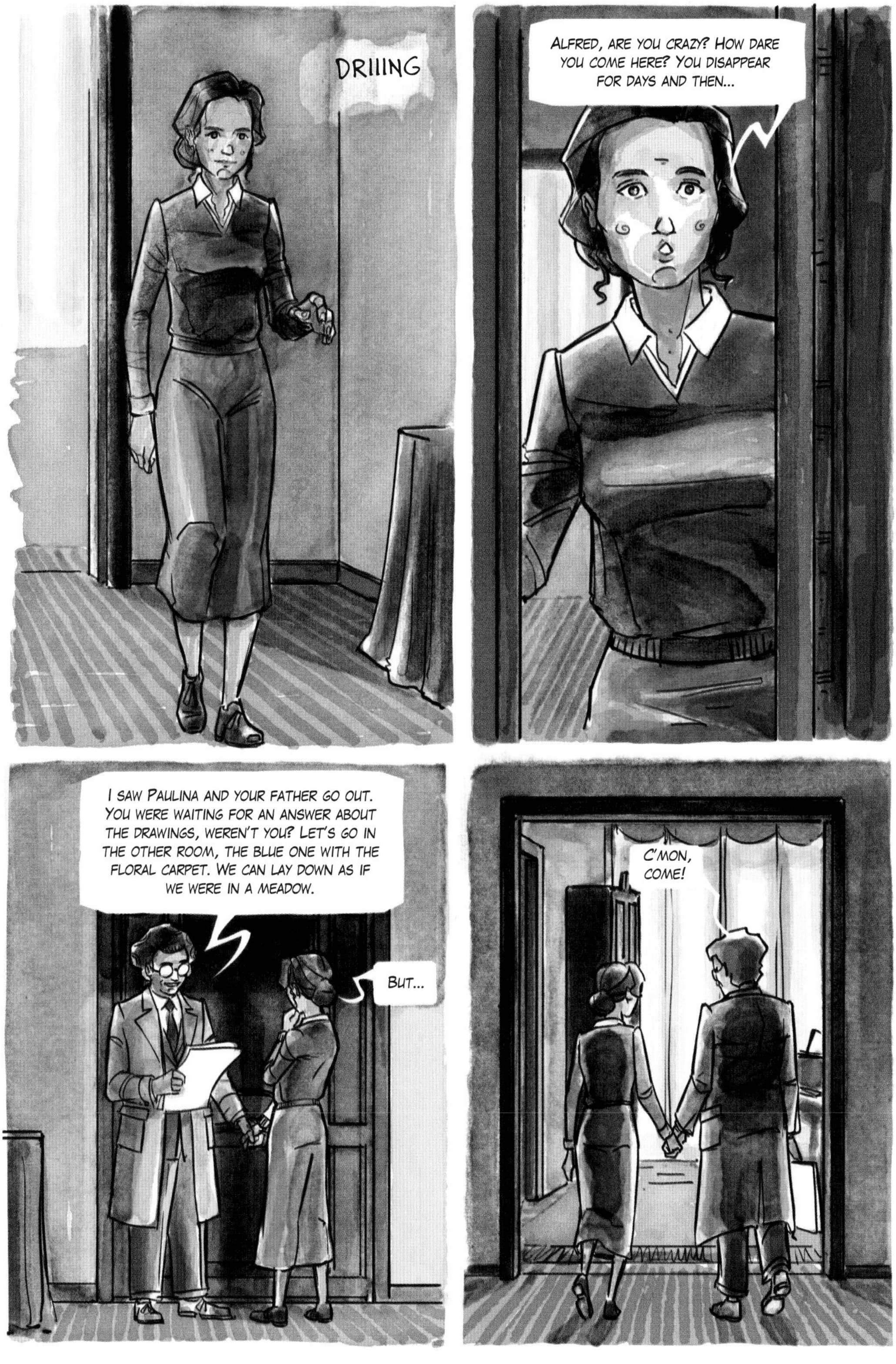
DRIIING
ALFRED, ARE YOU CRAZY? HOW DARE YOU COME HERE? YOU DISAPPEAR FOR DAYS AND THEN...
I SAW PAULINA AND YOUR FATHER GO OUT. YOU WERE WAITING FOR AN ANSWER ABOUT THE DRAWINGS, WEREN'T YOU? LET'S GO IN THE OTHER ROOM, THE BLUE ONE WITH THE FLORAL CARPET. WE CAN LAY DOWN AS IF WE WERE IN A MEADOW.
BUT...
C'MON, COME!

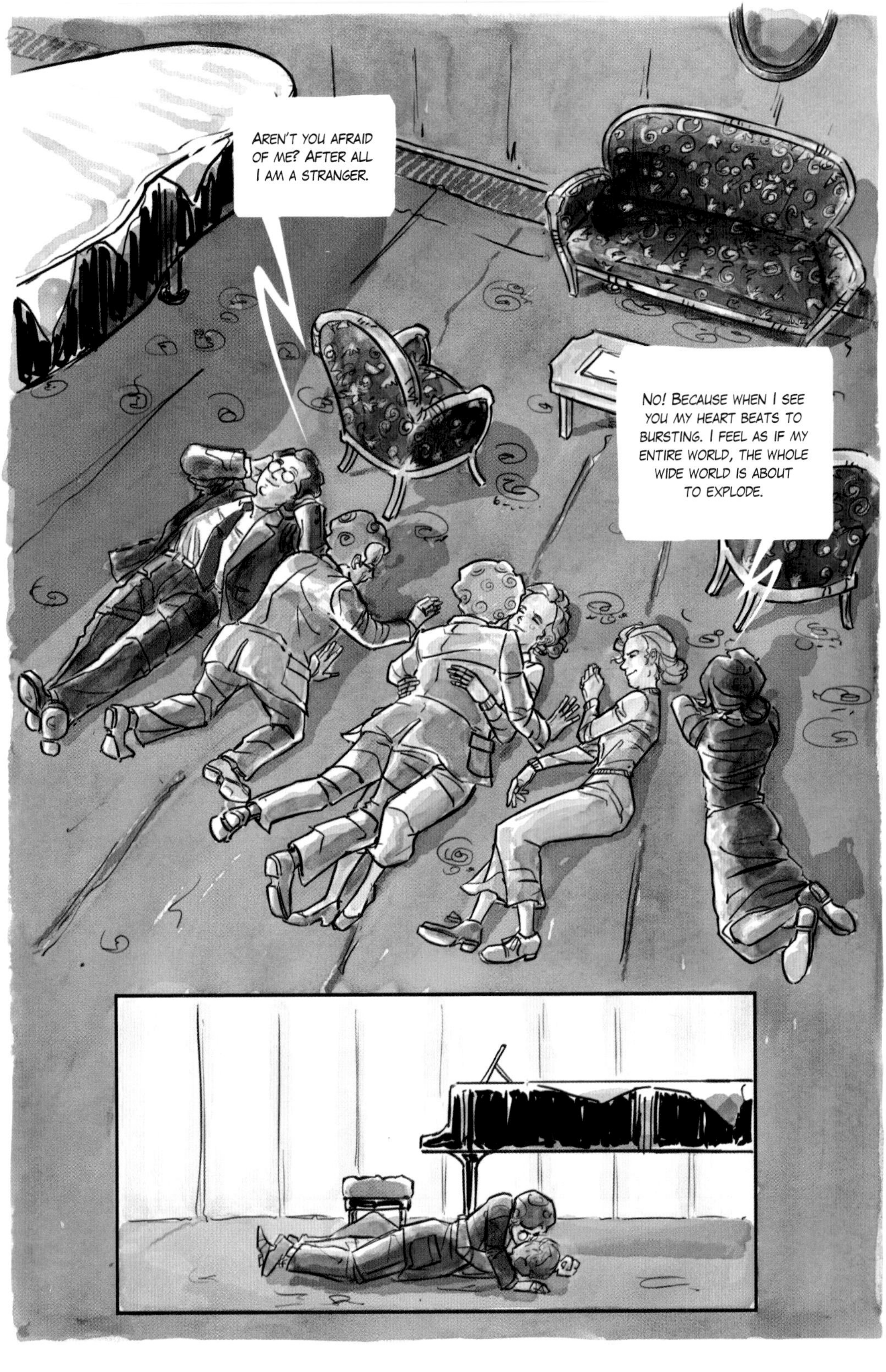
AREN'T YOU AFRAID OF ME? AFTER ALL I AM A STRANGER.
NO! BECAUSE WHEN I SEE YOU MY HEART BEATS TO BURSTING. I FEEL AS IF MY ENTIRE WORLD, THE WHOLE WIDE WORLD IS ABOUT TO EXPLODE.

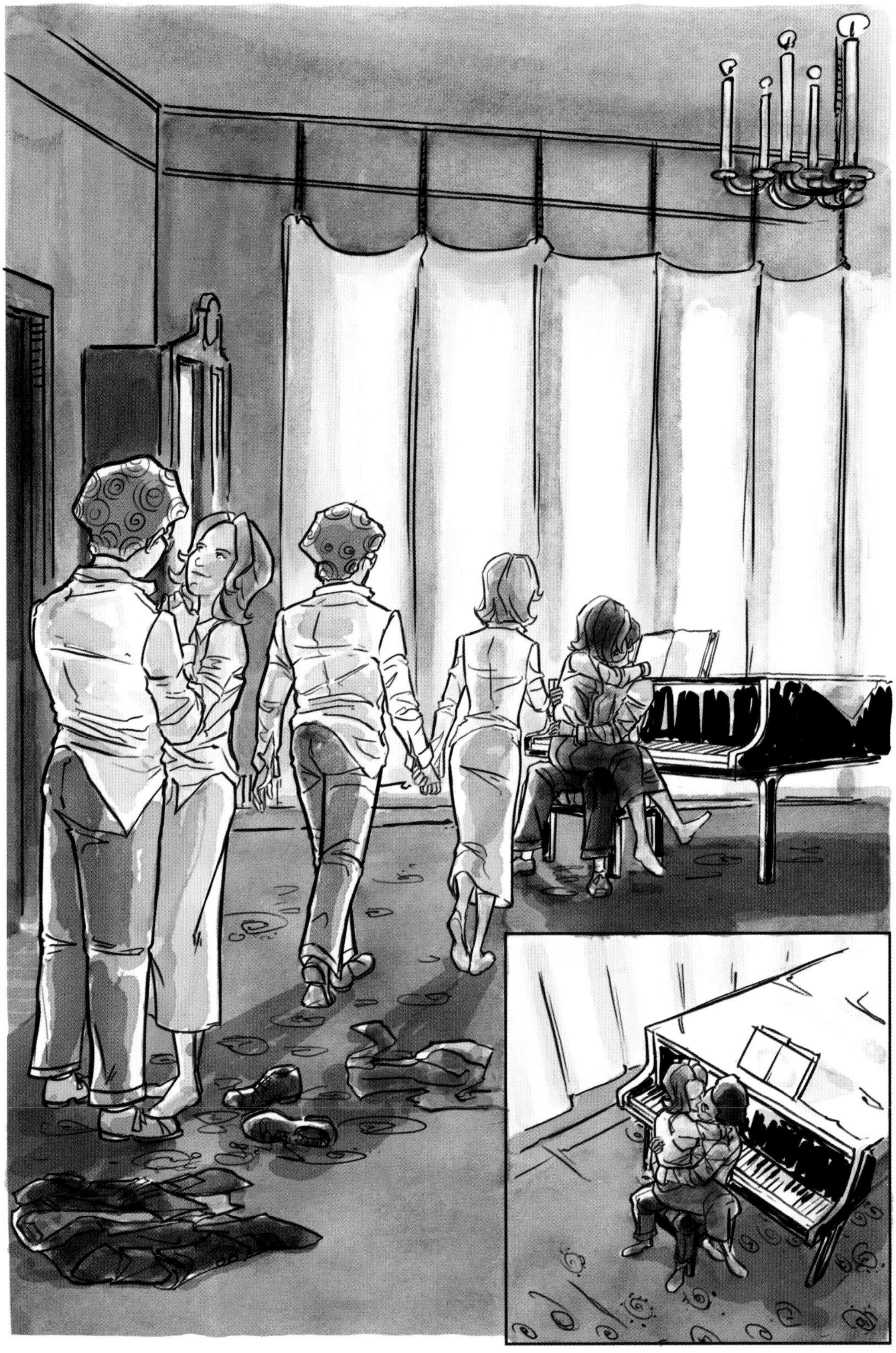

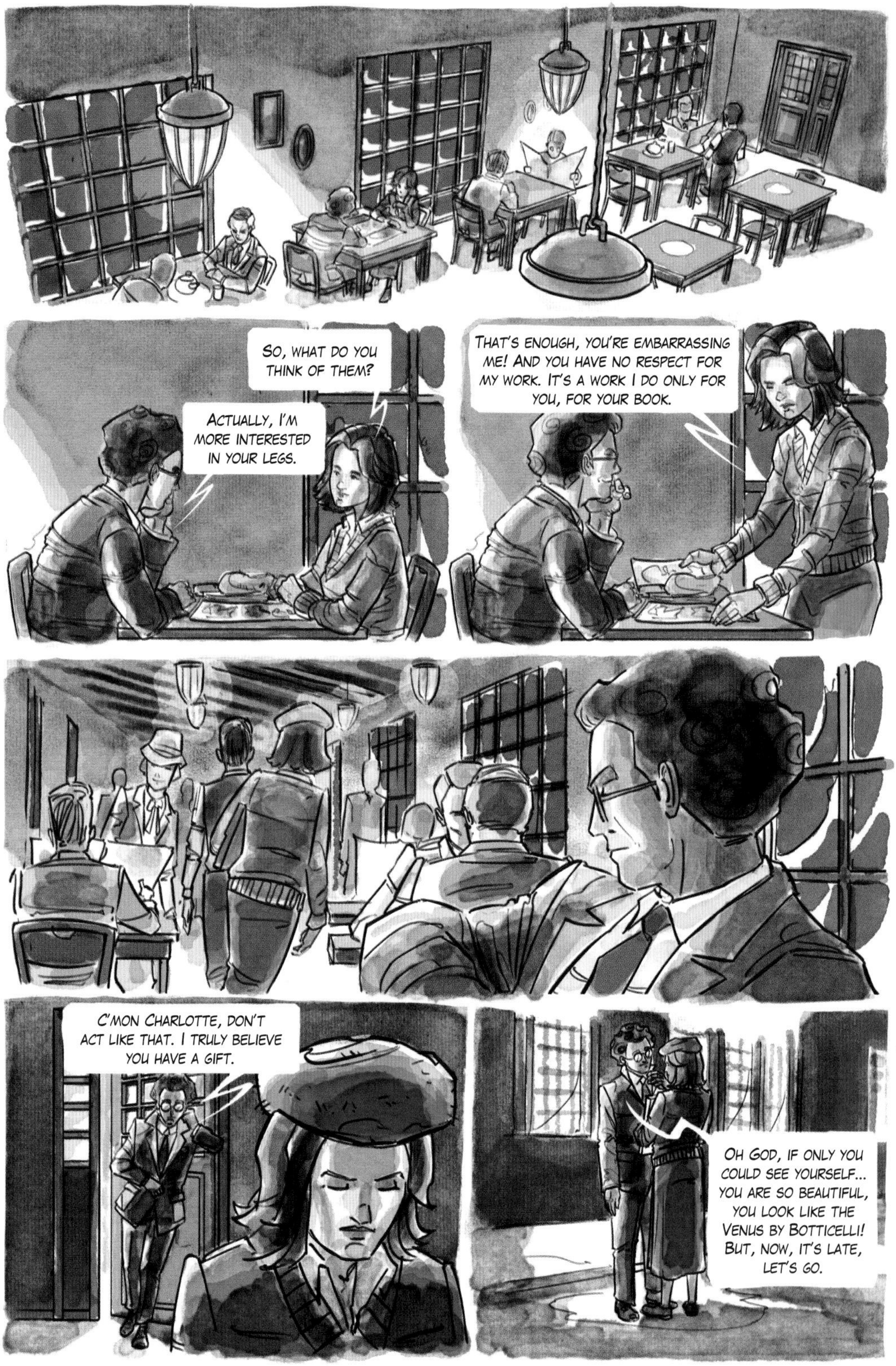
So, what do you think of them?
Actually, I'm more interested in your legs.
That's enough, you're embarrassing me! And you have no respect for my work. It's a work I do only for you, for your book.
C'mon Charlotte, don't act like that. I truly believe you have a gift.
Oh God, if only you could see yourself... you are so beautiful, you look like the Venus by Botticelli! But, now, it's late, let's go.

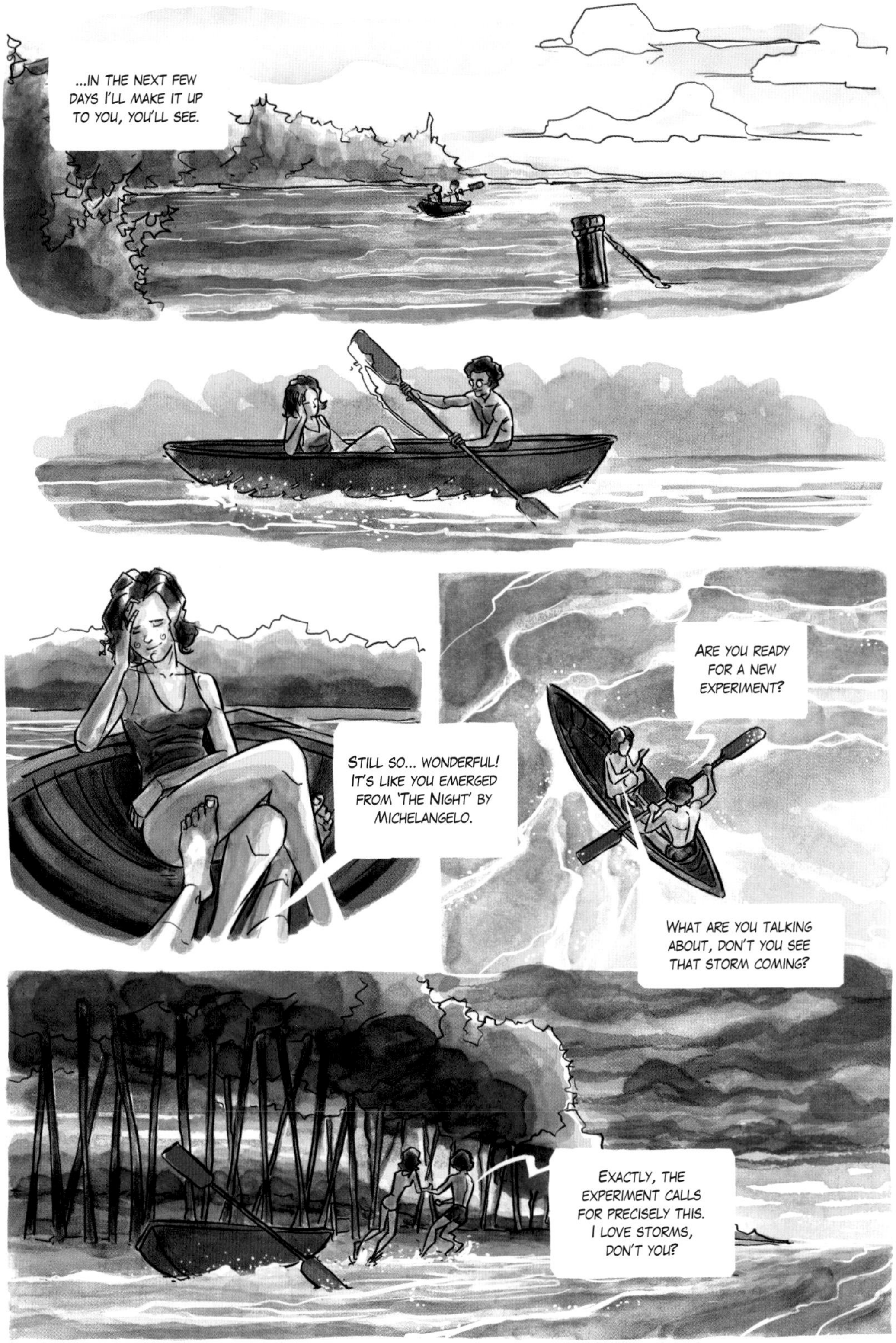
...IN THE NEXT FEW DAYS I'LL MAKE IT UP TO YOU, YOU'LL SEE.
STILL SO... WONDERFUL! IT'S LIKE YOU EMERGED FROM 'THE NIGHT' BY MICHELANGELO.
ARE YOU READY FOR A NEW EXPERIMENT?
WHAT ARE YOU TALKING ABOUT, DON'T YOU SEE THAT STORM COMING?
EXACTLY, THE EXPERIMENT CALLS FOR PRECISELY THIS. I LOVE STORMS, DON'T YOU?

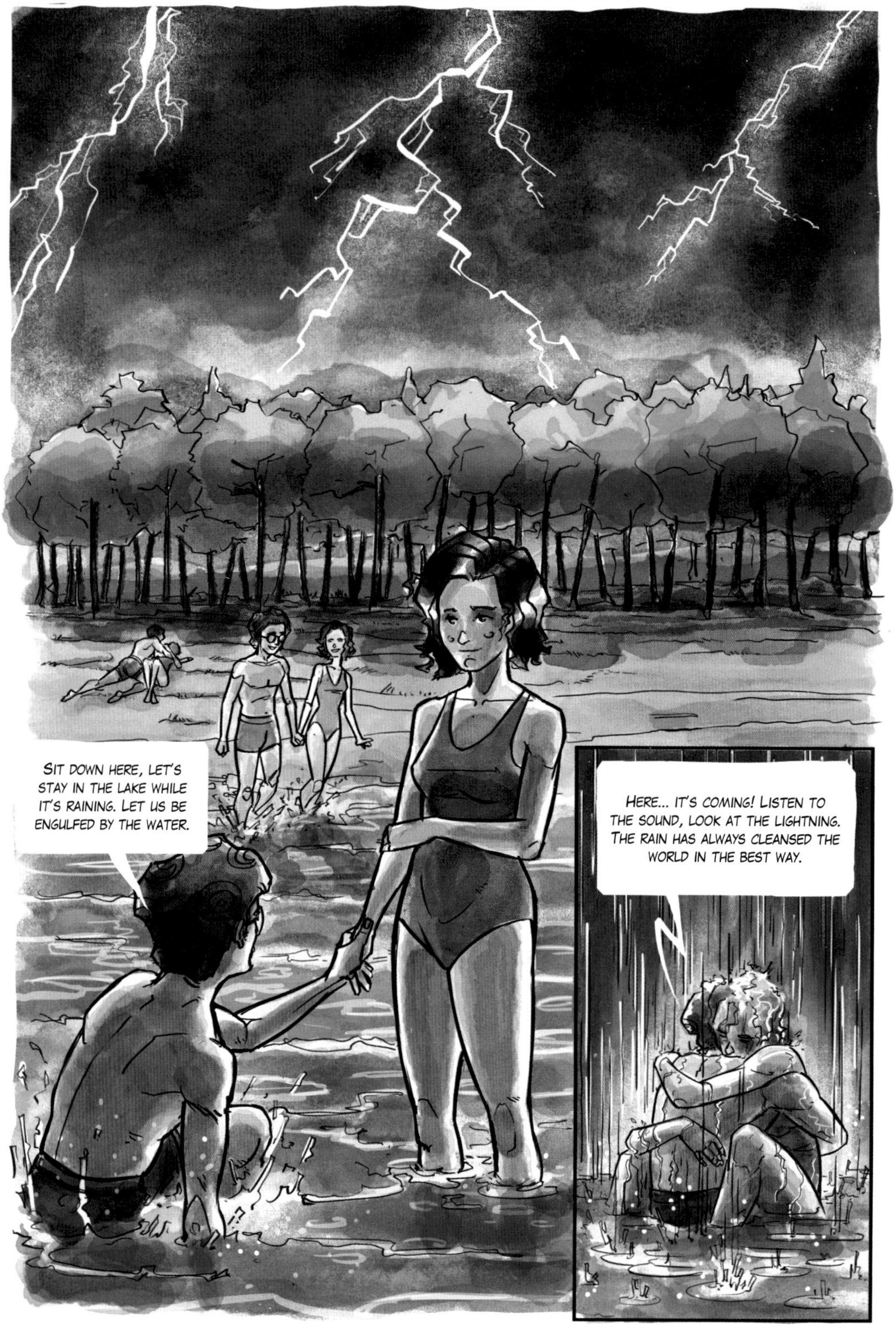
Sit down here, let's stay in the lake while it's raining. Let us be engulfed by the water.
Here... it's coming! Listen to the sound, look at the lightning. The rain has always cleansed the world in the best way.

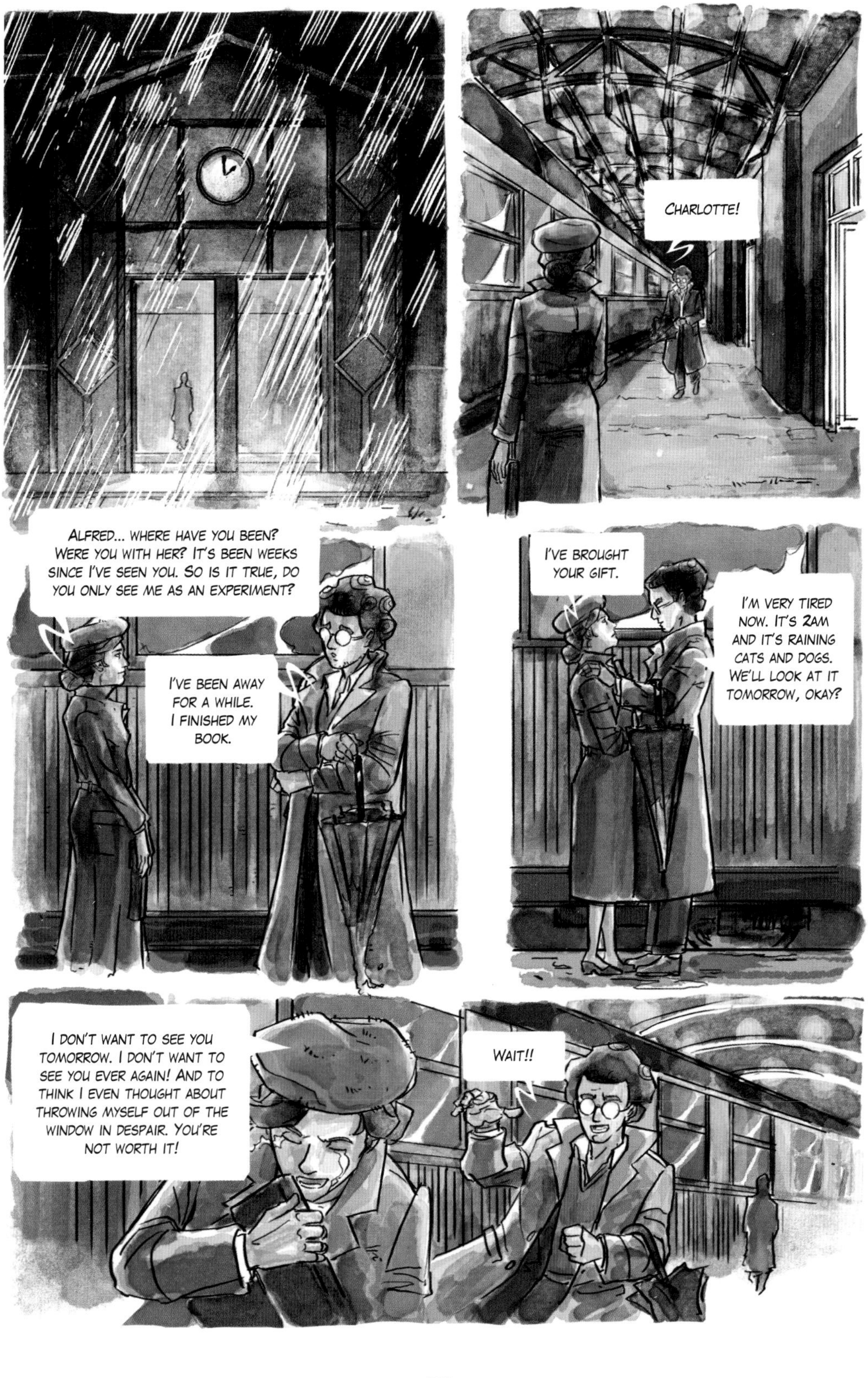
CHARLOTTE!
ALFRED... WHERE HAVE YOU BEEN? WERE YOU WITH HER? IT'S BEEN WEEKS SINCE I'VE SEEN YOU. SO IS IT TRUE, DO YOU ONLY SEE ME AS AN EXPERIMENT?
I'VE BEEN AWAY FOR A WHILE. I FINISHED MY BOOK.
I'VE BROUGHT YOUR GIFT.
I'M VERY TIRED NOW. IT'S 2AM AND IT'S RAINING CATS AND DOGS. WE'LL LOOK AT IT TOMORROW, OKAY?
I DON'T WANT TO SEE YOU TOMORROW. I DON'T WANT TO SEE YOU EVER AGAIN! AND TO THINK I EVEN THOUGHT ABOUT THROWING MYSELF OUT OF THE WINDOW IN DESPAIR. YOU'RE NOT WORTH IT!
WAIT!!

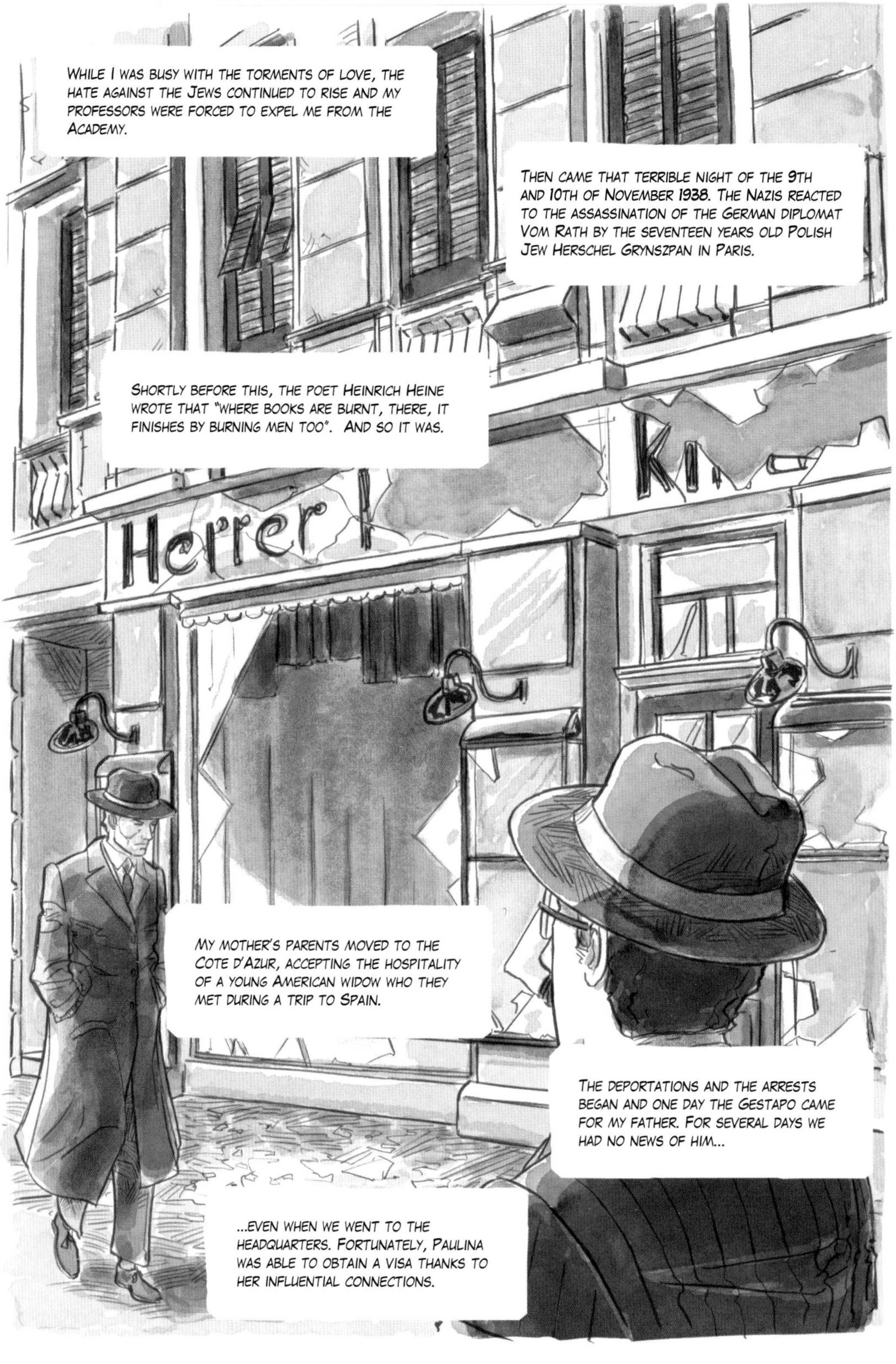
WHILE I WAS BUSY WITH THE TORMENTS OF LOVE, THE HATE AGAINST THE JEWS CONTINUED TO RISE AND MY PROFESSORS WERE FORCED TO EXPEL ME FROM THE ACADEMY.
THEN CAME THAT TERRIBLE NIGHT OF THE 9TH AND 10TH OF NOVEMBER 1938. THE NAZIS REACTED TO THE ASSASSINATION OF THE GERMAN DIPLOMAT VOM RATH BY THE SEVENTEEN YEARS OLD POLISH JEW HERSCHEL GRYNSZPAN IN PARIS.
SHORTLY BEFORE THIS, THE POET HEINRICH HEINE WROTE THAT "WHERE BOOKS ARE BURNT, THERE, IT FINISHES BY BURNING MEN TOO". AND SO IT WAS.
Herrer
MY MOTHER'S PARENTS MOVED TO THE COTE D'AZUR, ACCEPTING THE HOSPITALITY OF A YOUNG AMERICAN WIDOW WHO THEY MET DURING A TRIP TO SPAIN.
THE DEPORTATIONS AND THE ARRESTS BEGAN AND ONE DAY THE GESTAPO CAME FOR MY FATHER. FOR SEVERAL DAYS WE HAD NO NEWS OF HIM...
...EVEN WHEN WE WENT TO THE HEADQUARTERS. FORTUNATELY, PAULINA WAS ABLE TO OBTAIN A VISA THANKS TO HER INFLUENTIAL CONNECTIONS.

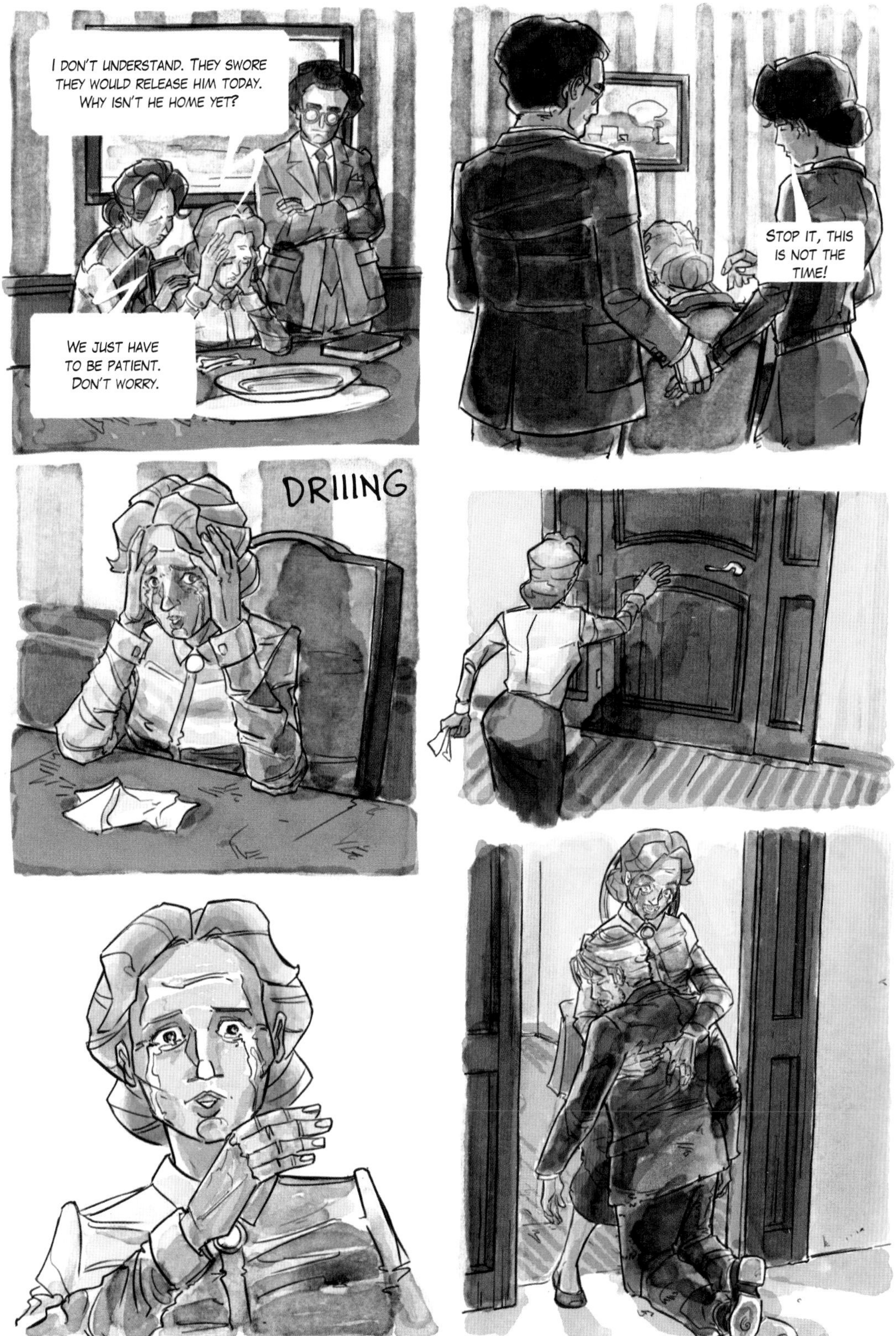
I DON'T UNDERSTAND. THEY SWORE THEY WOULD RELEASE HIM TODAY. WHY ISN'T HE HOME YET?
WE JUST HAVE TO BE PATIENT. DON'T WORRY.
STOP IT, THIS IS NOT THE TIME!
DRIIING

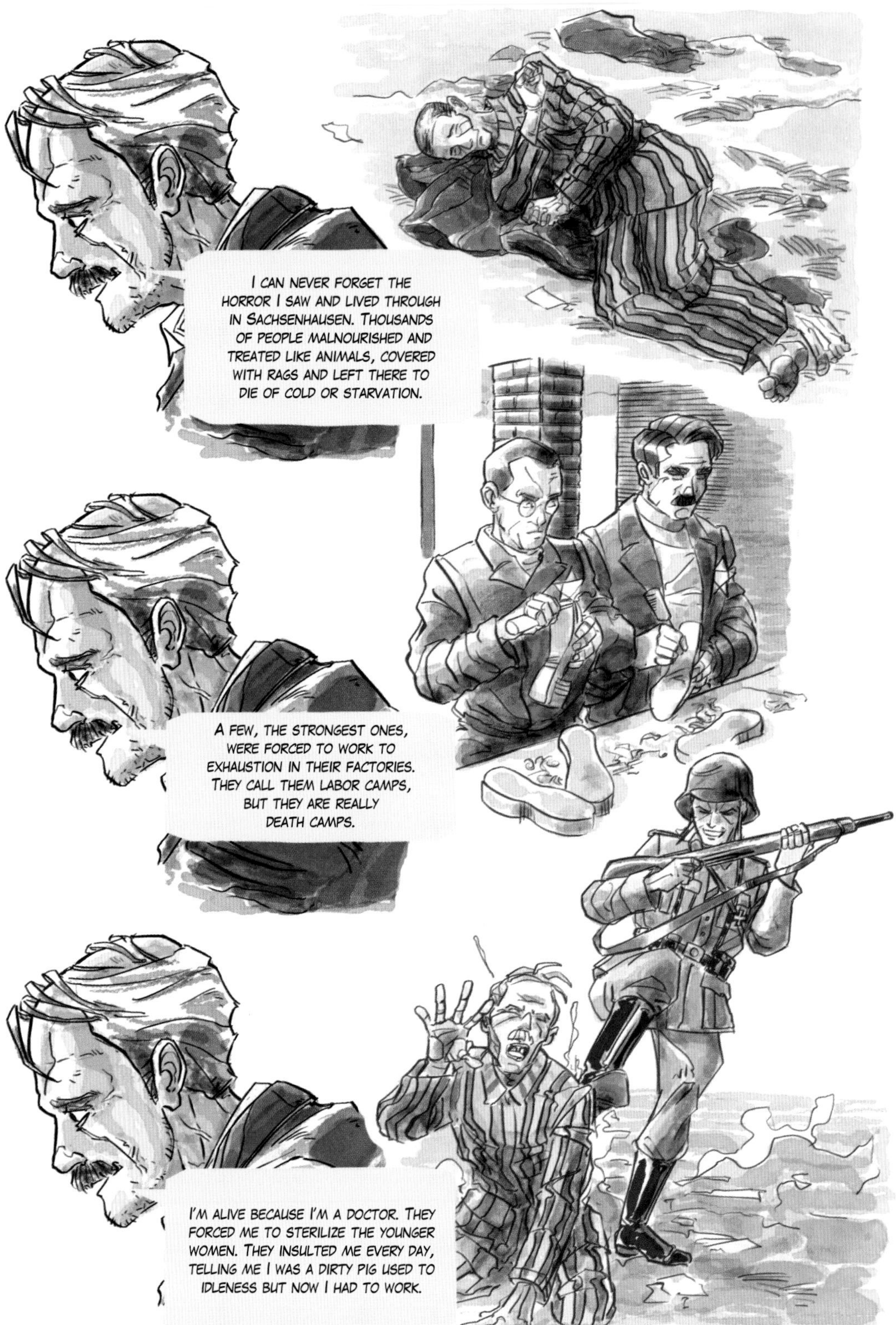
I CAN NEVER FORGET THE HORROR I SAW AND LIVED THROUGH IN SACHSENHAUSEN. THOUSANDS OF PEOPLE MALNOURISHED AND TREATED LIKE ANIMALS, COVERED WITH RAGS AND LEFT THERE TO DIE OF COLD OR STARVATION.
A FEW, THE STRONGEST ONES, WERE FORCED TO WORK TO EXHAUSTION IN THEIR FACTORIES. THEY CALL THEM LABOR CAMPS, BUT THEY ARE REALLY DEATH CAMPS.
I'M ALIVE BECAUSE I'M A DOCTOR. THEY FORCED ME TO STERILIZE THE YOUNGER WOMEN. THEY INSULTED ME EVERY DAY, TELLING ME I WAS A DIRTY PIG USED TO IDLENESS BUT NOW I HAD TO WORK.

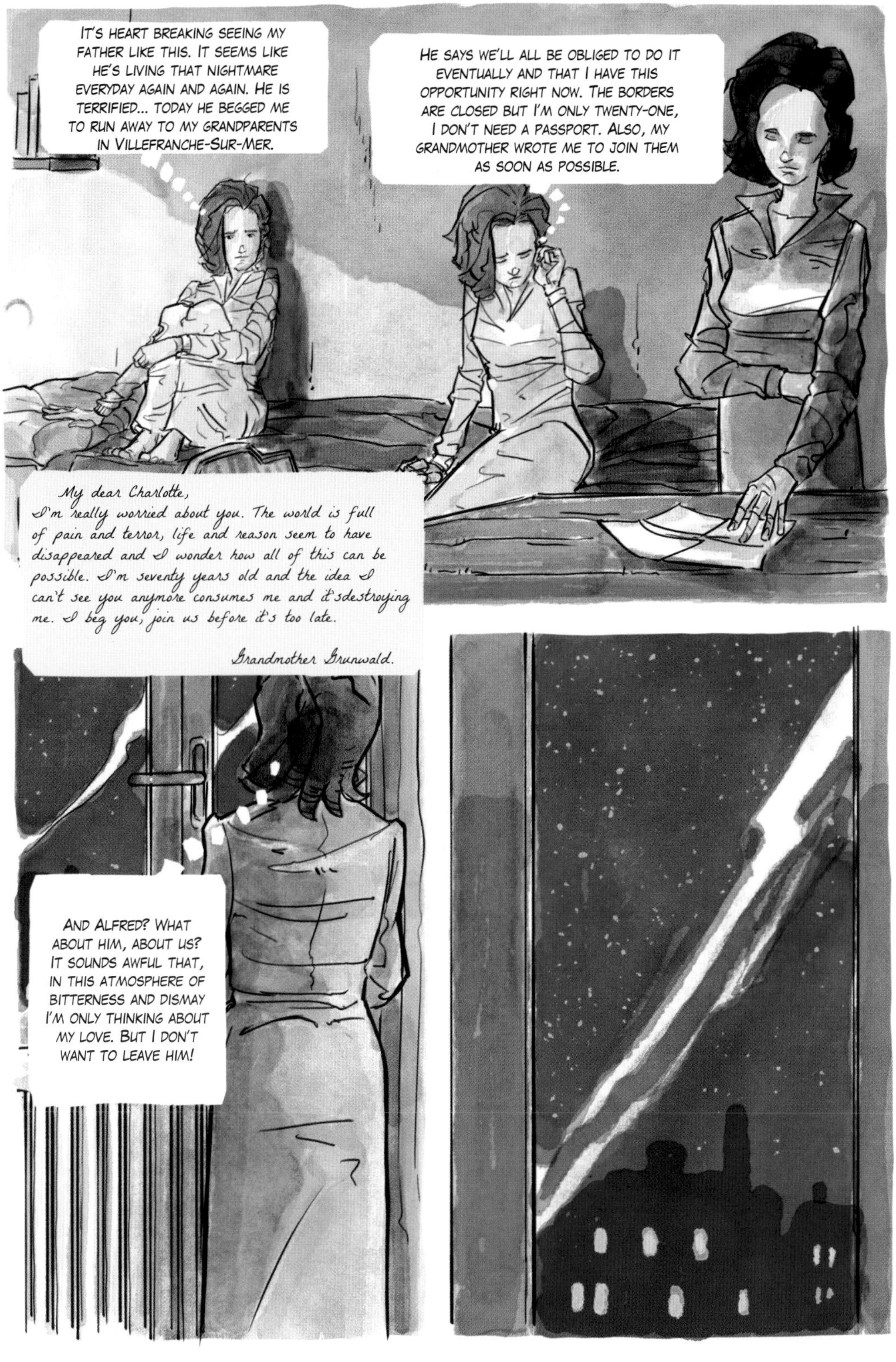
IT'S HEART BREAKING SEEING MY FATHER LIKE THIS. IT SEEMS LIKE HE'S LIVING THAT NIGHTMARE EVERYDAY AGAIN AND AGAIN. HE IS TERRIFIED... TODAY HE BEGGED ME TO RUN AWAY TO MY GRANDPARENTS IN VILLEFRANCHE-SUR-MER.
HE SAYS WE'LL ALL BE OBLIGED TO DO IT EVENTUALLY AND THAT I HAVE THIS OPPORTUNITY RIGHT NOW. THE BORDERS ARE CLOSED BUT I'M ONLY TWENTY-ONE, I DON'T NEED A PASSPORT. ALSO, MY GRANDMOTHER WROTE ME TO JOIN THEM AS SOON AS POSSIBLE.
My dear Charlotte,
I'm really worried about you. The world is full of pain and terror, life and reason seem to have disappeared and I wonder how all of this can be possible. I'm seventy years old and the idea I can't see you anymore consumes me and it'sdestroying me. I beg you, join us before it's too late.
Grandmother Grunwald.
AND ALFRED? WHAT ABOUT HIM, ABOUT US? IT SOUNDS AWFUL THAT, IN THIS ATMOSPHERE OF BITTERNESS AND DISMAY I'M ONLY THINKING ABOUT MY LOVE. BUT I DON'T WANT TO LEAVE HIM!

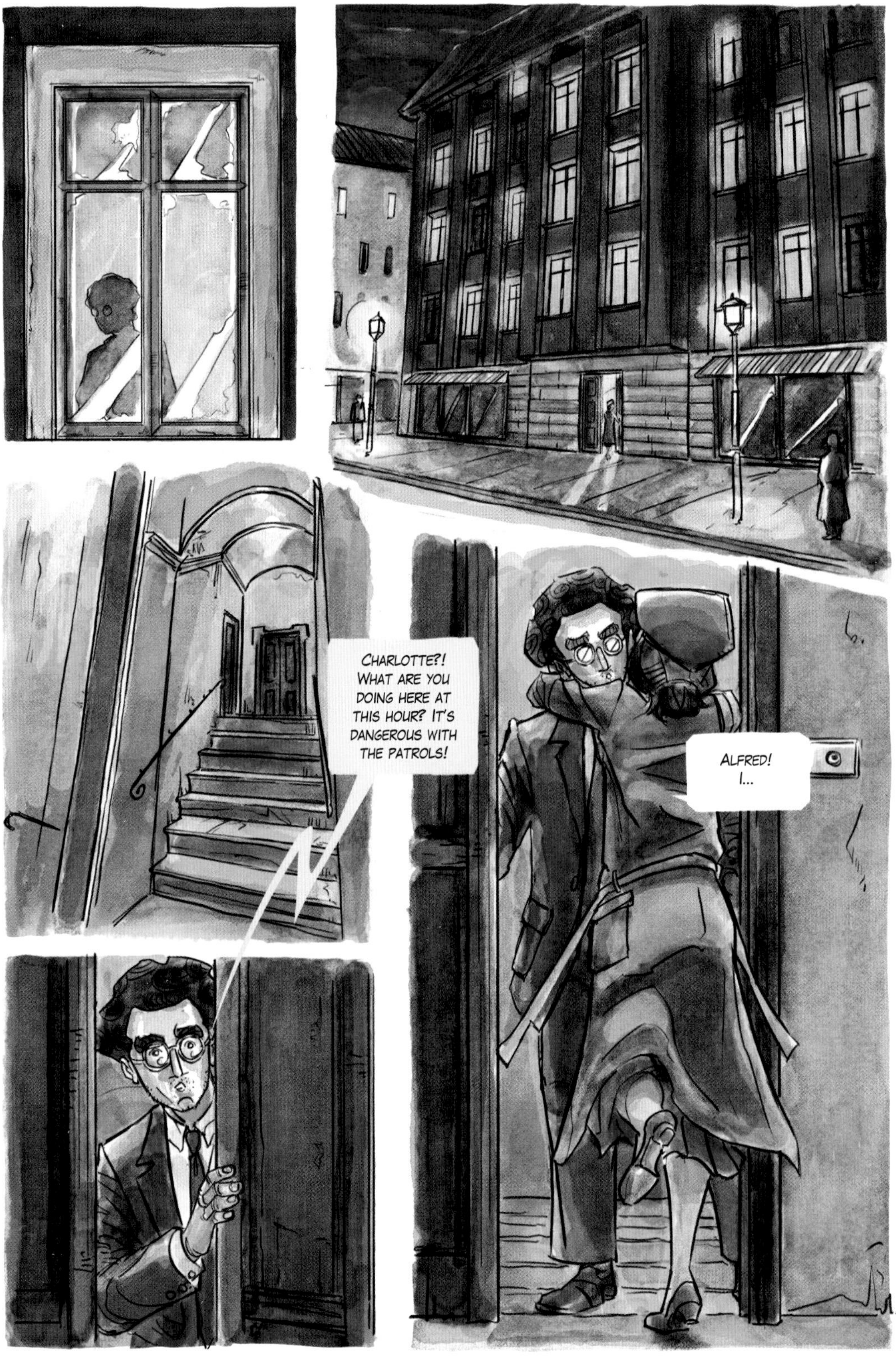
CHARLOTTE?! WHAT ARE YOU DOING HERE AT THIS HOUR? IT'S DANGEROUS WITH THE PATROLS!
ALFRED! I...

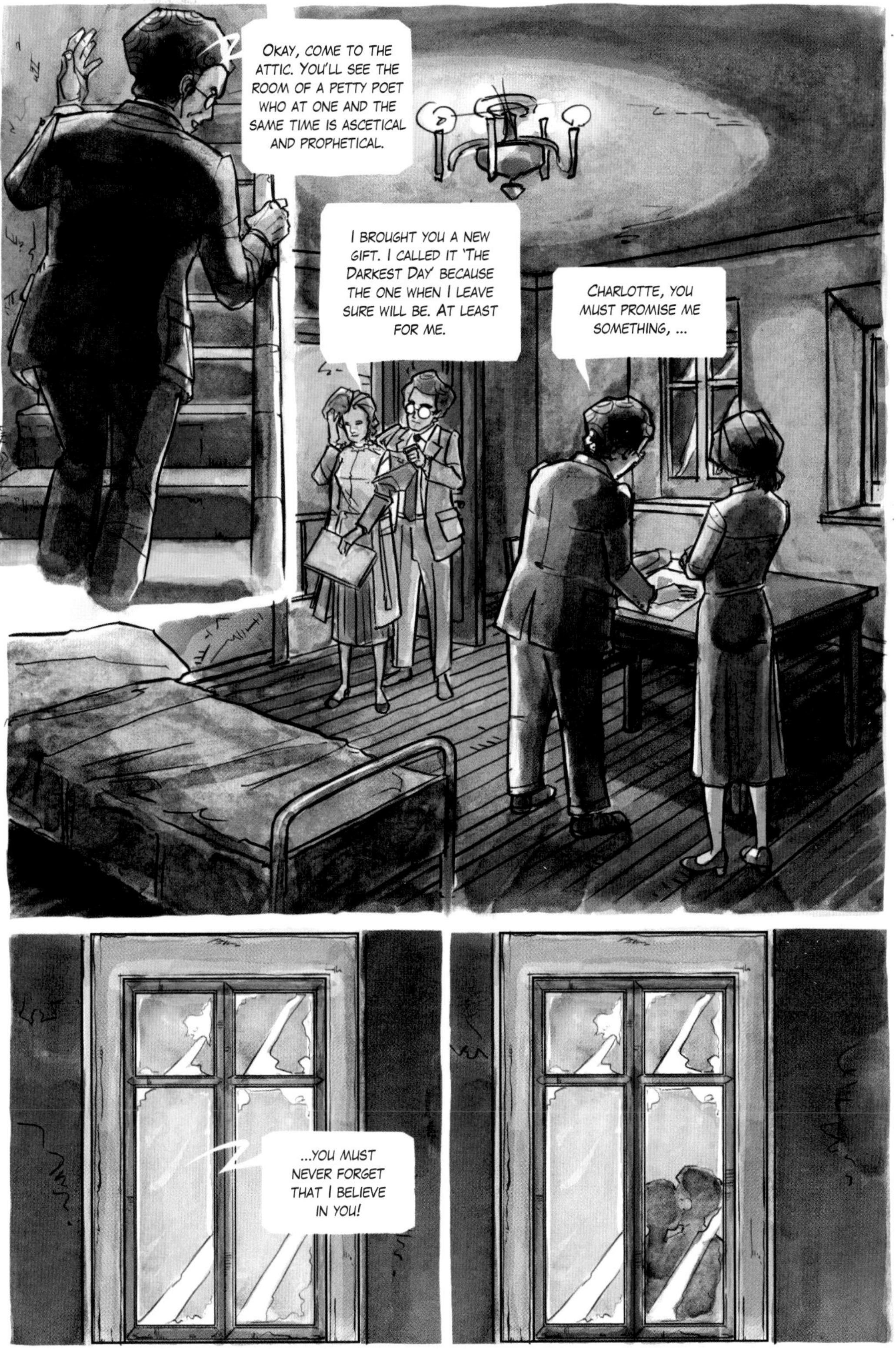
OKAY, COME TO THE ATTIC. YOU'LL SEE THE ROOM OF A PETTY POET WHO AT ONE AND THE SAME TIME IS ASCETICAL AND PROPHETICAL.
I BROUGHT YOU A NEW GIFT. I CALLED IT 'THE DARKEST DAY' BECAUSE THE ONE WHEN I LEAVE SURE WILL BE. AT LEAST FOR ME.
CHARLOTTE, YOU MUST PROMISE ME SOMETHING, ...
...YOU MUST NEVER FORGET THAT I BELIEVE IN YOU!

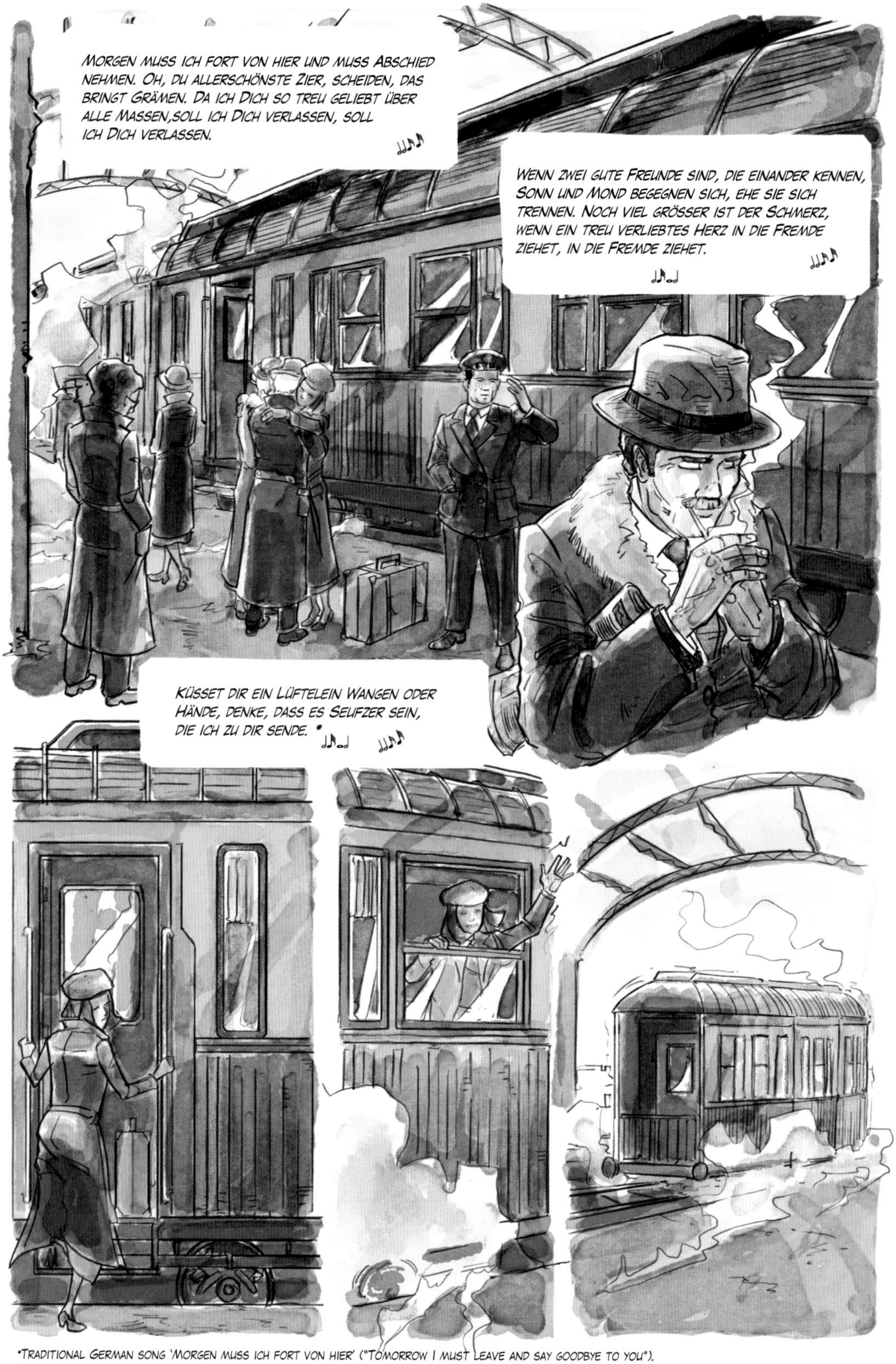
MORGEN MUSS ICH FORT VON HIER UND MUSS ABSCHIED NEHMEN. OH, DU ALLERSCHÖNSTE ZIER, SCHEIDEN, DAS BRINGT GRÄMEN. DA ICH DICH SO TREU GELIEBT ÜBER ALLE MASSEN,SOLL ICH DICH VERLASSEN, SOLL ICH DICH VERLASSEN.
WENN ZWEI GUTE FREUNDE SIND, DIE EINANDER KENNEN, SONN UND MOND BEGEGNEN SICH, EHE SIE SICH TRENNEN. NOCH VIEL GRÖSSER IST DER SCHMERZ, WENN EIN TREU VERLIEBTES HERZ IN DIE FREMDE ZIEHET, IN DIE FREMDE ZIEHET.
KÜSSET DIR EIN LÜFTELEIN WANGEN ODER HÄNDE, DENKE, DASS ES SEUFZER SEIN, DIE ICH ZU DIR SENDE. *

*TRADITIONAL GERMAN SONG 'MORGEN MUSS ICH FORT VON HIER' ("TOMORROW I MUST LEAVE AND SAY GOODBYE TO YOU").

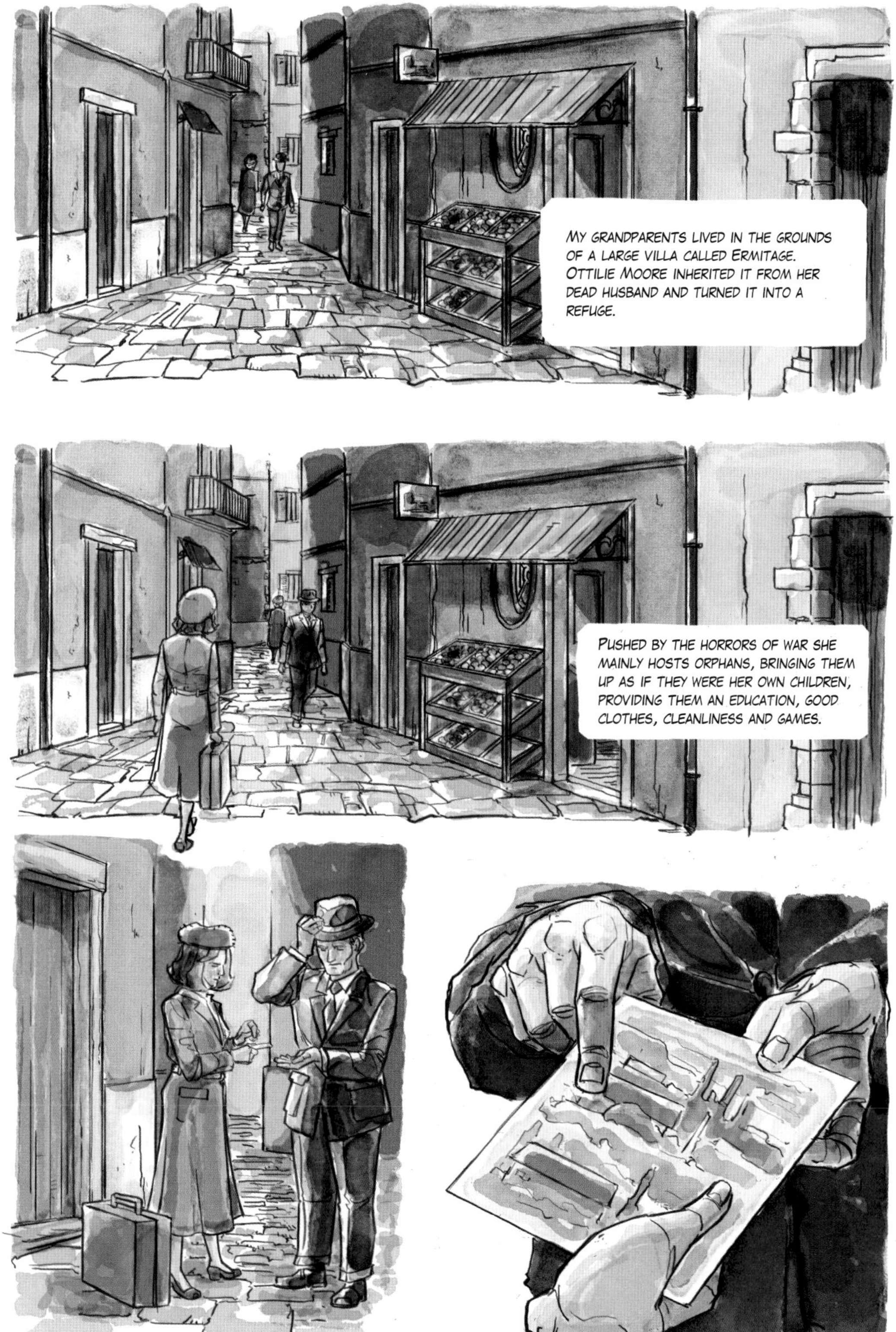
MY GRANDPARENTS LIVED IN THE GROUNDS OF A LARGE VILLA CALLED ERMITAGE. OTTILIE MOORE INHERITED IT FROM HER DEAD HUSBAND AND TURNED IT INTO A REFUGE.
PUSHED BY THE HORRORS OF WAR SHE MAINLY HOSTS ORPHANS, BRINGING THEM UP AS IF THEY WERE HER OWN CHILDREN, PROVIDING THEM AN EDUCATION, GOOD CLOTHES, CLEANLINESS AND GAMES.

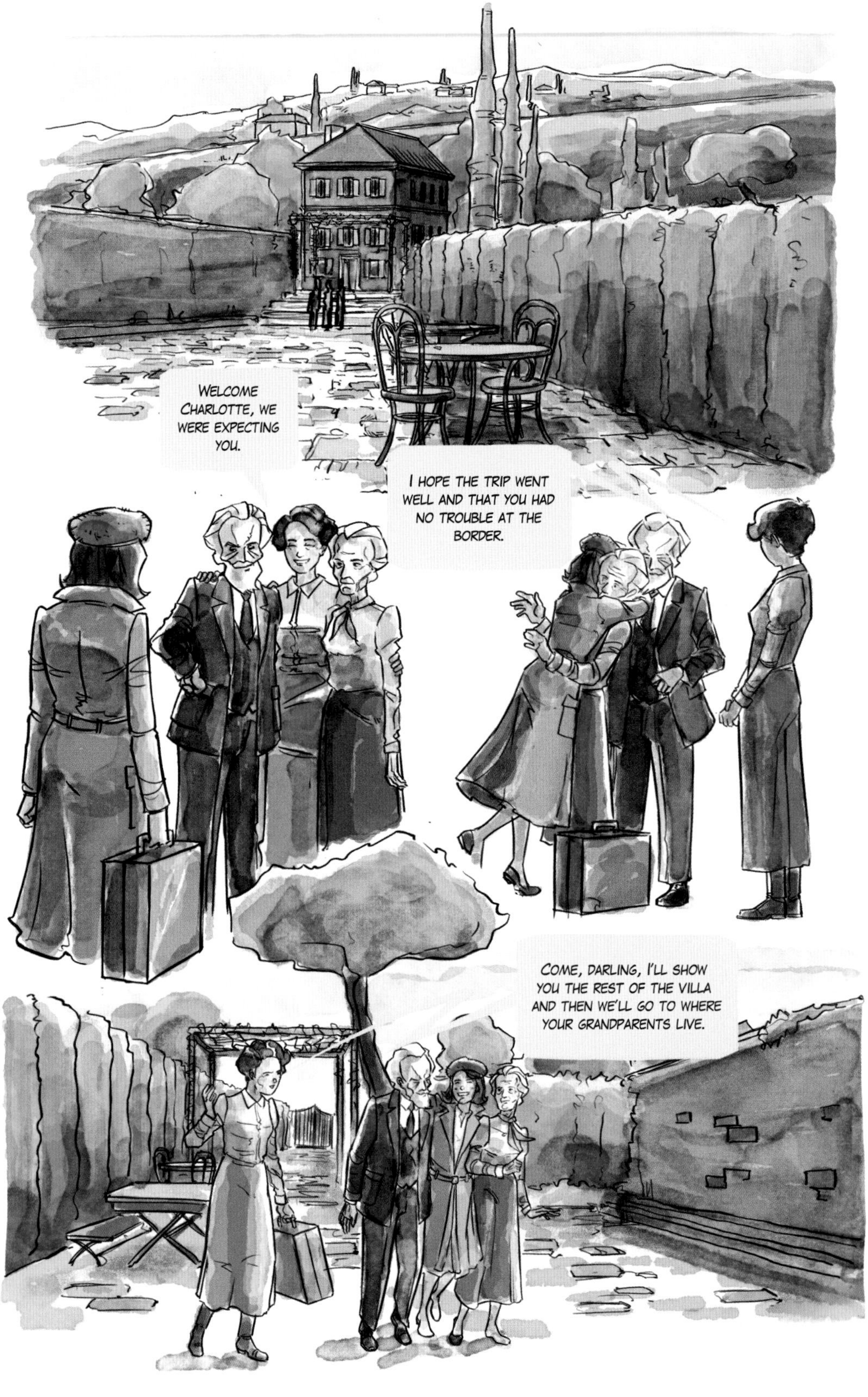
WELCOME CHARLOTTE, WE WERE EXPECTING YOU.
I HOPE THE TRIP WENT WELL AND THAT YOU HAD NO TROUBLE AT THE BORDER.
COME, DARLING, I'LL SHOW YOU THE REST OF THE VILLA AND THEN WE'LL GO TO WHERE YOUR GRANDPARENTS LIVE.

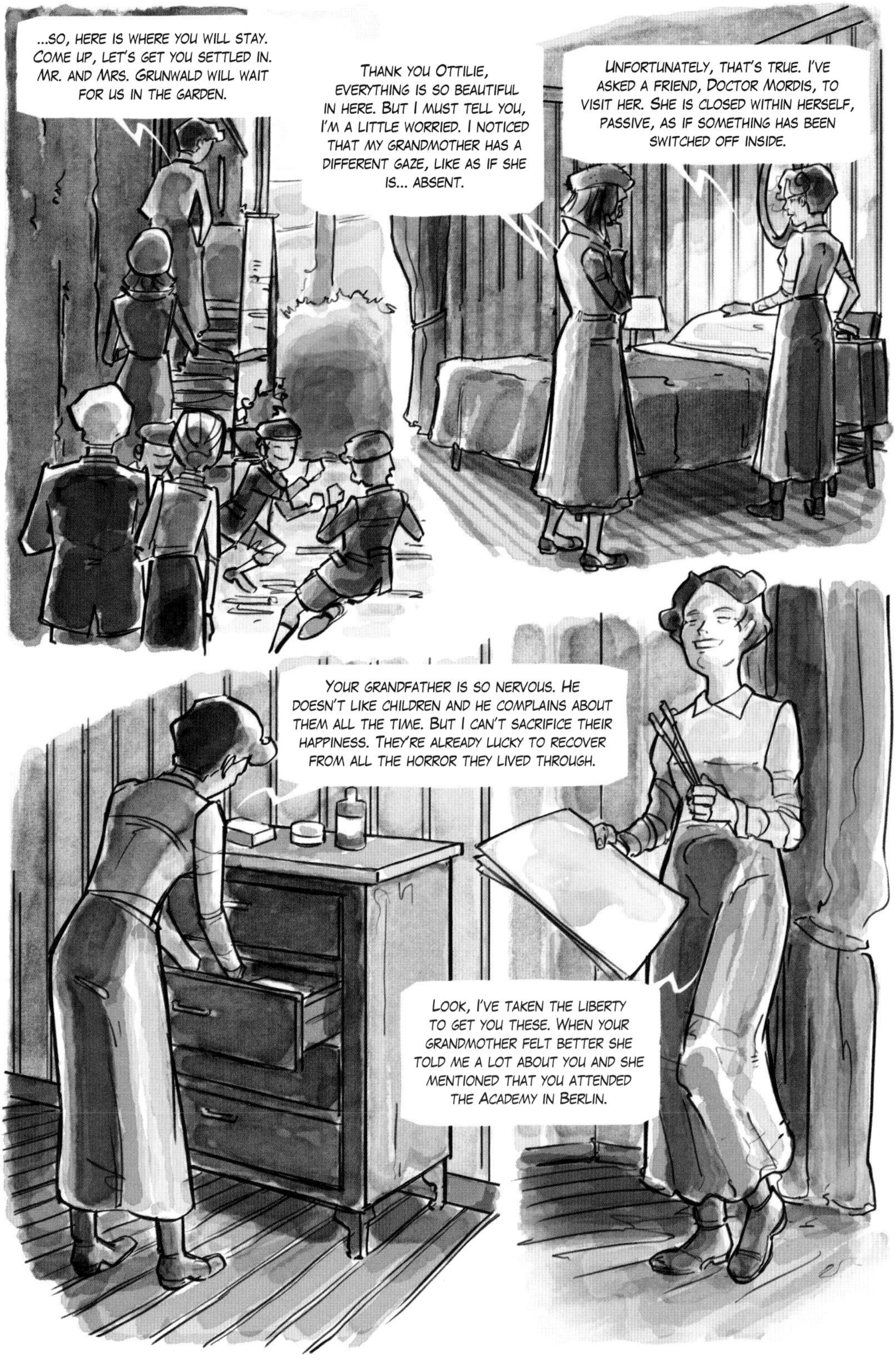
...SO, HERE IS WHERE YOU WILL STAY. COME UP, LET'S GET YOU SETTLED IN. MR. AND MRS. GRUNWALD WILL WAIT FOR US IN THE GARDEN.
THANK YOU OTTILIE, EVERYTHING IS SO BEAUTIFUL IN HERE. BUT I MUST TELL YOU, I'M A LITTLE WORRIED. I NOTICED THAT MY GRANDMOTHER HAS A DIFFERENT GAZE, LIKE AS IF SHE IS... ABSENT.
UNFORTUNATELY, THAT'S TRUE. I'VE ASKED A FRIEND, DOCTOR MORDIS, TO VISIT HER. SHE IS CLOSED WITHIN HERSELF, PASSIVE, AS IF SOMETHING HAS BEEN SWITCHED OFF INSIDE.
YOUR GRANDFATHER IS SO NERVOUS. HE DOESN'T LIKE CHILDREN AND HE COMPLAINS ABOUT THEM ALL THE TIME. BUT I CAN'T SACRIFICE THEIR HAPPINESS. THEY'RE ALREADY LUCKY TO RECOVER FROM ALL THE HORROR THEY LIVED THROUGH.
LOOK, I'VE TAKEN THE LIBERTY TO GET YOU THESE. WHEN YOUR GRANDMOTHER FELT BETTER SHE TOLD ME A LOT ABOUT YOU AND SHE MENTIONED THAT YOU ATTENDED THE ACADEMY IN BERLIN.

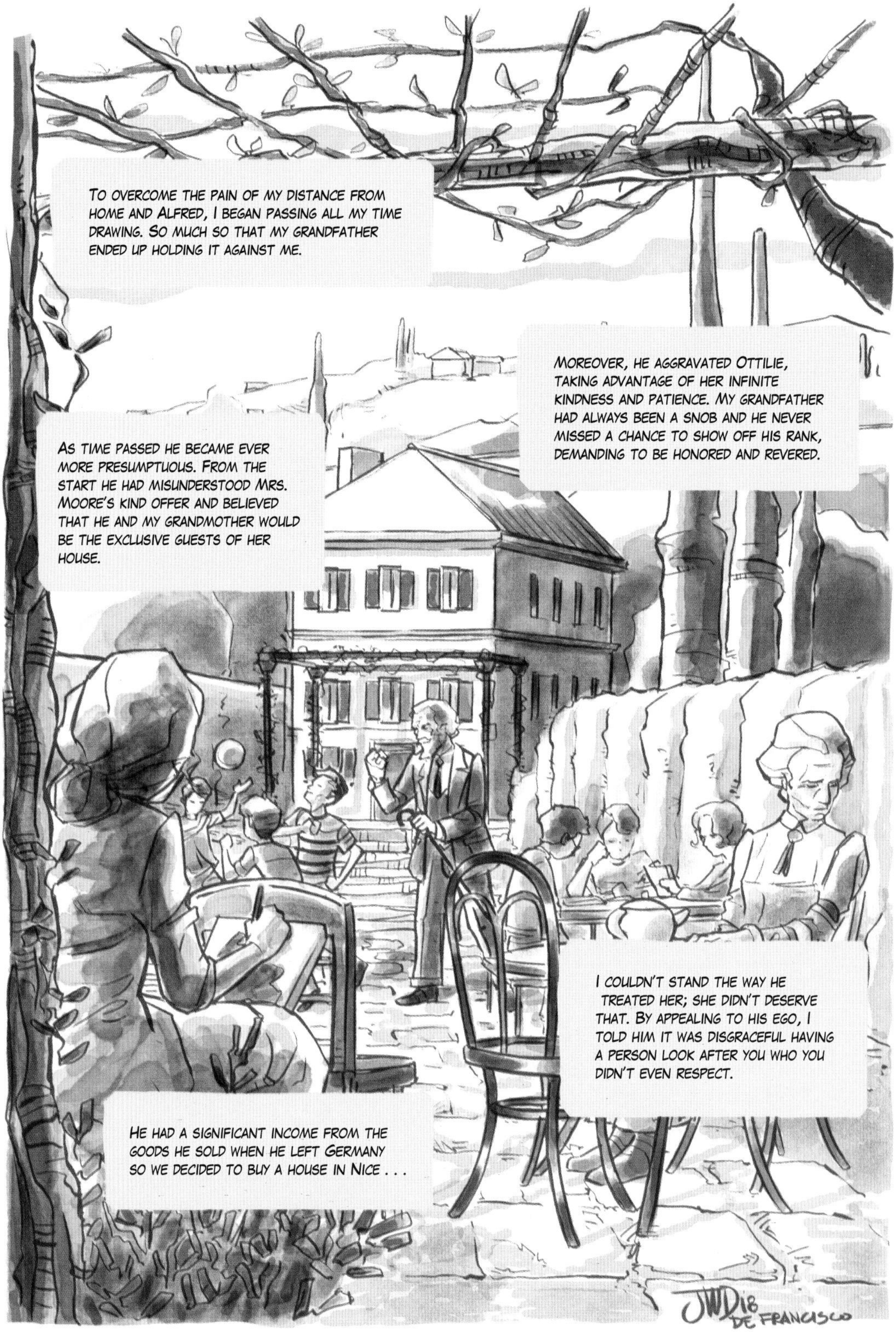
To overcome the pain of my distance from home and Alfred, I began passing all my time drawing. So much so that my grandfather ended up holding it against me.
As time passed he became ever more presumptuous. From the start he had misunderstood Mrs. Moore's kind offer and believed that he and my grandmother would be the exclusive guests of her house.
Moreover, he aggravated Ottilie, taking advantage of her infinite kindness and patience. My grandfather had always been a snob and he never missed a chance to show off his rank, demanding to be honored and revered.
I couldn't stand the way he treated her; she didn't deserve that. By appealing to his ego, I told him it was disgraceful having a person look after you who you didn't even respect.
He had a significant income from the goods he sold when he left Germany so we decided to buy a house in Nice . . .
JWD18
De Francisco

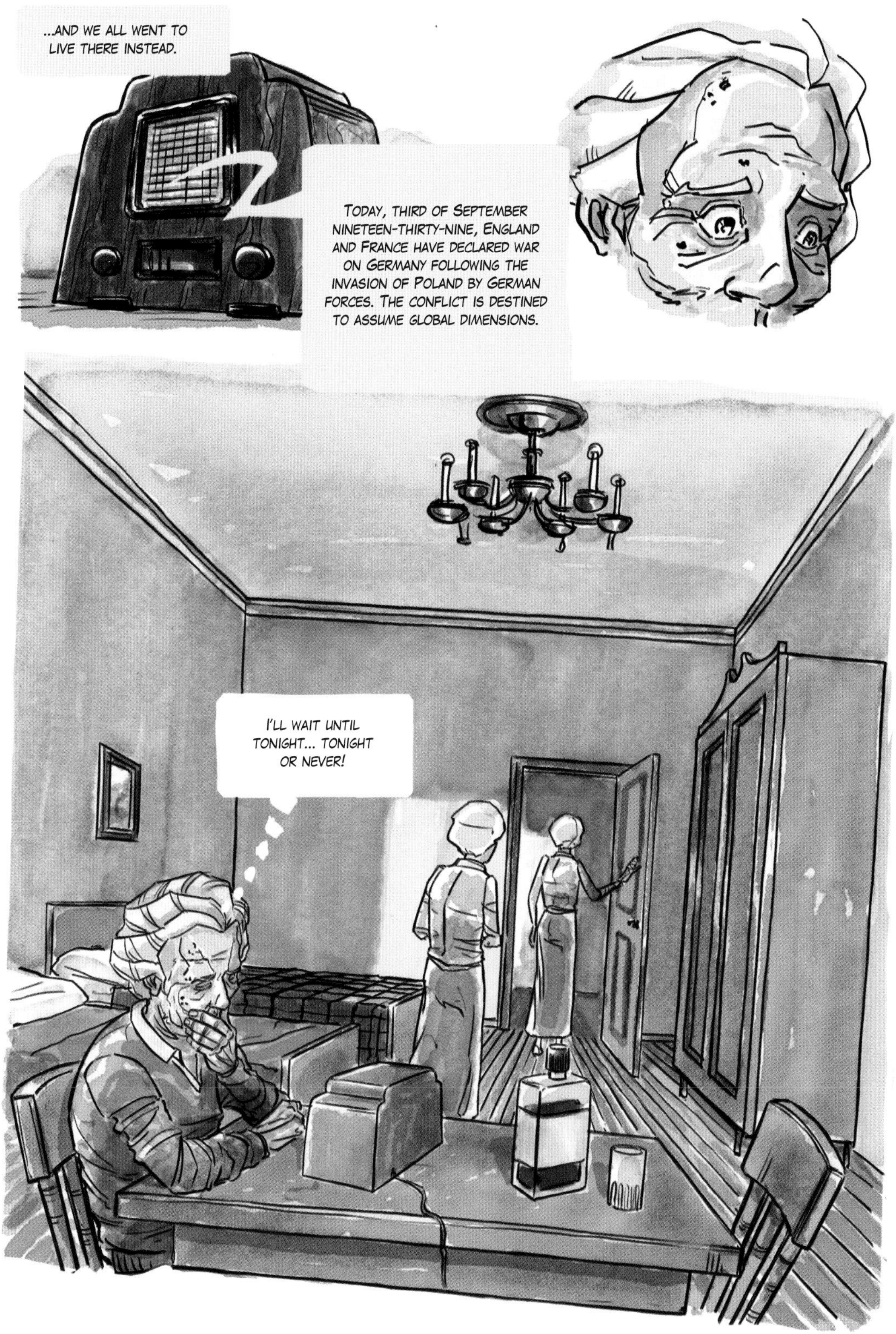
...AND WE ALL WENT TO LIVE THERE INSTEAD.
TODAY, THIRD OF SEPTEMBER NINETEEN-THIRTY-NINE, ENGLAND AND FRANCE HAVE DECLARED WAR ON GERMANY FOLLOWING THE INVASION OF POLAND BY GERMAN FORCES. THE CONFLICT IS DESTINED TO ASSUME GLOBAL DIMENSIONS.
I'LL WAIT UNTIL TONIGHT... TONIGHT OR NEVER!

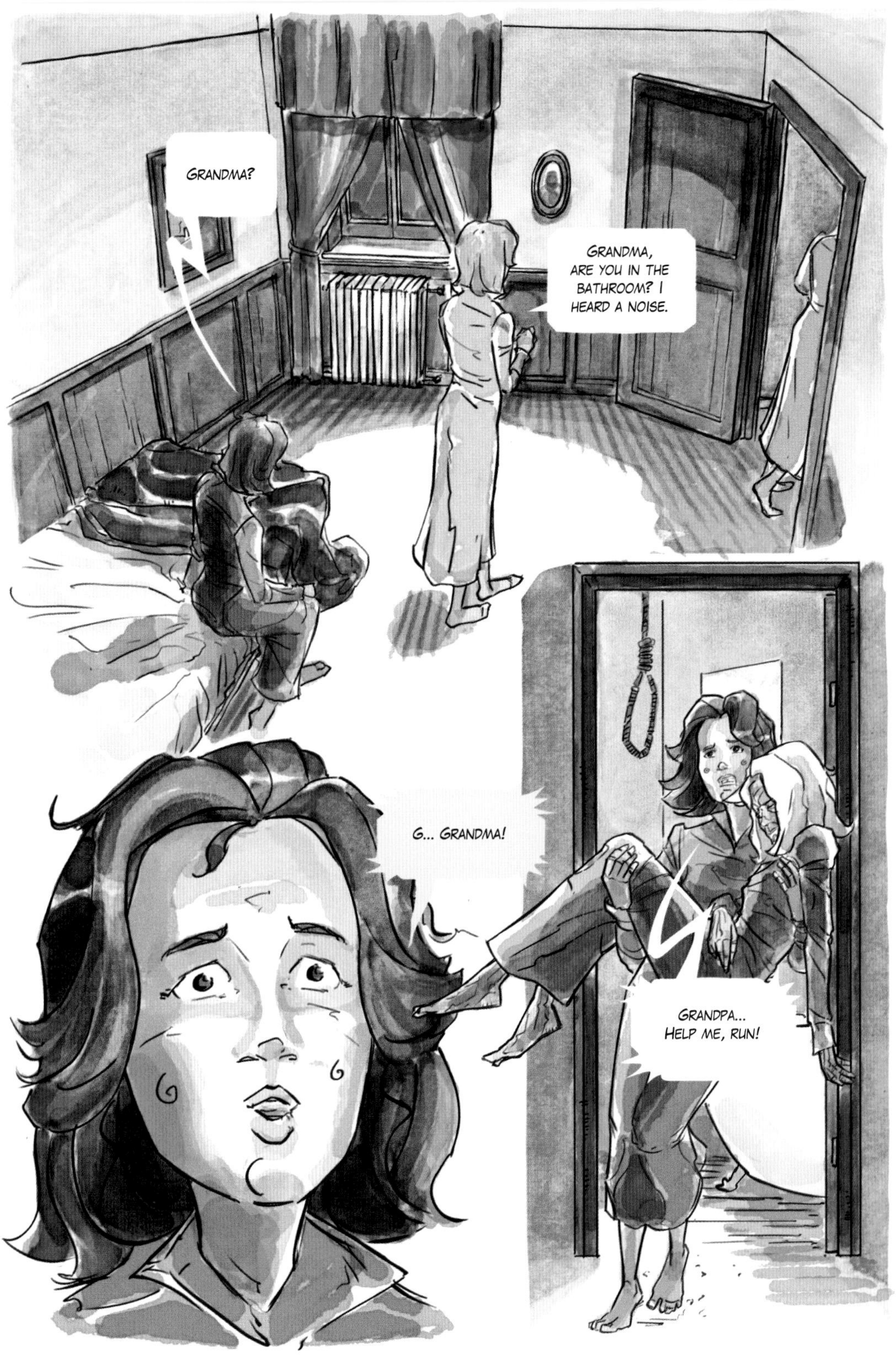
GRANDMA?
GRANDMA, ARE YOU IN THE BATHROOM? I HEARD A NOISE.
G... GRANDMA!
GRANDPA... HELP ME, RUN!

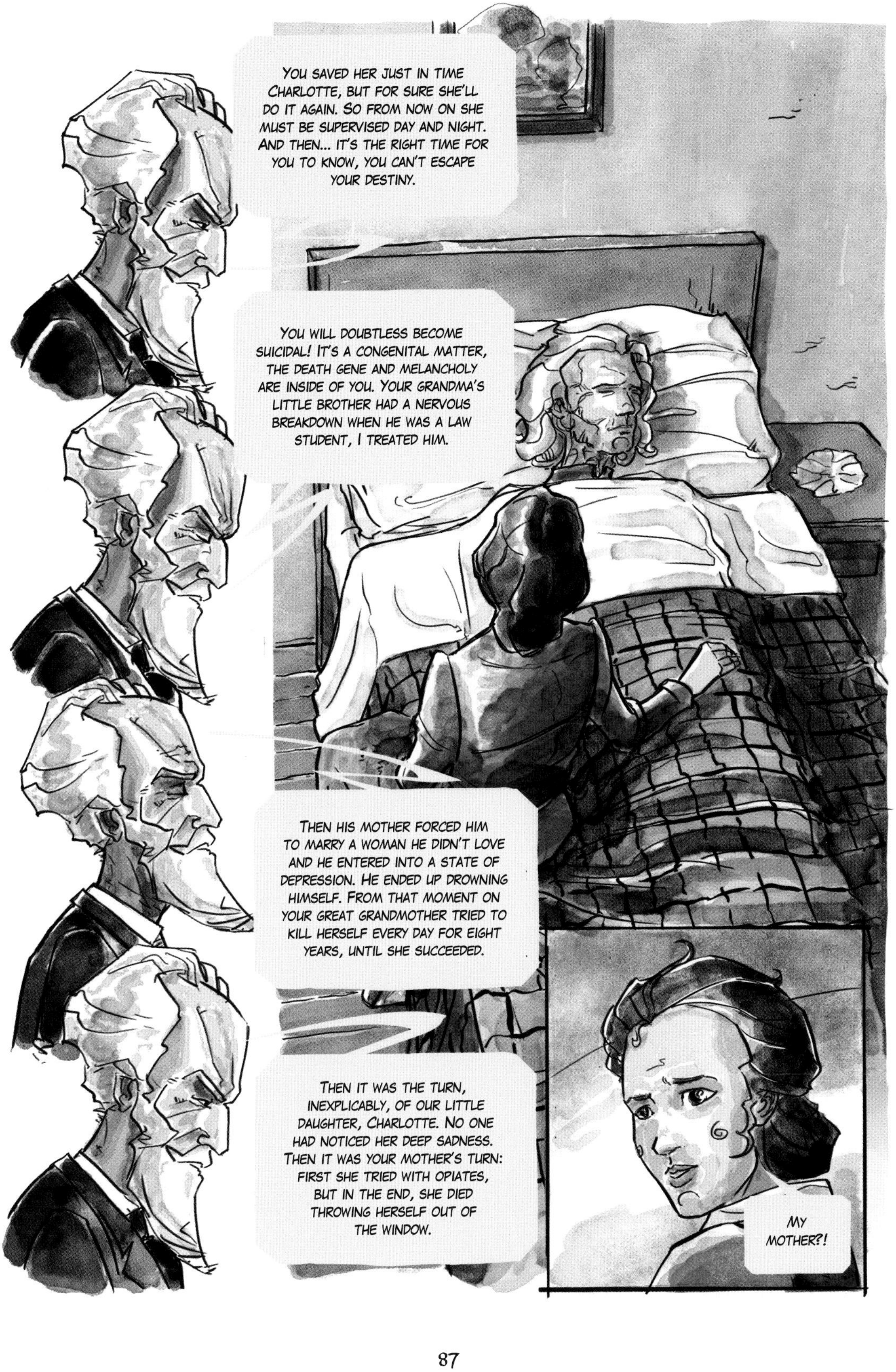

YOU SAVED HER JUST IN TIME CHARLOTTE, BUT FOR SURE SHE'LL DO IT AGAIN. SO FROM NOW ON SHE MUST BE SUPERVISED DAY AND NIGHT. AND THEN... IT'S THE RIGHT TIME FOR YOU TO KNOW, YOU CAN'T ESCAPE YOUR DESTINY.
YOU WILL DOUBTLESS BECOME SUICIDAL! IT'S A CONGENITAL MATTER, THE DEATH GENE AND MELANCHOLY ARE INSIDE OF YOU. YOUR GRANDMA'S LITTLE BROTHER HAD A NERVOUS BREAKDOWN WHEN HE WAS A LAW STUDENT, I TREATED HIM.
THEN HIS MOTHER FORCED HIM TO MARRY A WOMAN HE DIDN'T LOVE AND HE ENTERED INTO A STATE OF DEPRESSION. HE ENDED UP DROWNING HIMSELF. FROM THAT MOMENT ON YOUR GREAT GRANDMOTHER TRIED TO KILL HERSELF EVERY DAY FOR EIGHT YEARS, UNTIL SHE SUCCEEDED.
THEN IT WAS THE TURN, INEXPLICABLY, OF OUR LITTLE DAUGHTER, CHARLOTTE. NO ONE HAD NOTICED HER DEEP SADNESS. THEN IT WAS YOUR MOTHER'S TURN: FIRST SHE TRIED WITH OPIATES, BUT IN THE END, SHE DIED THROWING HERSELF OUT OF THE WINDOW.
MY MOTHER?!

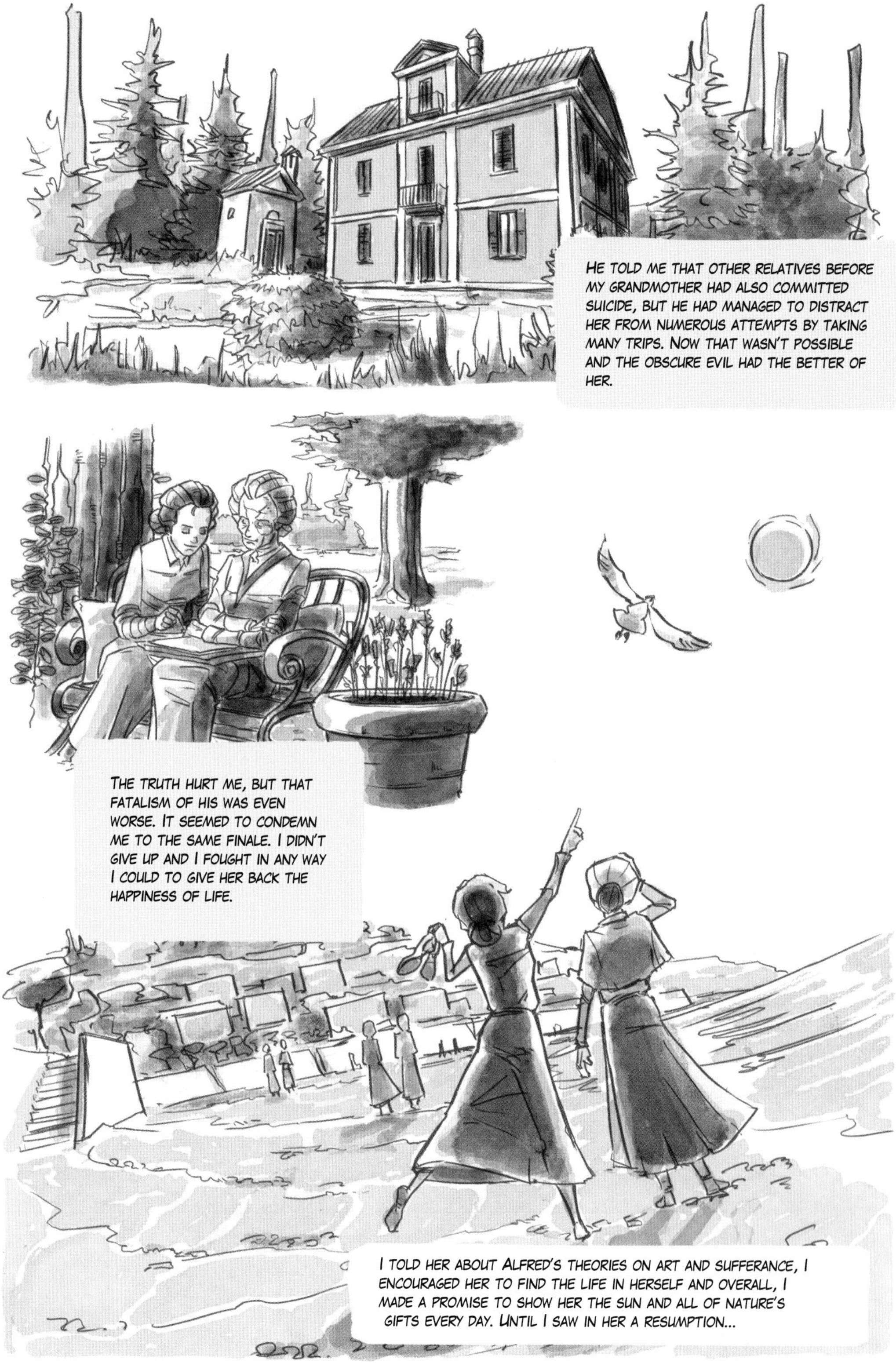
HE TOLD ME THAT OTHER RELATIVES BEFORE MY GRANDMOTHER HAD ALSO COMMITTED SUICIDE, BUT HE HAD MANAGED TO DISTRACT HER FROM NUMEROUS ATTEMPTS BY TAKING MANY TRIPS. NOW THAT WASN'T POSSIBLE AND THE OBSCURE EVIL HAD THE BETTER OF HER.
THE TRUTH HURT ME, BUT THAT FATALISM OF HIS WAS EVEN WORSE. IT SEEMED TO CONDEMN ME TO THE SAME FINALE. I DIDN'T GIVE UP AND I FOUGHT IN ANY WAY I COULD TO GIVE HER BACK THE HAPPINESS OF LIFE.
I TOLD HER ABOUT ALFRED'S THEORIES ON ART AND SUFFERANCE, I ENCOURAGED HER TO FIND THE LIFE IN HERSELF AND OVERALL, I MADE A PROMISE TO SHOW HER THE SUN AND ALL OF NATURE'S GIFTS EVERY DAY. UNTIL I SAW IN HER A RESUMPTION...

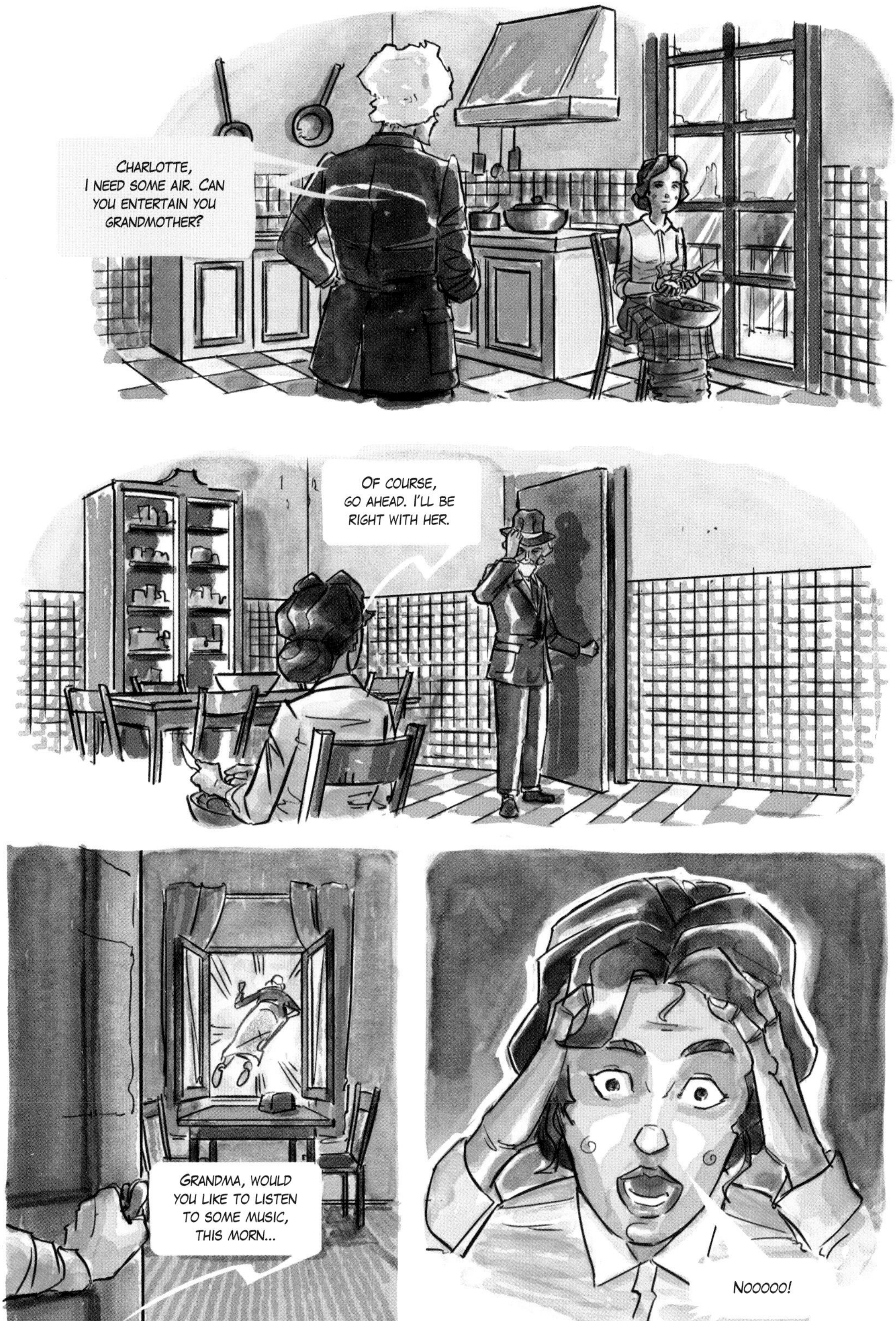
CHARLOTTE, I NEED SOME AIR. CAN YOU ENTERTAIN YOU GRANDMOTHER?
OF COURSE, GO AHEAD. I'LL BE RIGHT WITH HER.
GRANDMA, WOULD YOU LIKE TO LISTEN TO SOME MUSIC, THIS MORN...
NOOOOO!

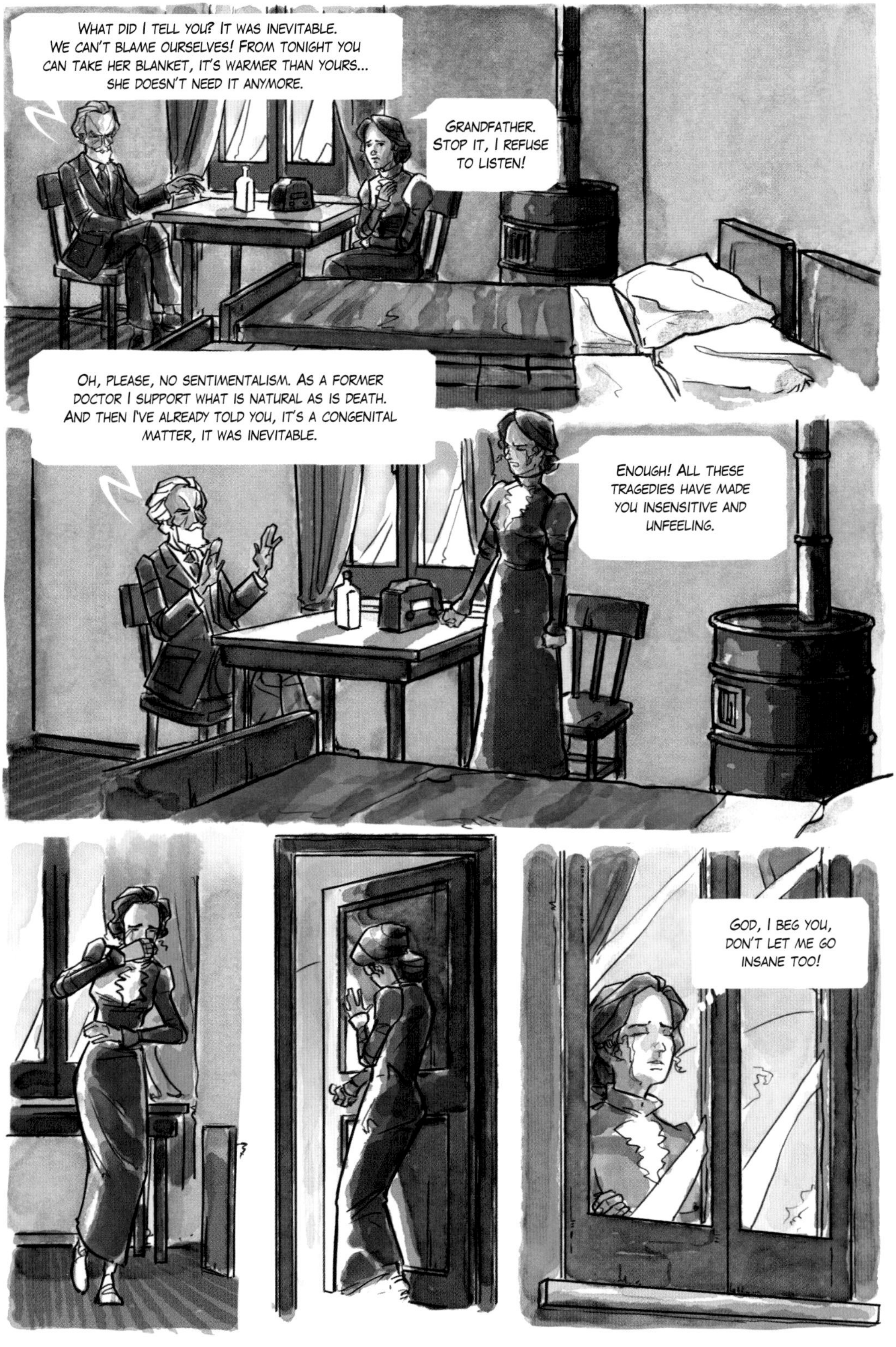
WHAT DID I TELL YOU? IT WAS INEVITABLE. WE CAN'T BLAME OURSELVES! FROM TONIGHT YOU CAN TAKE HER BLANKET, IT'S WARMER THAN YOURS... SHE DOESN'T NEED IT ANYMORE.
GRANDFATHER. STOP IT, I REFUSE TO LISTEN!
OH, PLEASE, NO SENTIMENTALISM. AS A FORMER DOCTOR I SUPPORT WHAT IS NATURAL AS IS DEATH. AND THEN I'VE ALREADY TOLD YOU, IT'S A CONGENITAL MATTER, IT WAS INEVITABLE.
ENOUGH! ALL THESE TRAGEDIES HAVE MADE YOU INSENSITIVE AND UNFEELING.
GOD, I BEG YOU, DON'T LET ME GO INSANE TOO!

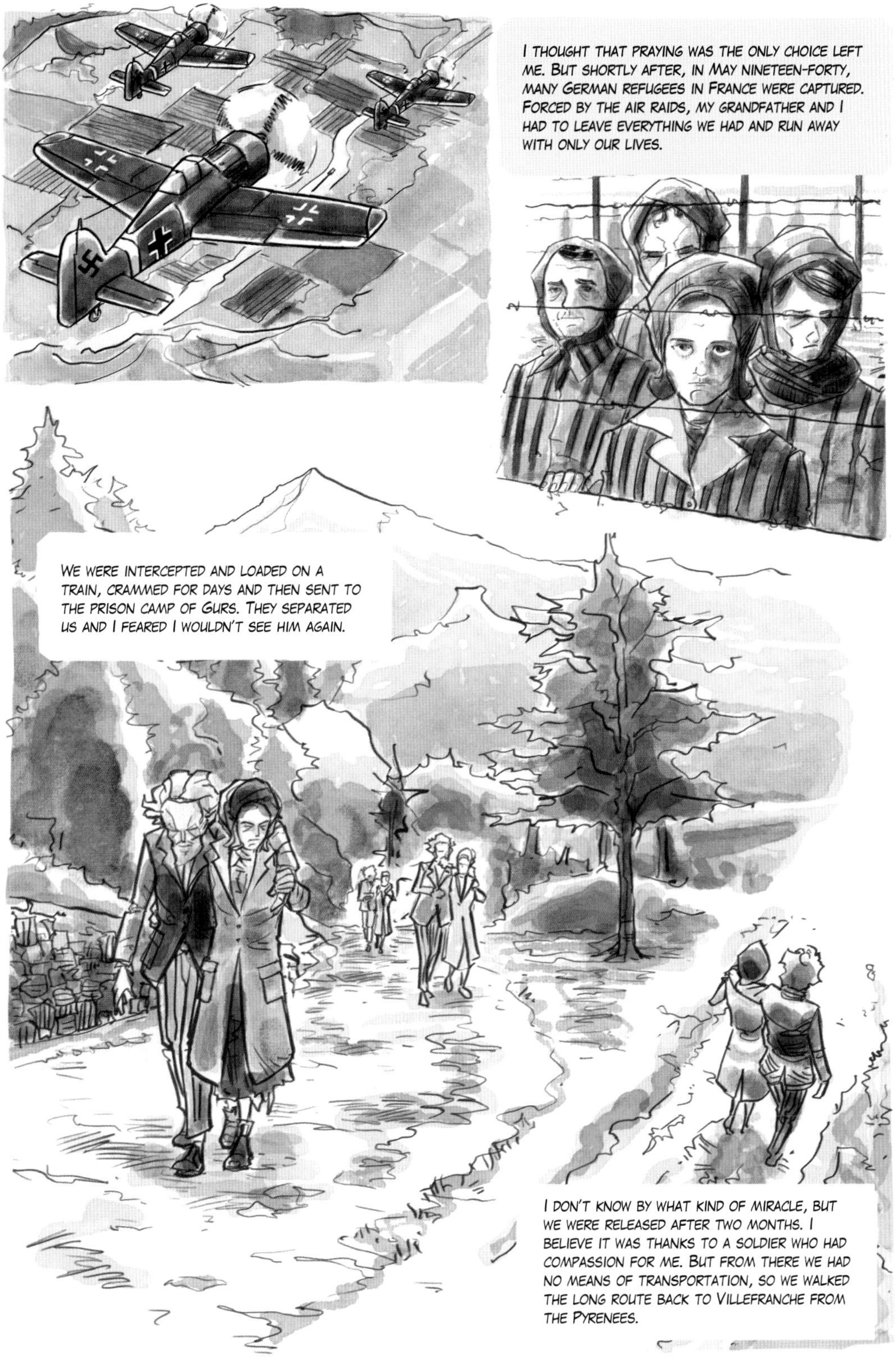
I THOUGHT THAT PRAYING WAS THE ONLY CHOICE LEFT ME. BUT SHORTLY AFTER, IN MAY NINETEEN-FORTY, MANY GERMAN REFUGEES IN FRANCE WERE CAPTURED. FORCED BY THE AIR RAIDS, MY GRANDFATHER AND I HAD TO LEAVE EVERYTHING WE HAD AND RUN AWAY WITH ONLY OUR LIVES.
WE WERE INTERCEPTED AND LOADED ON A TRAIN, CRAMMED FOR DAYS AND THEN SENT TO THE PRISON CAMP OF GURS. THEY SEPARATED US AND I FEARED I WOULDN'T SEE HIM AGAIN.
I DON'T KNOW BY WHAT KIND OF MIRACLE, BUT WE WERE RELEASED AFTER TWO MONTHS. I BELIEVE IT WAS THANKS TO A SOLDIER WHO HAD COMPASSION FOR ME. BUT FROM THERE WE HAD NO MEANS OF TRANSPORTATION, SO WE WALKED THE LONG ROUTE BACK TO VILLEFRANCHE FROM THE PYRENEES.

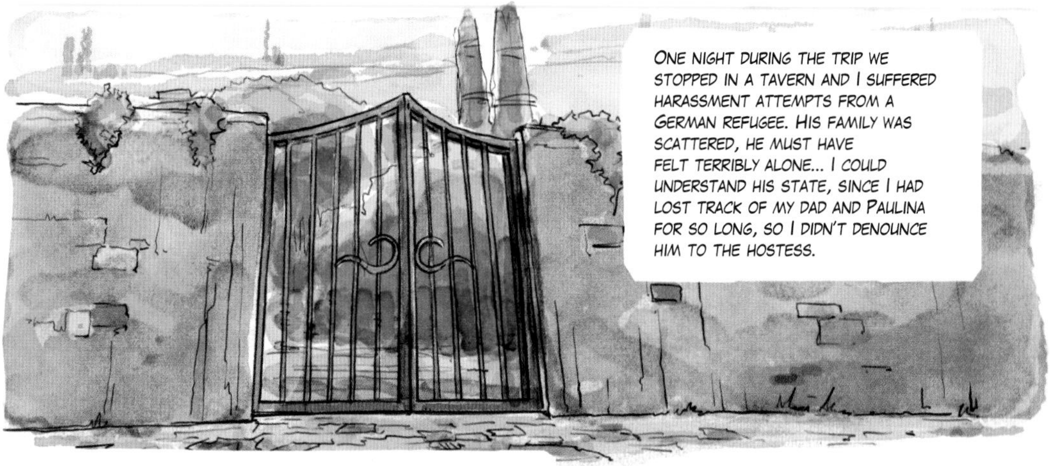
One night during the trip we stopped in a tavern and I suffered harassment attempts from a German refugee. His family was scattered, he must have felt terribly alone... I could understand his state, since I had lost track of my dad and Paulina for so long, so I didn't denounce him to the hostess.

But worse was that my grandfather had no proper attitude towards me. After the horror of the camp, he lost lucidity and sometimes he seemed to not even recognize me.

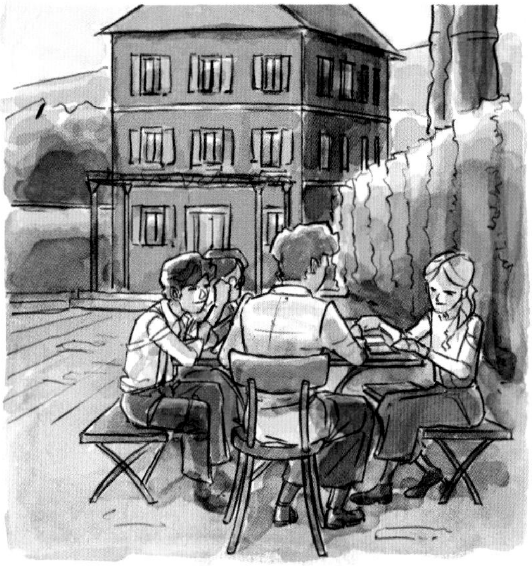

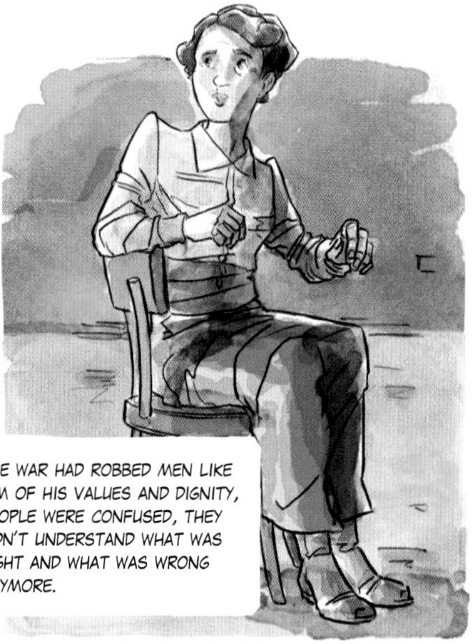
The war had robbed men like him of his values and dignity, people were confused, they didn't understand what was right and what was wrong anymore.

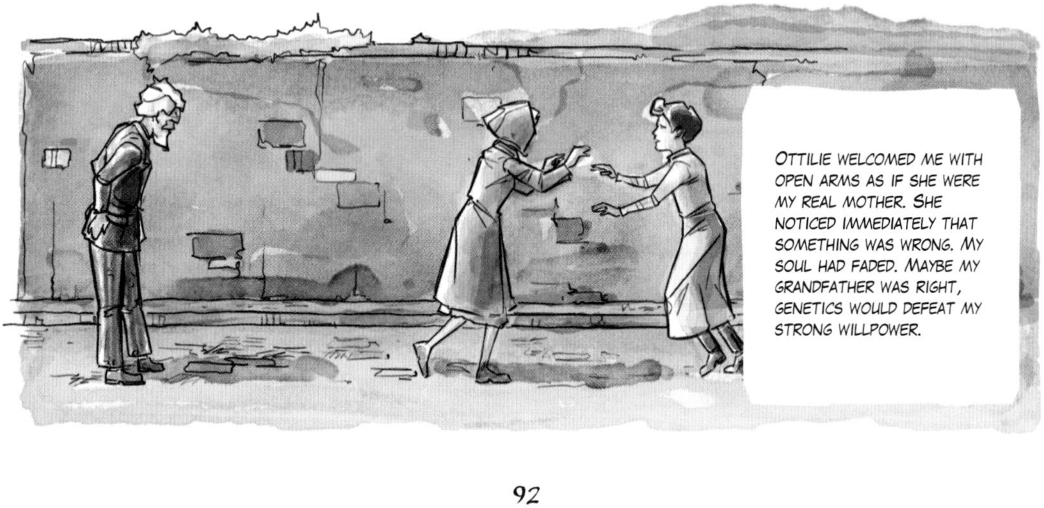
Ottilie welcomed me with open arms as if she were my real mother. She noticed immediately that something was wrong. My soul had faded. Maybe my grandfather was right, genetics would defeat my strong willpower.

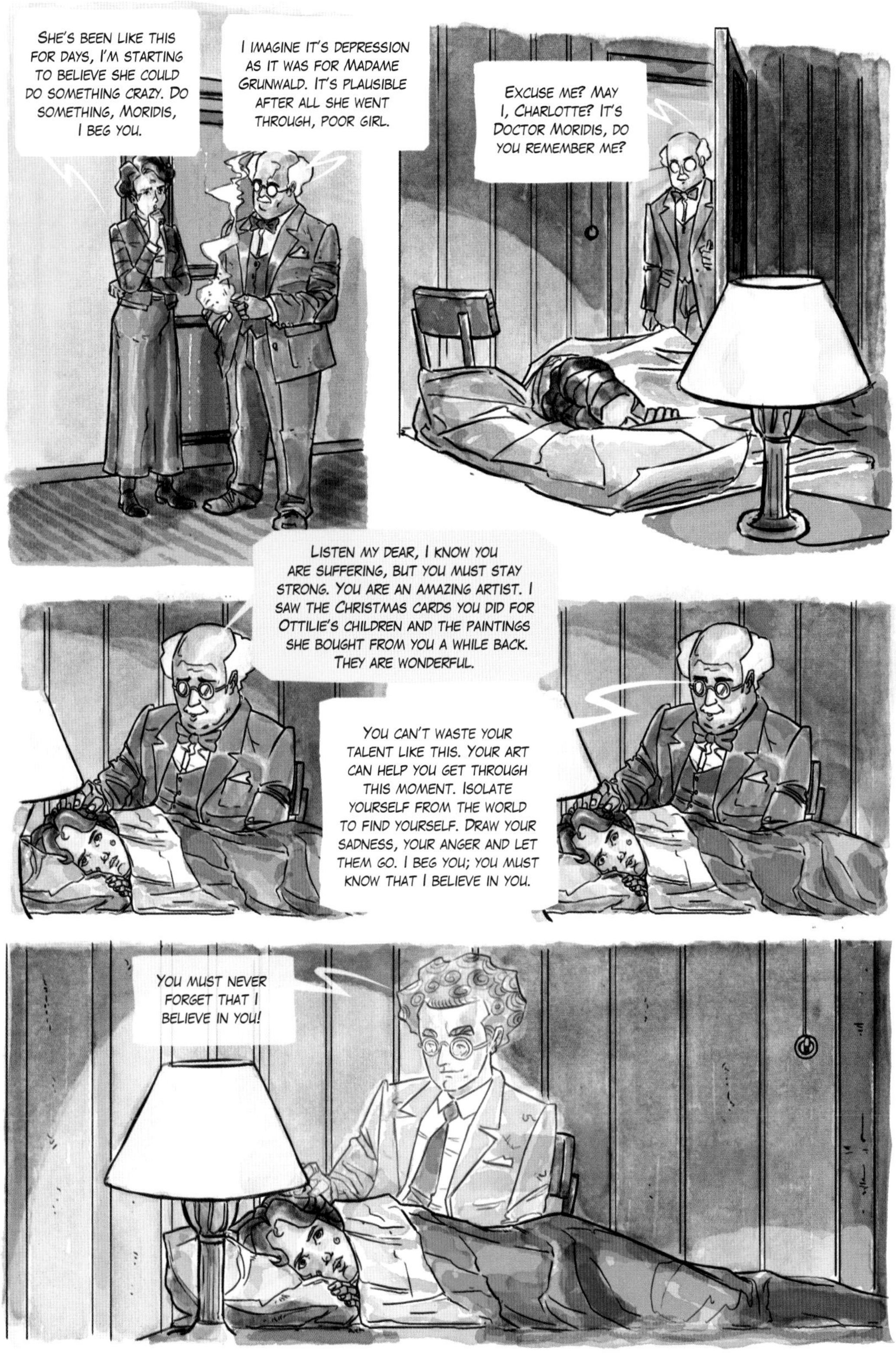
SHE'S BEEN LIKE THIS FOR DAYS, I'M STARTING TO BELIEVE SHE COULD DO SOMETHING CRAZY. DO SOMETHING, MORIDIS, I BEG YOU.
I IMAGINE IT'S DEPRESSION AS IT WAS FOR MADAME GRUNWALD. IT'S PLAUSIBLE AFTER ALL SHE WENT THROUGH, POOR GIRL.
EXCUSE ME? MAY I, CHARLOTTE? IT'S DOCTOR MORIDIS, DO YOU REMEMBER ME?
LISTEN MY DEAR, I KNOW YOU ARE SUFFERING, BUT YOU MUST STAY STRONG. YOU ARE AN AMAZING ARTIST. I SAW THE CHRISTMAS CARDS YOU DID FOR OTTILIE'S CHILDREN AND THE PAINTINGS SHE BOUGHT FROM YOU A WHILE BACK. THEY ARE WONDERFUL.
YOU CAN'T WASTE YOUR TALENT LIKE THIS. YOUR ART CAN HELP YOU GET THROUGH THIS MOMENT. ISOLATE YOURSELF FROM THE WORLD TO FIND YOURSELF. DRAW YOUR SADNESS, YOUR ANGER AND LET THEM GO. I BEG YOU; YOU MUST KNOW THAT I BELIEVE IN YOU.
YOU MUST NEVER FORGET THAT I BELIEVE IN YOU!

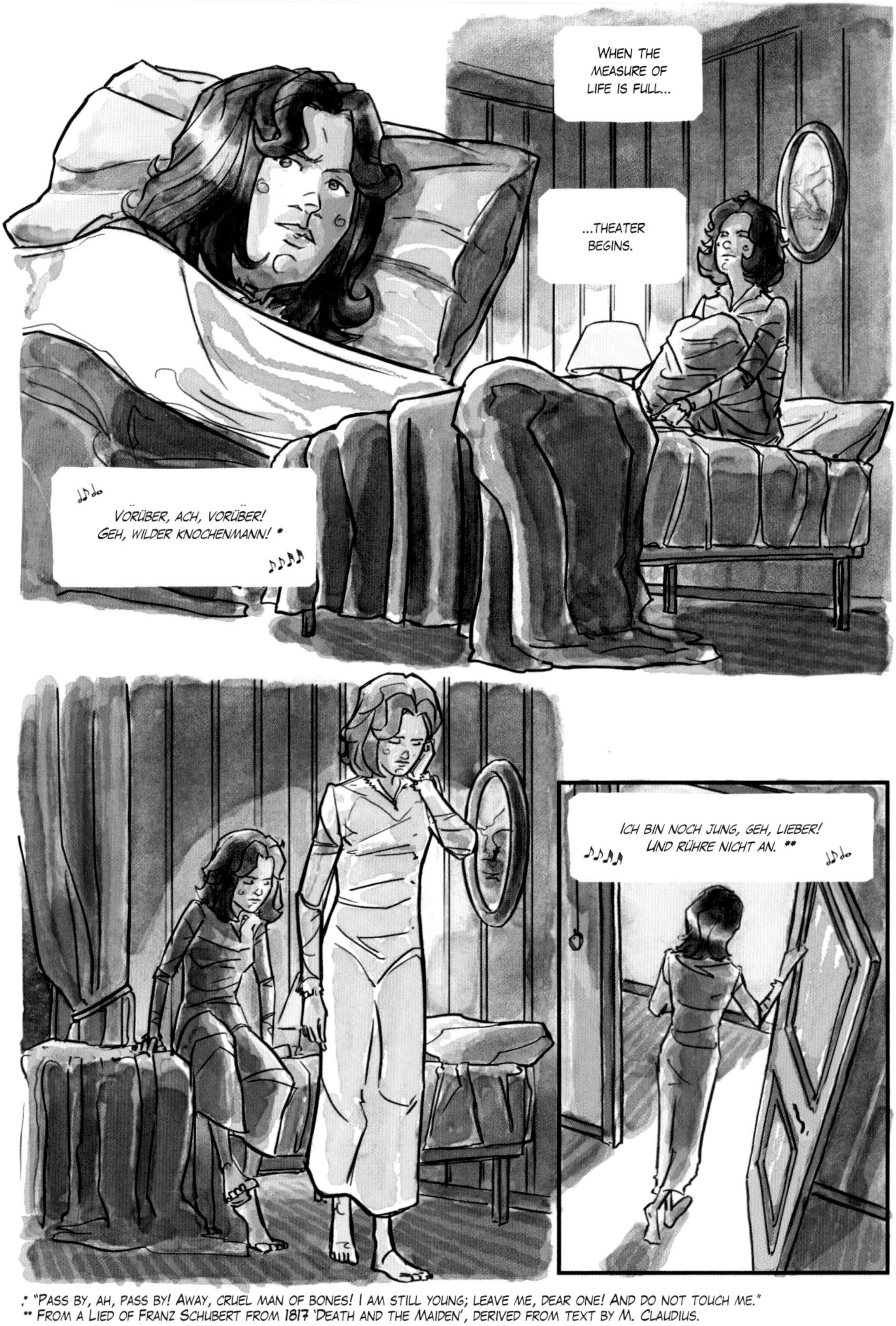
WHEN THE MEASURE OF LIFE IS FULL...
...THEATER BEGINS.
VORÜBER, ACH, VORÜBER! GEH, WILDER KNOCHENMANN! *
ICH BIN NOCH JUNG, GEH, LIEBER! UND RÜHRE NICHT AN. **

* "PASS BY, AH, PASS BY! AWAY, CRUEL MAN OF BONES! I AM STILL YOUNG; LEAVE ME, DEAR ONE! AND DO NOT TOUCH ME."
** FROM A LIED OF FRANZ SCHUBERT FROM 1817 'DEATH AND THE MAIDEN', DERIVED FROM TEXT BY M. CLAUDIUS.

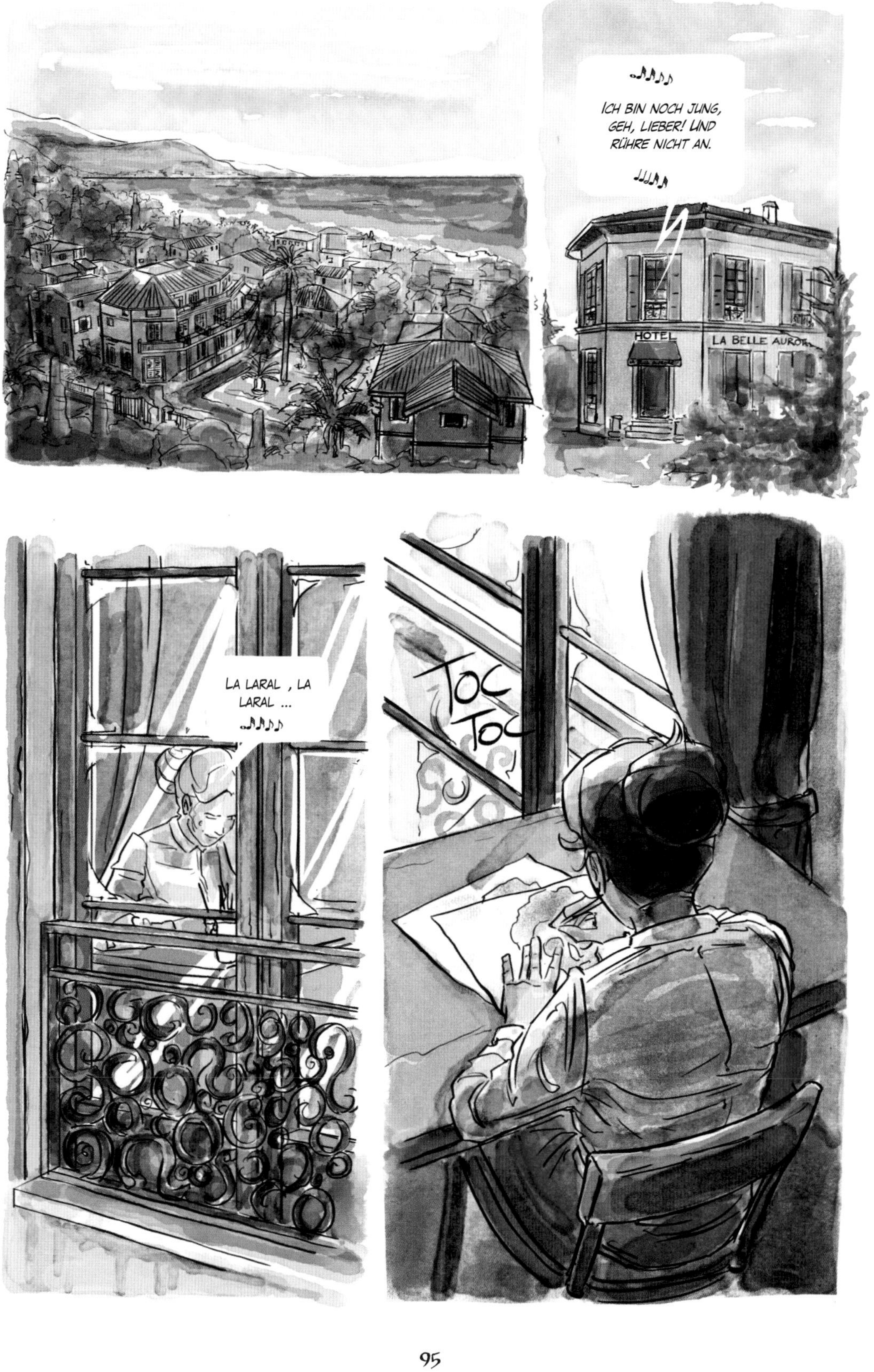
ICH BIN NOCH JUNG, GEH, LIEBER! UND RÜHRE NICHT AN.
HOTEL
LA BELLE AUROR
LA LARAL , LA LARAL ...
TOC TOC

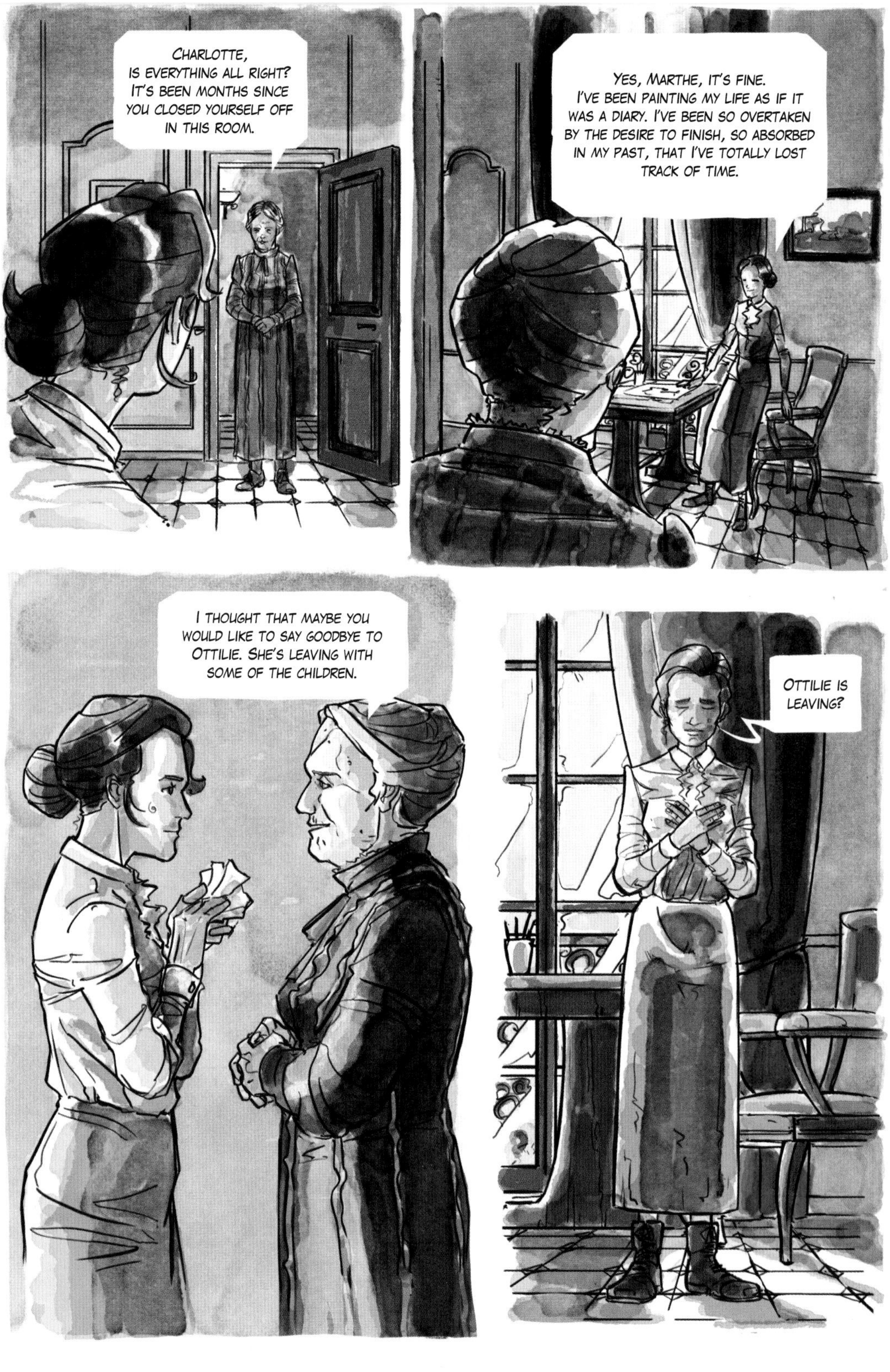
CHARLOTTE, IS EVERYTHING ALL RIGHT? IT'S BEEN MONTHS SINCE YOU CLOSED YOURSELF OFF IN THIS ROOM.
YES, MARTHE, IT'S FINE. I'VE BEEN PAINTING MY LIFE AS IF IT WAS A DIARY. I'VE BEEN SO OVERTAKEN BY THE DESIRE TO FINISH, SO ABSORBED IN MY PAST, THAT I'VE TOTALLY LOST TRACK OF TIME.
I THOUGHT THAT MAYBE YOU WOULD LIKE TO SAY GOODBYE TO OTTILIE. SHE'S LEAVING WITH SOME OF THE CHILDREN.
OTTILIE IS LEAVING?

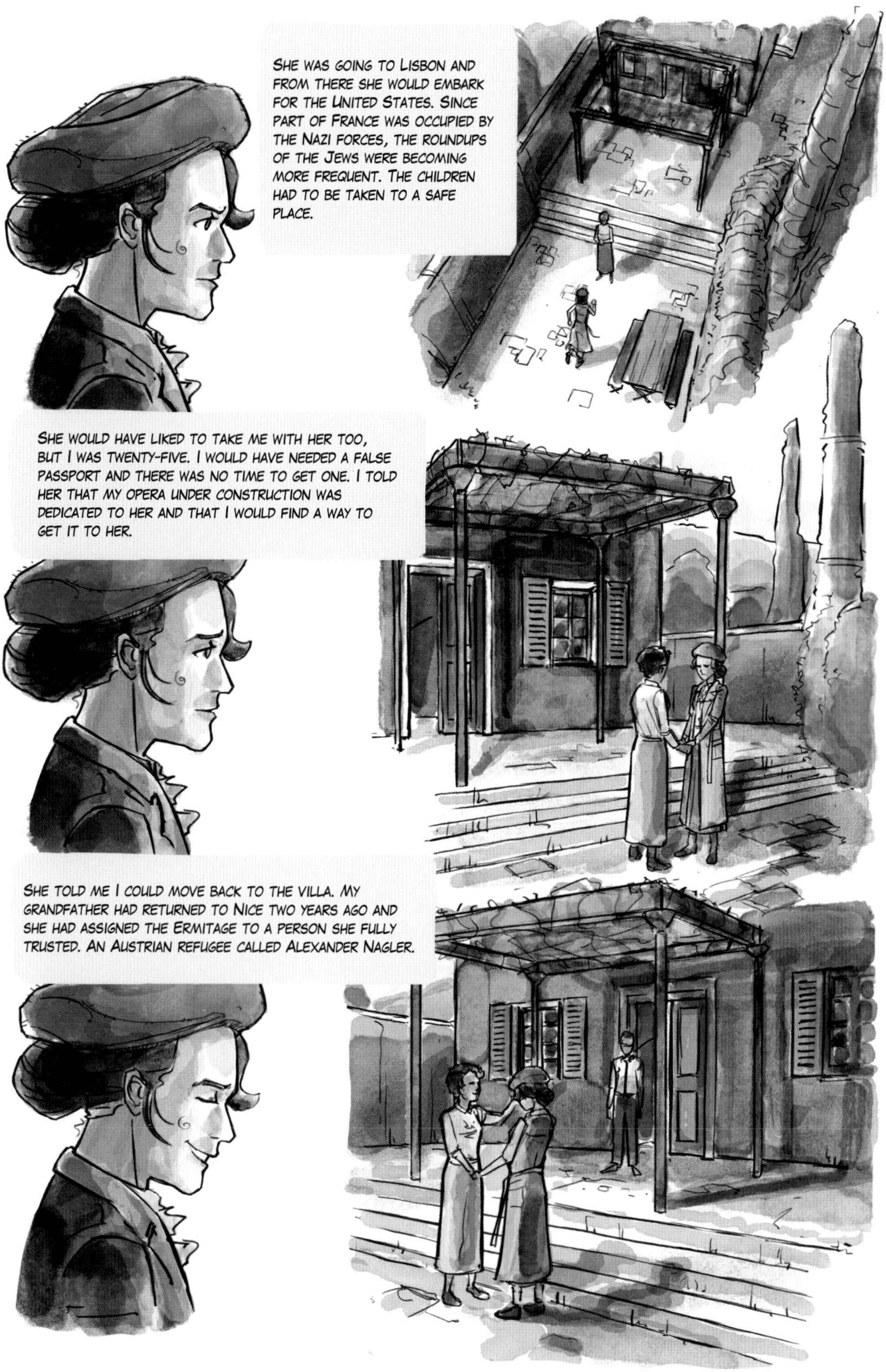
SHE WAS GOING TO LISBON AND FROM THERE SHE WOULD EMBARK FOR THE UNITED STATES. SINCE PART OF FRANCE WAS OCCUPIED BY THE NAZI FORCES, THE ROUNDUPS OF THE JEWS WERE BECOMING MORE FREQUENT. THE CHILDREN HAD TO BE TAKEN TO A SAFE PLACE.
SHE WOULD HAVE LIKED TO TAKE ME WITH HER TOO, BUT I WAS TWENTY-FIVE. I WOULD HAVE NEEDED A FALSE PASSPORT AND THERE WAS NO TIME TO GET ONE. I TOLD HER THAT MY OPERA UNDER CONSTRUCTION WAS DEDICATED TO HER AND THAT I WOULD FIND A WAY TO GET IT TO HER.
SHE TOLD ME I COULD MOVE BACK TO THE VILLA. MY GRANDFATHER HAD RETURNED TO NICE TWO YEARS AGO AND SHE HAD ASSIGNED THE ERMITAGE TO A PERSON SHE FULLY TRUSTED. AN AUSTRIAN REFUGEE CALLED ALEXANDER NAGLER.

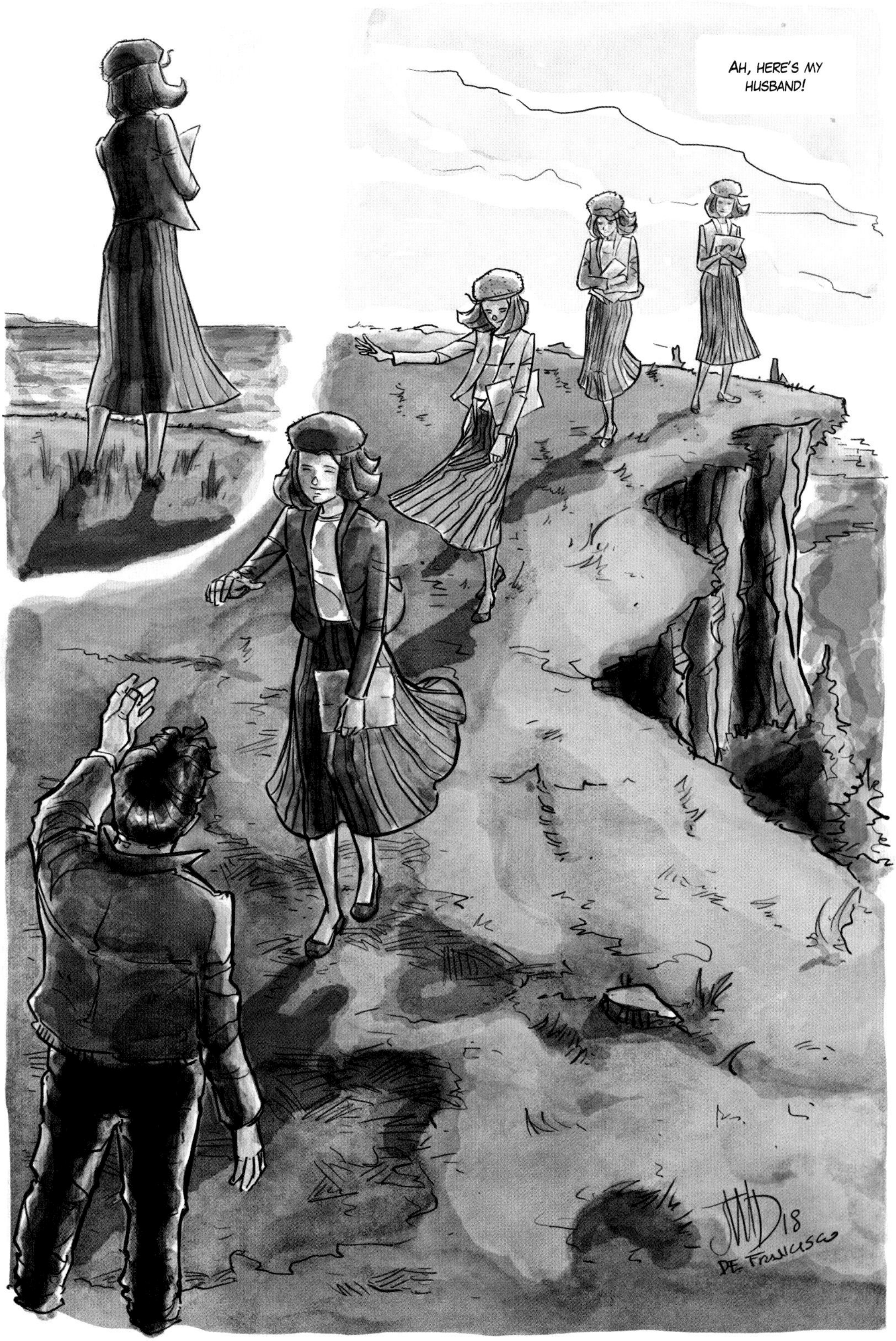
AH, HERE'S MY HUSBAND!
JWD 18
DE FRANCISCO

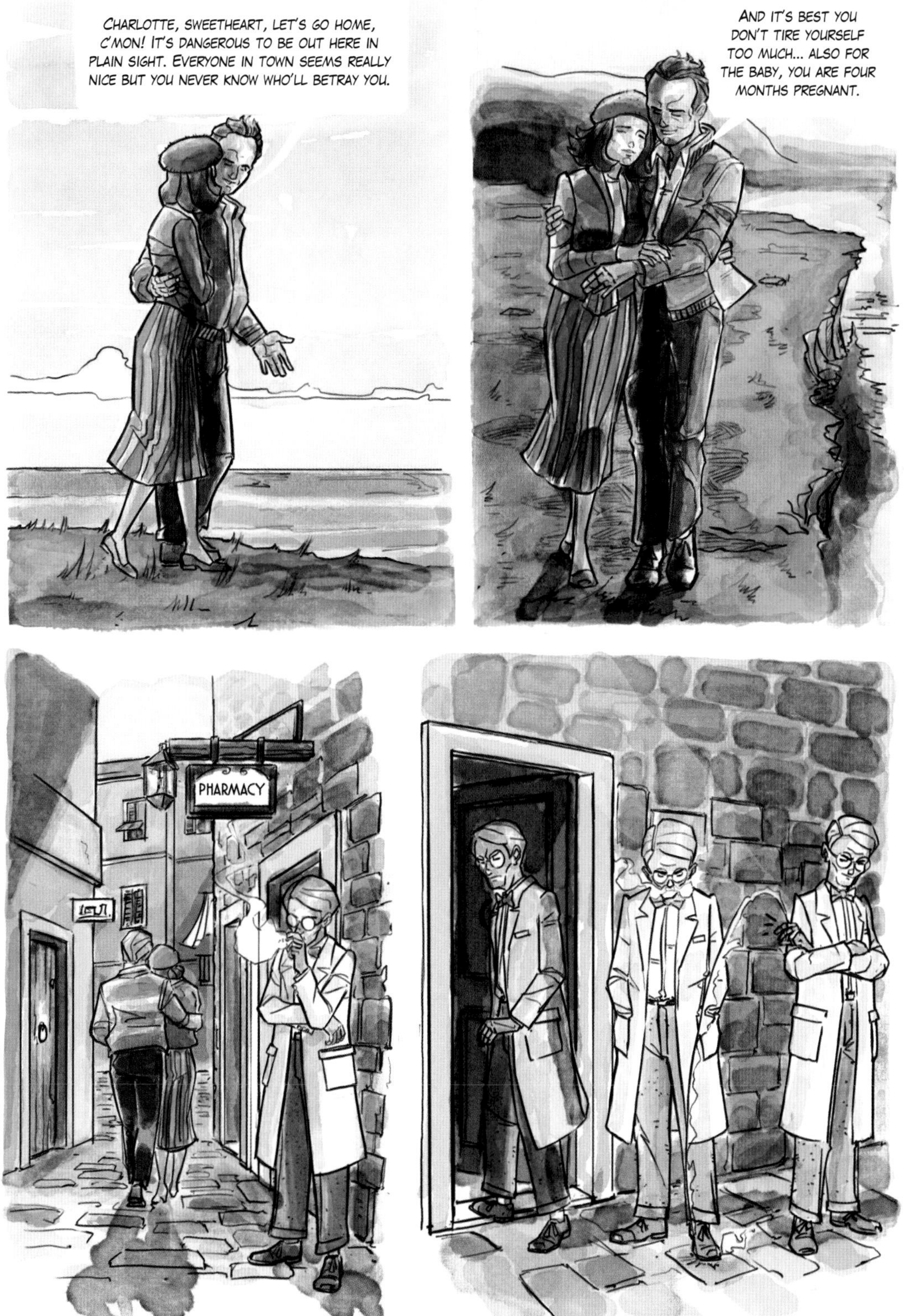
CHARLOTTE, SWEETHEART, LET'S GO HOME, C'MON! IT'S DANGEROUS TO BE OUT HERE IN PLAIN SIGHT. EVERYONE IN TOWN SEEMS REALLY NICE BUT YOU NEVER KNOW WHO'LL BETRAY YOU.
AND IT'S BEST YOU DON'T TIRE YOURSELF TOO MUCH... ALSO FOR THE BABY, YOU ARE FOUR MONTHS PREGNANT.
PHARMACY

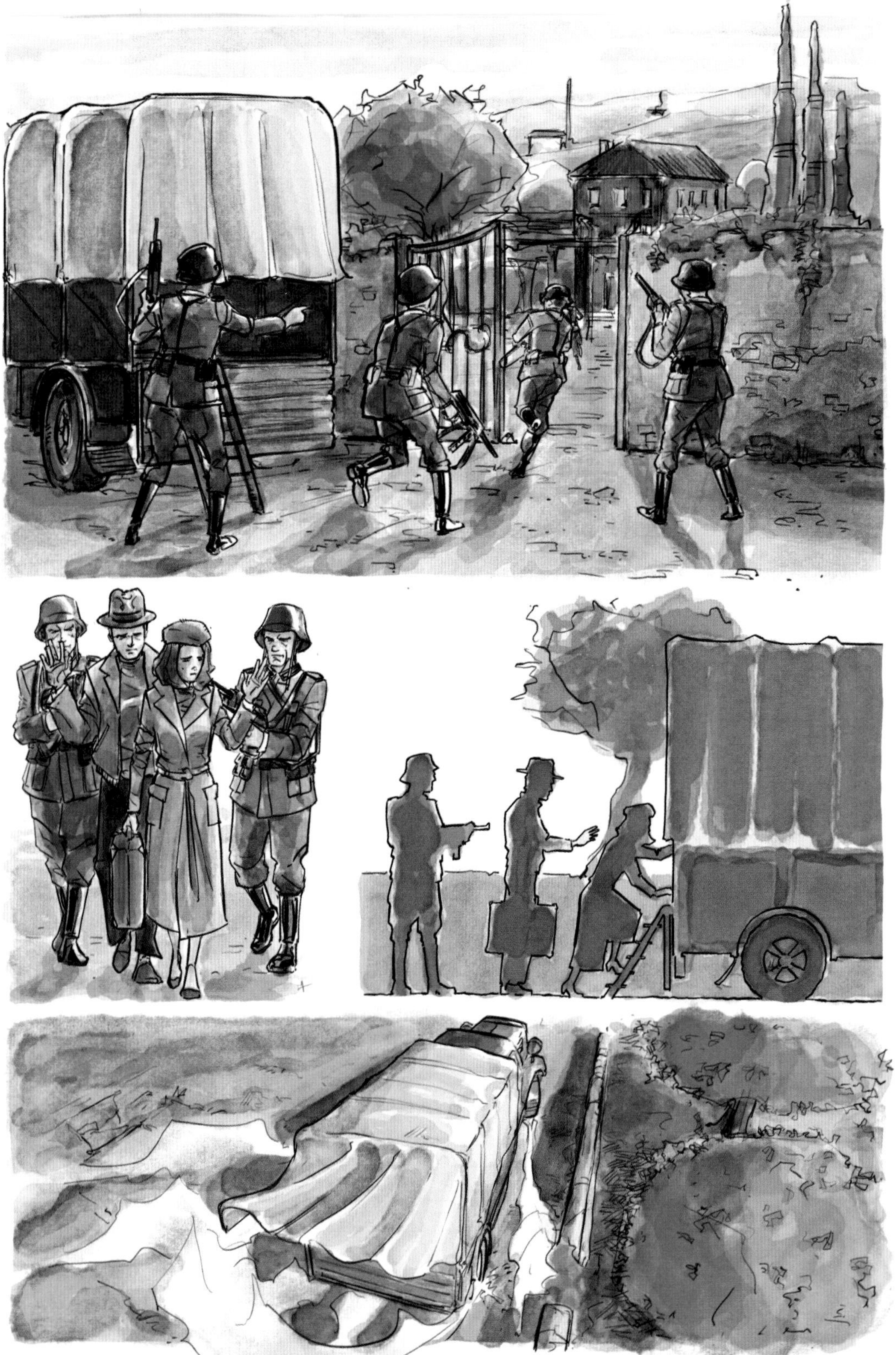

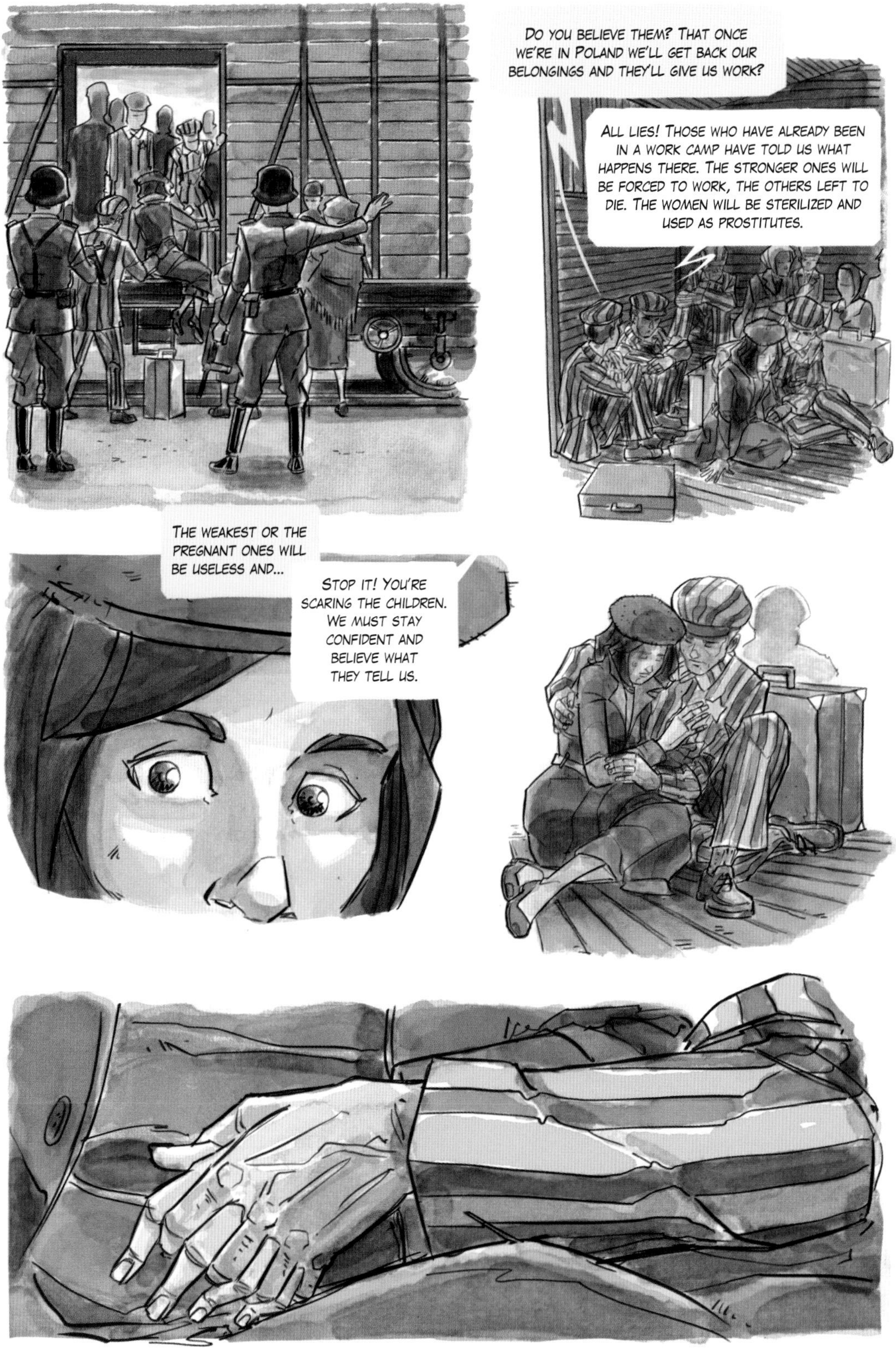
Do you believe them? That once we're in Poland we'll get back our belongings and they'll give us work?
All lies! Those who have already been in a work camp have told us what happens there. The stronger ones will be forced to work, the others left to die. The women will be sterilized and used as prostitutes.
The weakest or the pregnant ones will be useless and...
Stop it! You're scaring the children. We must stay confident and believe what they tell us.

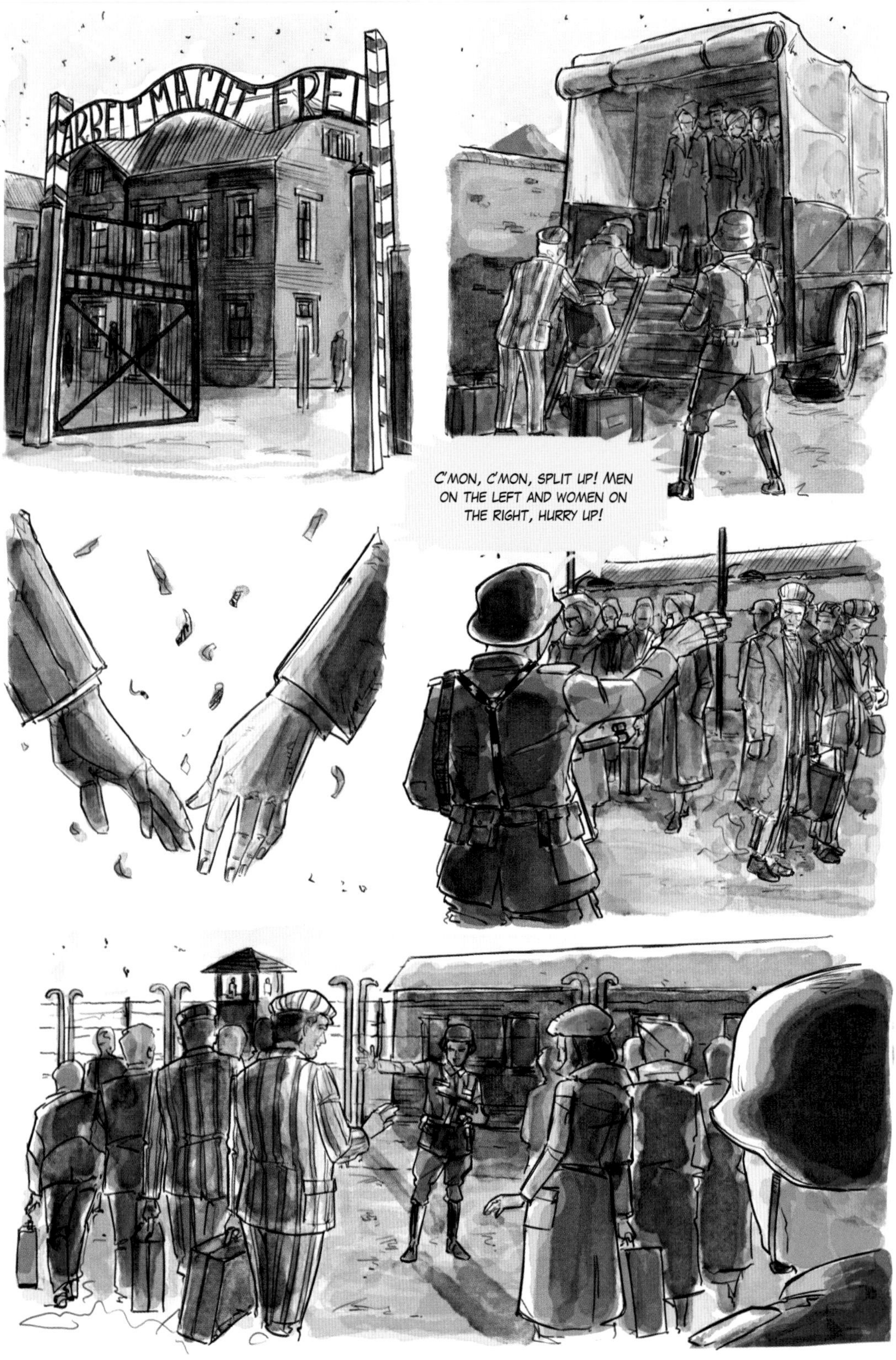
ARBEIT MACHT FREI
C'MON, C'MON, SPLIT UP! MEN ON THE LEFT AND WOMEN ON THE RIGHT, HURRY UP!

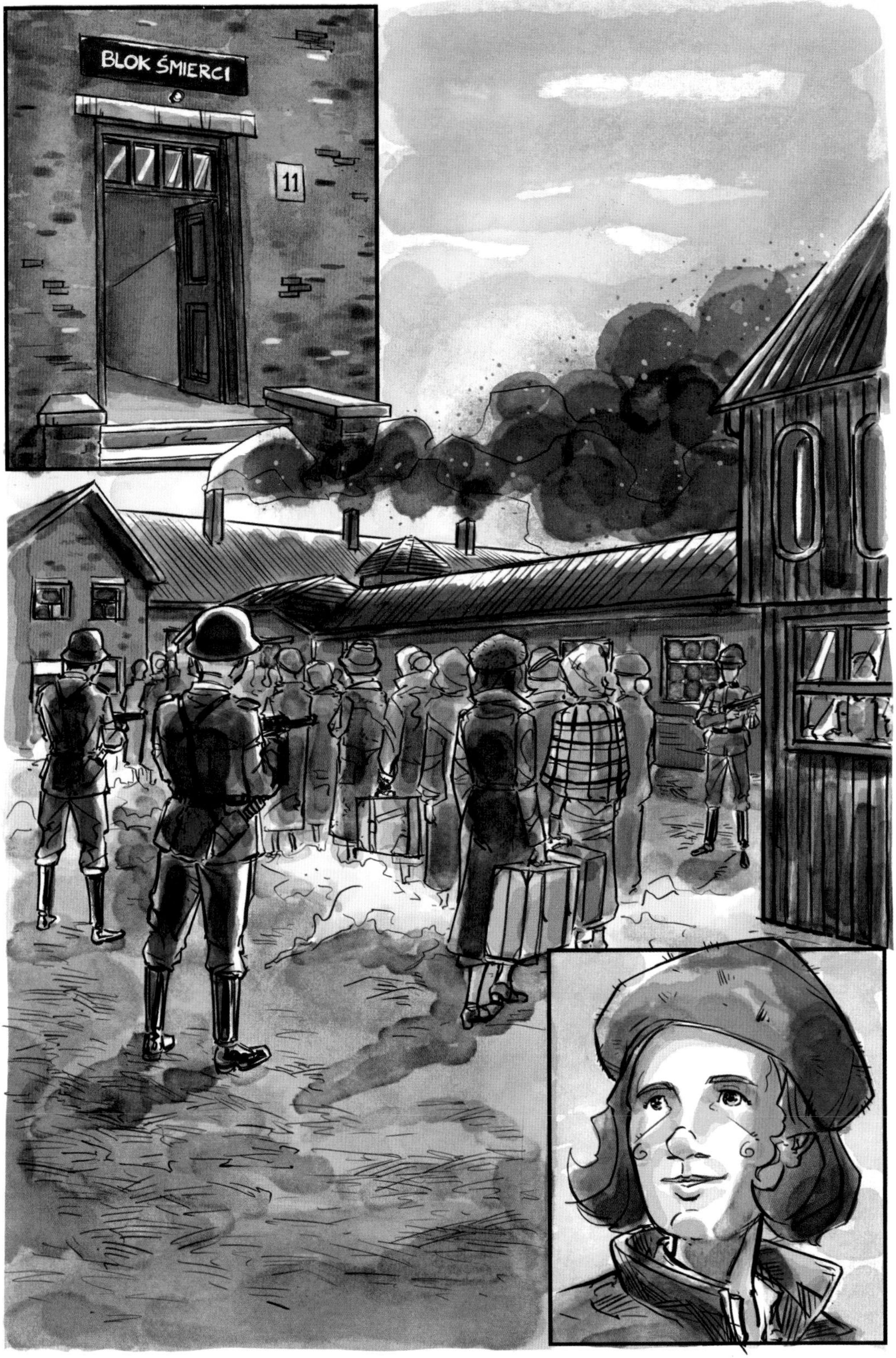
BLOK ŚMIERCI
11

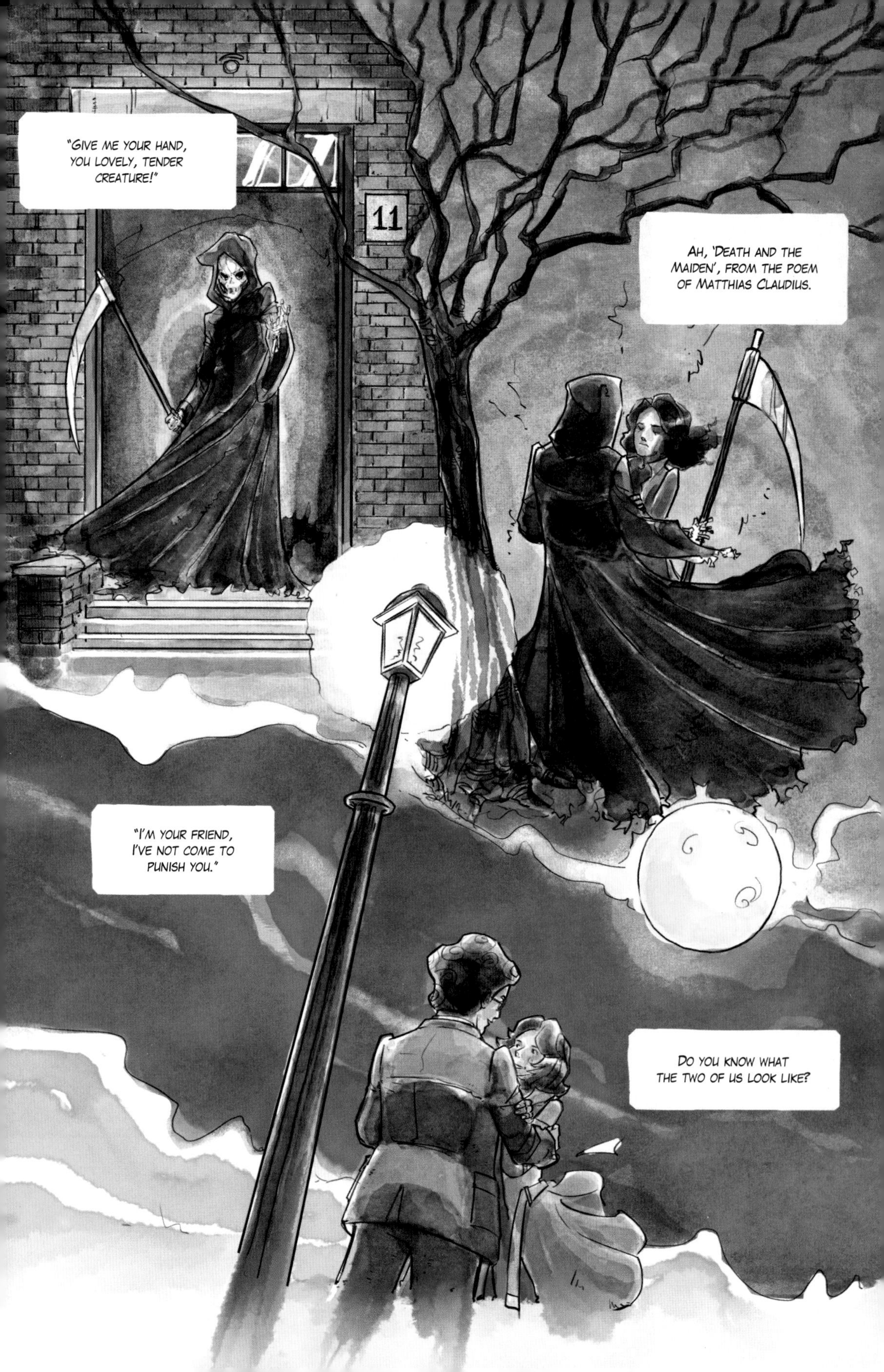
"GIVE ME YOUR HAND, YOU LOVELY, TENDER CREATURE!"
AH, 'DEATH AND THE MAIDEN', FROM THE POEM OF MATTHIAS CLAUDIUS.
"I'M YOUR FRIEND, I'VE NOT COME TO PUNISH YOU."
DO YOU KNOW WHAT THE TWO OF US LOOK LIKE?

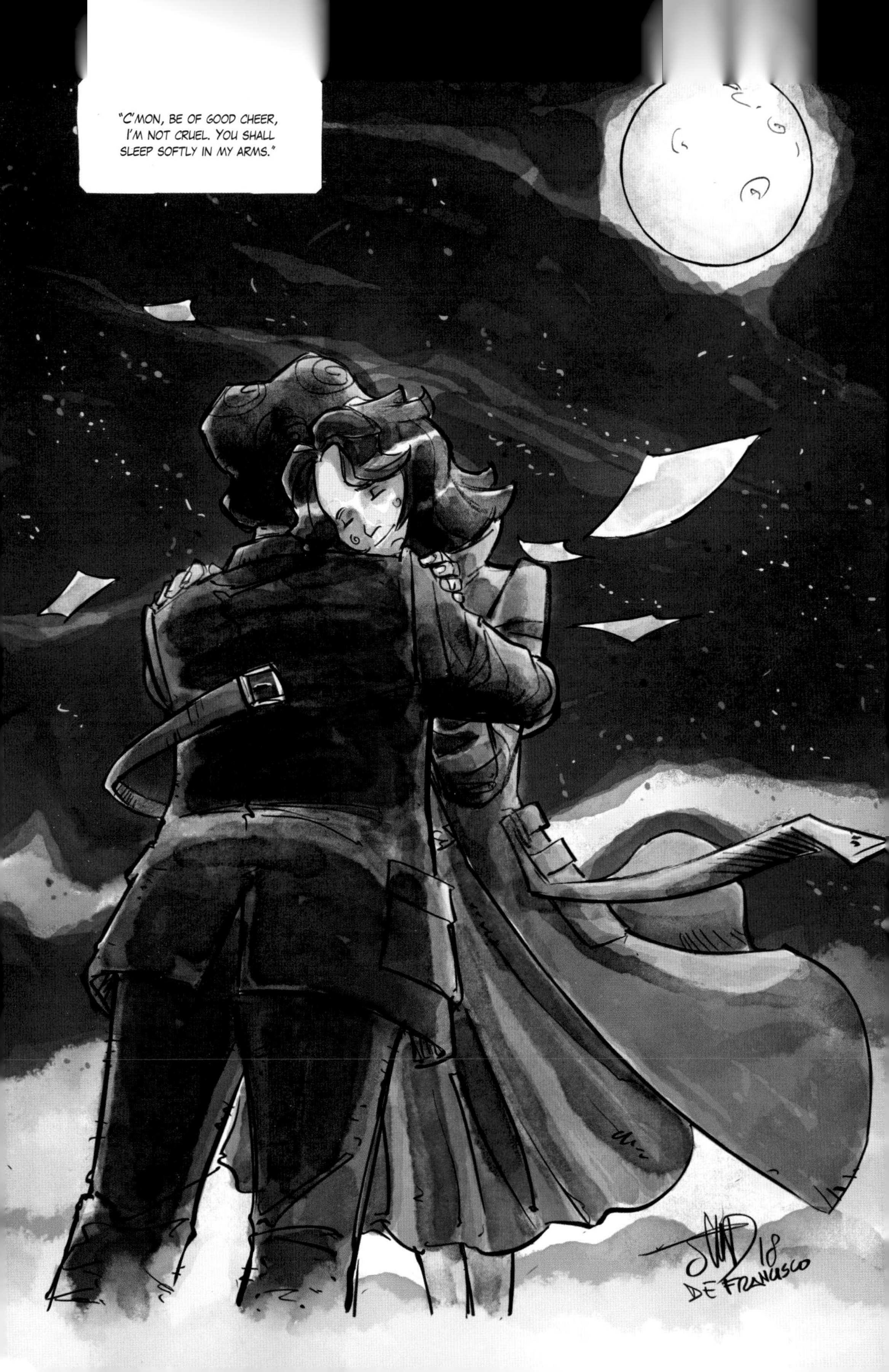
"C'MON, BE OF GOOD CHEER,
I'M NOT CRUEL. YOU SHALL
SLEEP SOFTLY IN MY ARMS."
DE FRANCISCO

Notes on the script
by Ilaria Ferramosca

Learned about the story of Charlotte Salomon one day by accident, while chatting with Maddalena Castegnaro, a friend of mine who is a cultural operator and responsible for one of the "Presidi nazionali del Libro", dedicated to "Libro d'Artista".

On that occasion it would have been premature of me to think about making a script, even though the story had affected me. So the idea remained dormant inside of me to settle itself, enriched by critical and biographical readings. Among them there was one which compared the entire opera of Charlotte to a multi-media hypertext, considering it as the first in pre- Internet history. Charlotte's opera was able to skilfully unify images, text and music, although it was only suggested through the titles of the songs that the author herself considered appropriate for that specific *gouache*.

Moreover, "Life? Or Theater?" has been compared to a comic book, by using the concept of "sequential art" which is an official definition given to it.

Put in these terms, the works of Charlotte Salomon represents, full-fledged, the first comic book regarding the Shoah, preceding both "La bête est morte!", a French comic book from 1944 in two volumes, art by Edom-François Calvo and scripted by Victor Dancette with Jacques Zimmermann, and the more famous and several times translated "Maus" by Art Spiegelman, published in 1986. In fact, by analyzing all the gouaches, you can identify not only a temporal sequence of events, but in every page there are figure movements, the ones that in screenwriting are called sequence shots, in which we can see the character move and interact while there is only one setting in the background.

Sometimes, however, the gouache is divided into strips or sectors, as if there was an ideal grid for sharing the scenes. Add to all this the use of texts, in some cases similar to real dialogue and in others to explanatory captions.

For this reason the script of this story wanted to pay tribute to Charlotte's artistic work by maintaining unchanged the intent and trying to get as close as possible to her style, not so much in the painting (although we used mainly red, blue and yellow which characterize her gouaches) but in the structure.

From here the decision not to use a grid and, especially, to get as close as possible to the narrative choices of our artist, taking inspiration directly from the gouaches and reproducing some of them in a very similar way, although it has been adapted to our chosen medium of expression: the graphic novel.

So, here you have the progression of faces repeated horizontally and vertically and the movement of the figures. Moreover, these enclose a double tribute, on the one hand to the painter whose life is being told, and on the other to a master of the Italian comic art.

The title of the Charlotte's opera and its strict correlation to the theater evokes, in fact, Gianni De Luca, one the most important cartoonists who transposed into a comic Shakespeare's works by making the characters act while moving with only one setting in the background, as if they were on a theatrical stage.

This was the intent, both in the script and of the drawing and we hope, sincerely, to have succeeded.

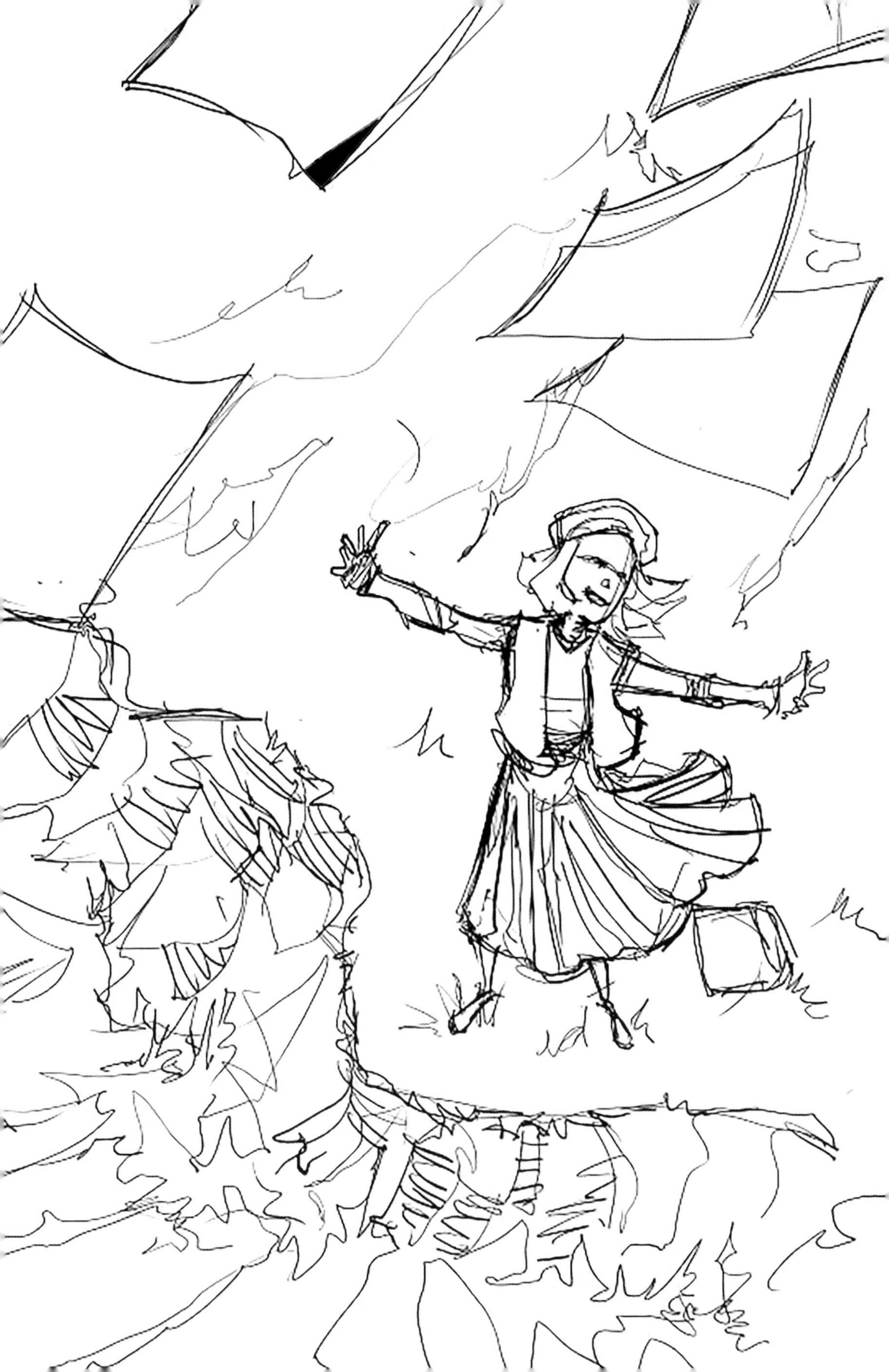

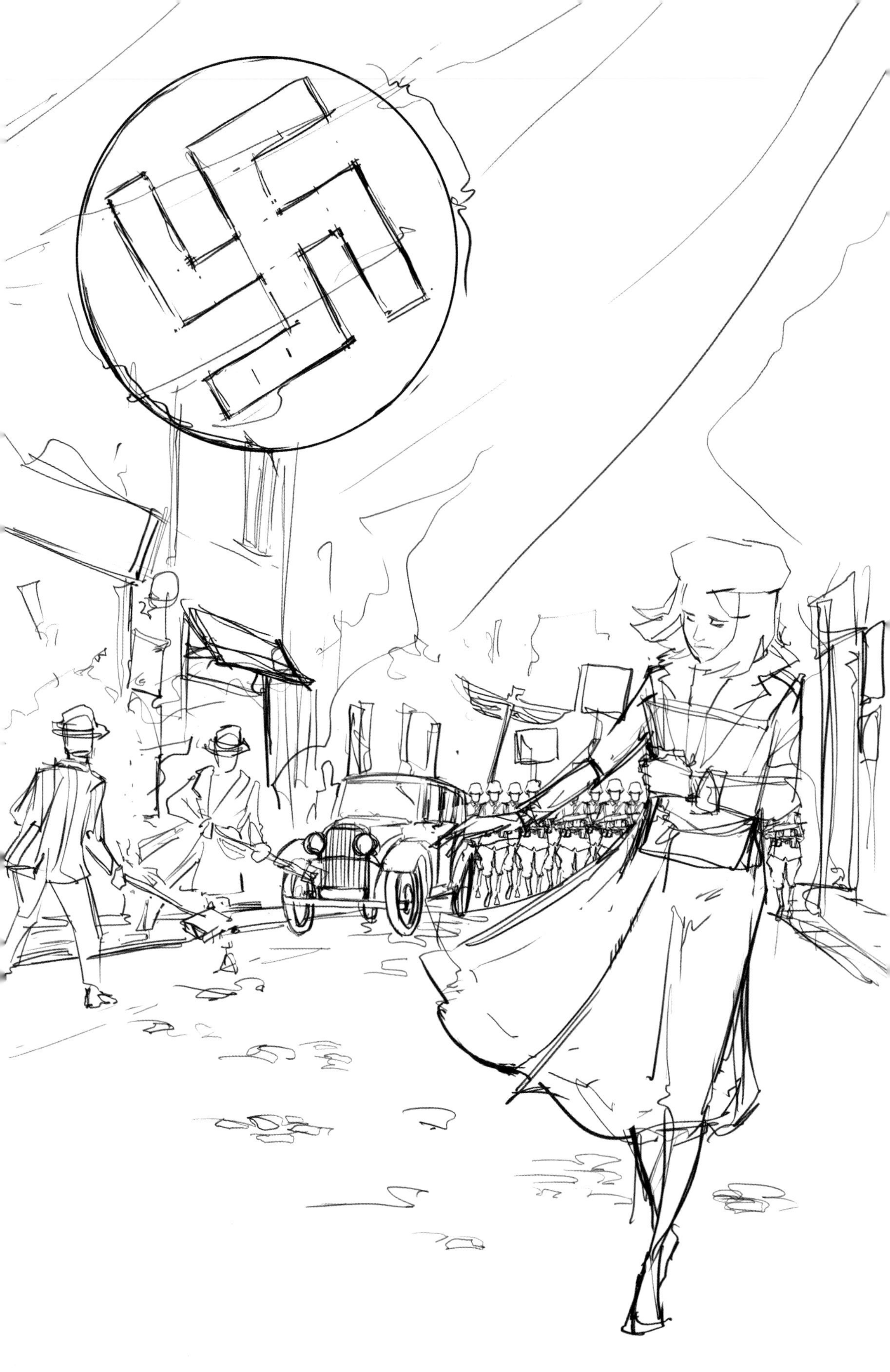

Short biography of Charlotte Salomon

by Ilaria Ferramosca

Charlotte Salomon was born on the 16th April 1917 to Albert Salomon, medical surgeon, and Franziska Grunwald, a young woman belonging to an aristocratic family of Berlin and in turn the daughter of a doctor. Franziska and Albert met each other during the First Great War while Franziska was serving as a volunteer nurse. She was trying to escape her suffering for the death of her little sister (also named Charlotte) who died from suicide at the age of eighteen by jumping off a bridge. A similar fate also occurs to little Charlotte's mother when she was only eight. Burdened by a strong depression, Franziska decided to free herself from her pain by throwing herself out of a window, although they told Charlotte she died from a fulminant form of flu virus.

Charlotte is entrusted to several different governesses' care and her moods alternate from moments of impatience and aggression to others of happiness. She ardently desires a maternal figure beside her because her father is often away, focused on his career as a surgeon and university professor. When Charlotte is almost thirteen, Albert finally decides to remarry with a famous opera singer: Paulina Lindberg. Charlotte has mixed feelings of admiration and morbid jealousy towards Paulina. She'd like to have her all for herself without sharing her affection with her father or her admirers. In 1933, Hitler rises to power and the existing racial campaigns against Jews become more violent. Soon, Charlotte is forced to leave school, but after some difficulties she is admitted to a school for Pure and Applied Arts in Berlin. She is the only Jewish student accepted that year and, in choosing her expressive style she seems influenced by modern art, and in particular by artists opposed by the regime such as Munch, Schiele, Kokosckha, Gauguin and van Gogh. Meanwhile, the intolerance of the German Nazi party towards the Jews was spreading and Charlotte's grandparents Grunwald decide to move to France, in Villefranche-sur-mer. In this period Charlotte meets Alfred Wolfsohn, Paulina's singing teacher with whom she falls in love.

The political situation, however, degenerates with the infamous "Crystal Night". From that moment numerous Jews are arrested and deported to concentration camps, Albert Salomon among them. He survives thanks to the influence his wife Paulina still exerts. Once home Albert seems to be a different man, he is anxious about his daughter's life, so he obliges her to leave Berlin and join her grandparents on the Côte d'Azur.

Once there Charlotte is welcomed by Ottilie Moore, an American benefactor who hosts Charlotte's grandparents and other refugees (in particular children) in an expansive villa: the Ermitage. Paulina and Albert are forced to leave Germany too and they move to the Netherlands. Communications are difficult due to the risk of being discovered by the SS, so Charlotte loses tracks of her relatives and also of her beloved Alfred.

Now in Nice with her grandparents, one night she prevents her grandmother's suicide who had fallen into depression obsessed by all the war and death. On that occasion her grandfather reveals to Charlotte her tragic past and the wave of suicides that weighs on her family as if it was a congenital matter. Soon the girl starts fearing for her own health and her thoughts become obsessive. She starts to feel marked by a destiny that she can't avoid. The situation gets worst after she is forced to spend some time in the concentration camp at Gurs in the foothills of the Pyrenees where she was deported together with her grandfather after a roundup. After the horror she lived through and the unorthodix behavior of her grandfather, who seems to have lost lucidity following his detention, she enters a depressive state that completely prostrates her.

At that point Ottilie Moore commends her to the care of Doctor Moridis. He pushes Charlotte to recover her love for art and painting and to use it as a therapy by putting in her work her memories, passions and fears.

She moves into an hotel room in order to isolate herself from the world and from her grandfather who has become more

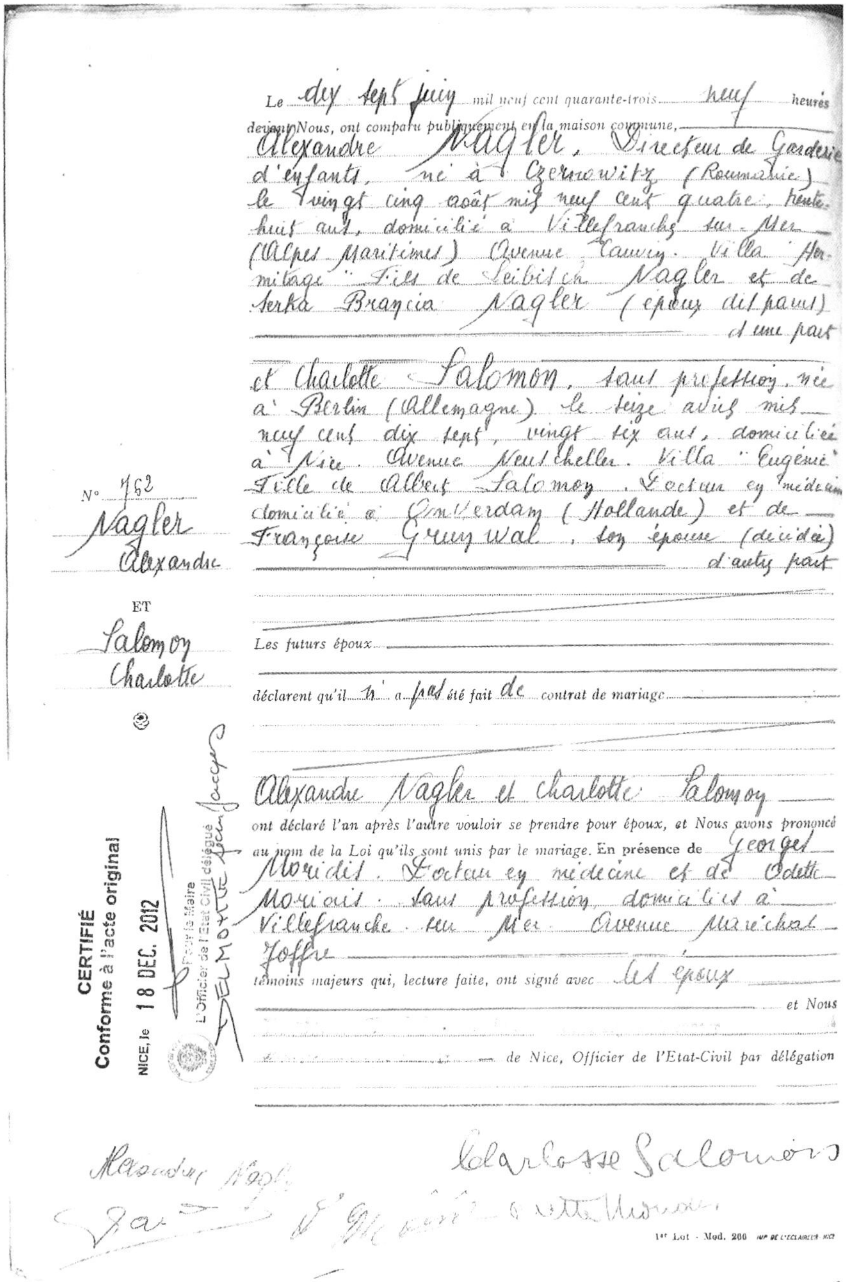

Le dix sept juin mil neuf cent quarante-trois neuf heures devant Nous, ont comparu publiquement en la maison commune, Alexandre Nagler, Directeur de Garderie d'enfants, né à Czernowitz (Roumanie) le vingt cinq août mil neuf cent quatre-vingt-huit ans, domicilié à Villefranche sur Mer (Alpes Maritimes) Avenue Lamy. Villa "Hermitage" Fils de Leibisch Nagler et de Perka Brancia Nagler (époux disparus) d'une part

et Charlotte Salomon, sans profession, née à Berlin (Allemagne) le seize avril mil neuf cent dix sept, vingt six ans, domiciliée à Nice Avenue Neuschellar. Villa "Eugénie" Fille de Albert Salomon, Docteur en médecin domicilié à Amsterdam (Hollande) et de Françoise Grunwal, son épouse (décédée) d'autre part

N° 762
Nagler Alexandre
ET
Salomon Charlotte

Les futurs époux

déclarent qu'il n' a pas été fait de contrat de mariage

Alexandre Nagler et Charlotte Salomon ont déclaré l'un après l'autre vouloir se prendre pour époux, et Nous avons prononcé au nom de la Loi qu'ils sont unis par le mariage. En présence de Georges Moridis. Docteur en médecine et de Odette Moridis. sans profession, domiciliés à Villefranche sur Mer Avenue Maréchal Joffre

témoins majeurs qui, lecture faite, ont signé avec les époux et Nous

de Nice, Officier de l'Etat-Civil par délégation

CERTIFIÉ
Conforme à l'acte original
NICE, le 18 DEC. 2012
Pour le Maire
L'Officier de l'Etat Civil délégué

Alexander Nagler
Charlotte Salomon

1er Lot - Mod. 200 IMP. DE L'ECLAIREUR NICE

Charlotte Salomon's marriage certificate.

aggressive and difficult to tolerate. For almost two years she devotes herself to painting, days and nights (from 1940 to 1942) and she creates the opera Life? Or Theater?: 769 illustrations using gouache technique and only the three primary colors (blue, red and yellow). Considering preparatory drawings and pages of notes these became more than 1300 pages.

She recounts her whole life and part of that of her family, identifying herself in her mother, grandmother, Paulina and also in her Alfred. She describes all his theories and dialogues in detail. But she does all this whilst maintaining a distance, as if they were the characters of a theater play. She becomes Charlotte Kann, her grandparents Grunwald and her mother Franziska become the Knarres; Paulina Lindberg becomes Paulinka Bimbam, and Alfred Wolfsohn is turned into Amadeus Daberlohn.

She completes her opera while the war is raging and leaves it in a suitcase with Doctor Moridis for safe keeping following her probable arrest. She asks him to give it to Ottilie if something serious happens to her. Ottilie, in fact, was forced to leave in order to save the Ermitage's children. She assigned the villa to an Austrian refugee that she trusts, Alexander Nagler. Charlotte and Alexander fall in love and marry but to do so he gives up his false documents, incriminating himself as a Jew. Some time later, Charlotte and Alexander are found by the Gestapo, probably because of a whistle blower. They are taken from Ottilie Moore's villa on the 21th September 1943 and deported to Auschwitz. They reach it on the 10th of October. That same day Charlotte is considered useless to work because she is four months pregnant and she is sent to a gas chamber.

When Ottilie Moore receives the suitcase with Charlotte's legacy, she tracks down Paulina and Albert Salomon in The Netherlands at war's end. In 1959 they donate the opera of Charlotte to the Rijksmuseum in Amsterdam; later it was relocated to the Joods Historisch Museum where it is still exhibited and held safe on behalf of the Charlotte Salomon Foundation.

Nom	Prénom	Convoi	Née	Date & lieu de naissance	Adresse
CAHEN-MOLINA	Gerard	60		13.12.11 Paris	63 Prom des Anglais
CHAPIRO	Abraham			11.09.92 Kowel	26 rue de Paris
DRORI	Pinchas			03.10.04 Kowel	St Martin d'Heres
EBLIN	Simone	60		16.04.19 Paris	St Martin
EDWABOSKI	Ernestine	60	Appel	20.11.72 Kattowitz	86, rue Mal Joffre
EWSELMANN	Colette	60		09.05.26 Nice	12 av Mchl Foch
EWSELMANN	Eugene	60		19.11.85 Moscou	12 av Mchl Foch
EWSELMANN	Irene	60	Koch	10.01.97 Marmoutier	12 av Mchl Foch
FISCHBEIN	Elie	60		29.11.97 Stryj	34 av des Acacias
FISCHER	Maurice	60		02.04.06 Gegewy	39 r Hotel-des-Postes
GLASS	Alexandre			15.12.06 Oran	10 r Mace, Cannes
GLOWICZOVER	Abram			23.07.07 Varsovie	42 av des Acacias
GORENBUCH	Moise	60		22.01.99 Kichineff	23 rue d'Italie
GRINBERT	Leon	60		10.11.97 Paris	25 rue Gounod
GRINBERT	Yvonne	60	Dosik	21.03.01 Dunkerque	25 rue Gounod
HAAS	Ruth	60	Schmitz	01.03.11 Coblence	Hotel de la Plata
HATSHONDO	Charles			28.01.25 Colombes	Villa Desir, St Martin
HERSCHENSOHN	David	62		24.08.02 Mourorany	37 bis Prom des Anglais
ICKOWICZ	Koppel	60		13.07.96 Szekociny	26 rue de Paris
KAHN	Arthur	62		23.10.74 Paris	42 av des Acacias
KAHN	Heinz	60		20.06.07 Stuttgart	2 ter rue Spitalieri
KARWASSER	Hiroz	60		07.07.92 Varsovie	42 av des Acacias
KARWASSER	Majem	60	Brajterman	14.06.00 Varsovie	42 av des Acacias
KLIMOWITZKI	Georges	60		13.07.02 Paris	Villa Madone - Cannes
KRANZLER	Edith	60	Stern	29.01.08 Vienne	Hotel Massiglia
KRANZLER	Heinz	60		13.10.37 Vienne	Hotel Massiglia
KRANZLER	Leib	60		18.06.99 Blazowa	Hotel Massiglia
KUPERWASSER	Annette	60		24.04.24 Paris	34 av des Acacias
KUPERWASSER	Eljusz	60		12.11.97 Belzyce	34 av des Acacias
LEVIN	Willy	60		19.10.09 Rotterdam	Hot Chateau du Four, Cannes
LEVY	Arthur	60		12.07.84 Hochfelden	42 av des Acacias
LEVY	Toni	60	Stein	03.11.93 Bale	42 av des Acacias
LIKIER	Joseph	60		26.02.91 Varsovie	60 bd Carnot, Cannes
MARKUS	Friedrich	61		23.07.02 Vienne	34 av des Acacias
MENASCH	Roger	60		20.01.88 Rodi	St-Jean-Cap-Ferrat
MEYER	Sylvain	61		19.07.91 Colmar	St-Jean-Cap-Ferrat
MIRELMAN	Celine	60	Brieffel	10.04.95 Cracovie	34 av des Acacias
MIRELMAN	Julia	60		05.02.28 Anvers	34 av des Acacias
MIRELMAN	Szymon	60		09.04.88 Pypin	34 av des Acacias
MORE	Albert	60		22.03.29 Paris	St Martin
NAGLER	Alexandre	60		25.08.04 Cernowitz	Villefranche
NAGLER	Charlotte	60	Salomon	16.04.17 Berlin	V Hermitage, Villefranche
REINACH	Julien			03.04.92 Paris	Villa Grecque, Beaulieu
SCHNERB	Rene	61		21.09.95 Paris	Hot Residence, Cannes
SCHUMACHER	Sarah	60	Lehman	11.09.76 Paris	6 rue Palerme
SCHWOB	Jacques	60		09.07.81 Hericourt	2 r Shakespeare, Cannes
SURMANI	Salvatore	60		12.10.03 Lodi	V Rocca, St Jean
SZAPIRO	Abraham	60		11.12.92 Kowel	
WAHL	Leni	60	Mandel	02.11.06 Welkaberezna	42 av des Acacias
WEIL	Ronald			28.06.12 Londres	1 r Paul-Daumer Beaulieu
WEISZ	Norbert	60		02.09.96 Vienne	5 passage Martin

The list of deportations in which Charlotte Salomon was included under her husband's surname: Nagler.

Ici a séjourné de 1941 à 1942

Charlotte SALOMON
Artiste-peintre expressionniste allemande

née à Berlin le 16 avril 1917
et morte en déportation à Auschwitz
le 10 octobre 1943

The plaque on the wall of the hotel where
Charlotte started and finished her work.

To know more

Books and articles

Leben? Oder theater? by C. Salomon, Special Collection of the Jewish Historical Museum. Available at this link: www.charlotte-salomon.nl/collection/specials/charlotte-salomon/leben-oder-theater

Charlotte by D. Foekinos (Mondadori, 2015)

Charlotte. The death and the girl by B. Pedretti (Skira, 2015)

Charlotte Salomon. The colors of the life by K. Ricci (Palomar, 2006)

Exhibitions. Charlotte's diary by N. Aspesi (La Repubblica, 1998)

The story of Charlotte Salomon: an attempt to go beyond a familiar trait of death, in an encounter with the destructiveness of the Holocaust by D. Gariglio (*Anamorphosis*, edited by W. and S. Cavalitto, Ananke, pp. 44-53, n.11, 2013)

Charlotte. Diary in images by Charlotte Salomon 1917-1943 by C. Levi and E. Strauss (Bompiani, 1963)

Commentary on the exhibition on Charlotte Salomon by A. Polito (Royal Academy, London, 1998)

Charlotte Salomon by L. Piras, *Women's Encyclopedia*. Available at this link: www.enciclopediadelledonne.it/niografie/charlotte-salomon

Brilliant Tempera. Charlotte Salomon by P. Cori, *In General*. Available at this link:
www.ingenere.it/rubrica/tempere-genia- li-charlotte-salomon

Charlotte Salomon: the Jew who took refuge in art by I. Baratta, Window on Art. Available at this link:
www.finestresullar-te.info/459n_charlotte-salomon-ebrea-che-si-rifugio-nell-arte. php#cookie-ok

Vita? O Teatro? by A. Iurilli Duhamel, Equilibri. Available at this link: www.equilibriarte.net/article/2772

History of Charlotte Salomon by D. Gariglio, Psychoanalysis and Science. Available at this link:
www.psico analysis.it/observatoio/3532

Documentaries

It's my whole life by R. Dindo (1992)

Charlotte by F. Weisz (1981)

Ilaria Ferramosca

Scenarist and writer. She made scripts for BeccoGiallo, Tunué, 001 Edizioni, Edizioni Voilier. Co-author and creator for Treccani of a didactic comic insert of grammar, she also created the screenplay for an animated short film for the Library of the Napoleonic Museums on the island of Elba. In fiction she has published short stories and anthologies, for which she has received several prizes and is among the recommended ones of the Italian National Calvin Prize (XXV edition). In 2014 she was among the ten finalists of the Tedeschi Prize for "Il Giallo Mondadori". She teaches screenwriting at the offices in Lecce and Taranto of the Grafite comic school, also taking care of teacher training there.

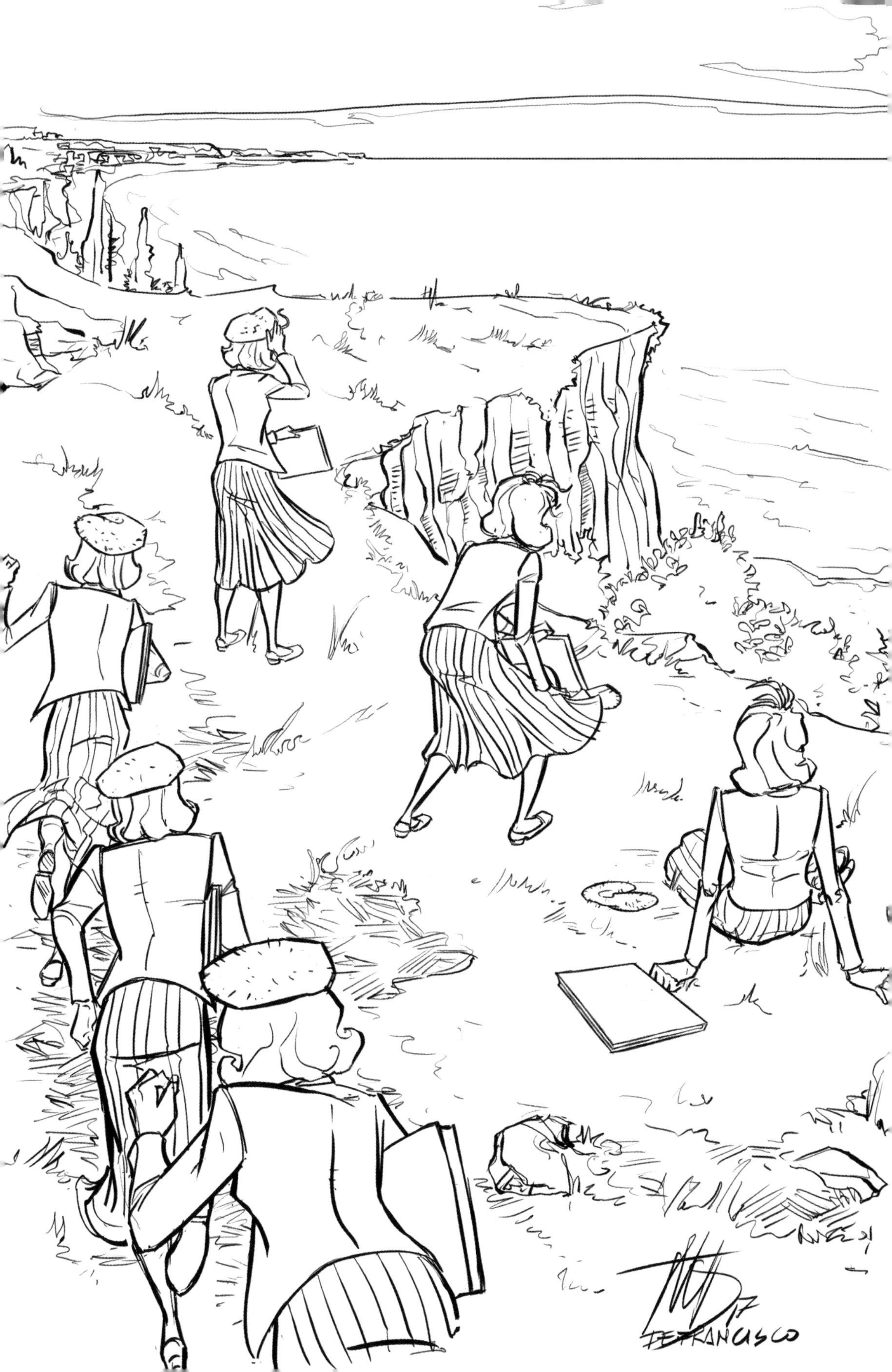
DEFRANCISCO

Gian Marco De Francisco

Architect, cartoonist and illustrator from Taranto has a collaboration on Zartana the sorcerer Blues (Cut Up Publishing) and the graphic novels Ragazzi di escort (BeccoGiallo), Our mother Renata Fonte (001 editions), A case of stalking (Voilier) and the comic book Da grande (Lilliput). As an illustrator on a national level, he collaborated with the magazine of Libera Narcomafie, creating some covers. In the Apulian territory he designed the signs for the Parco delle Civiltà di Grottaglie and, for the BCC Banca Credito Cooperativo di San Marzano di San Giuseppe, he created the illustrations for the 2015 Integrated Report. He is the creator and one of the two founders of the Apulian school of comics Grafite, in the territories of Taranto, Bari and Lecce, in fact creating in Puglia the first regional training center on the art of comics. To date he is the regional coordinator.

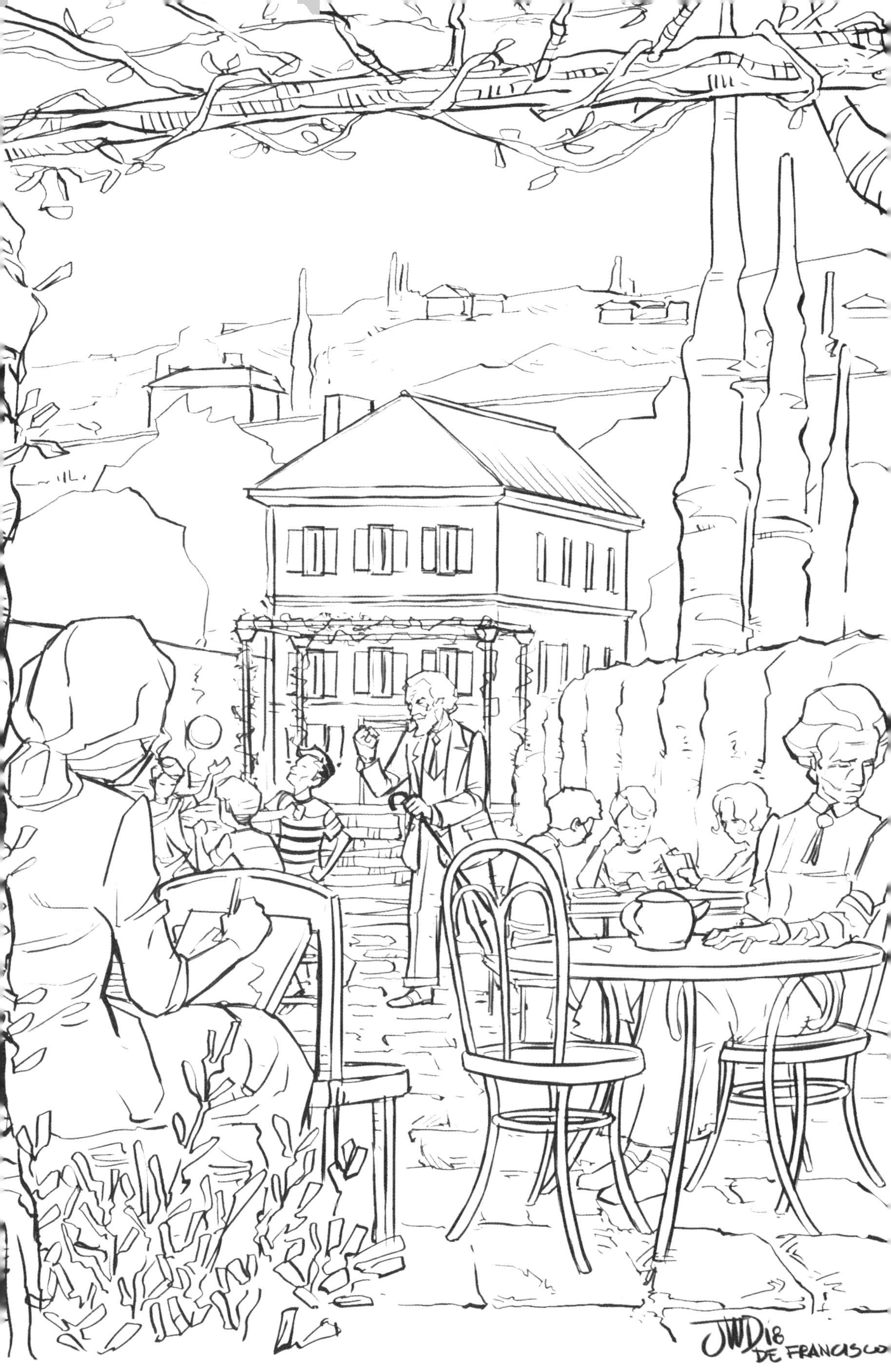
JWD18
DE FRANCISCO

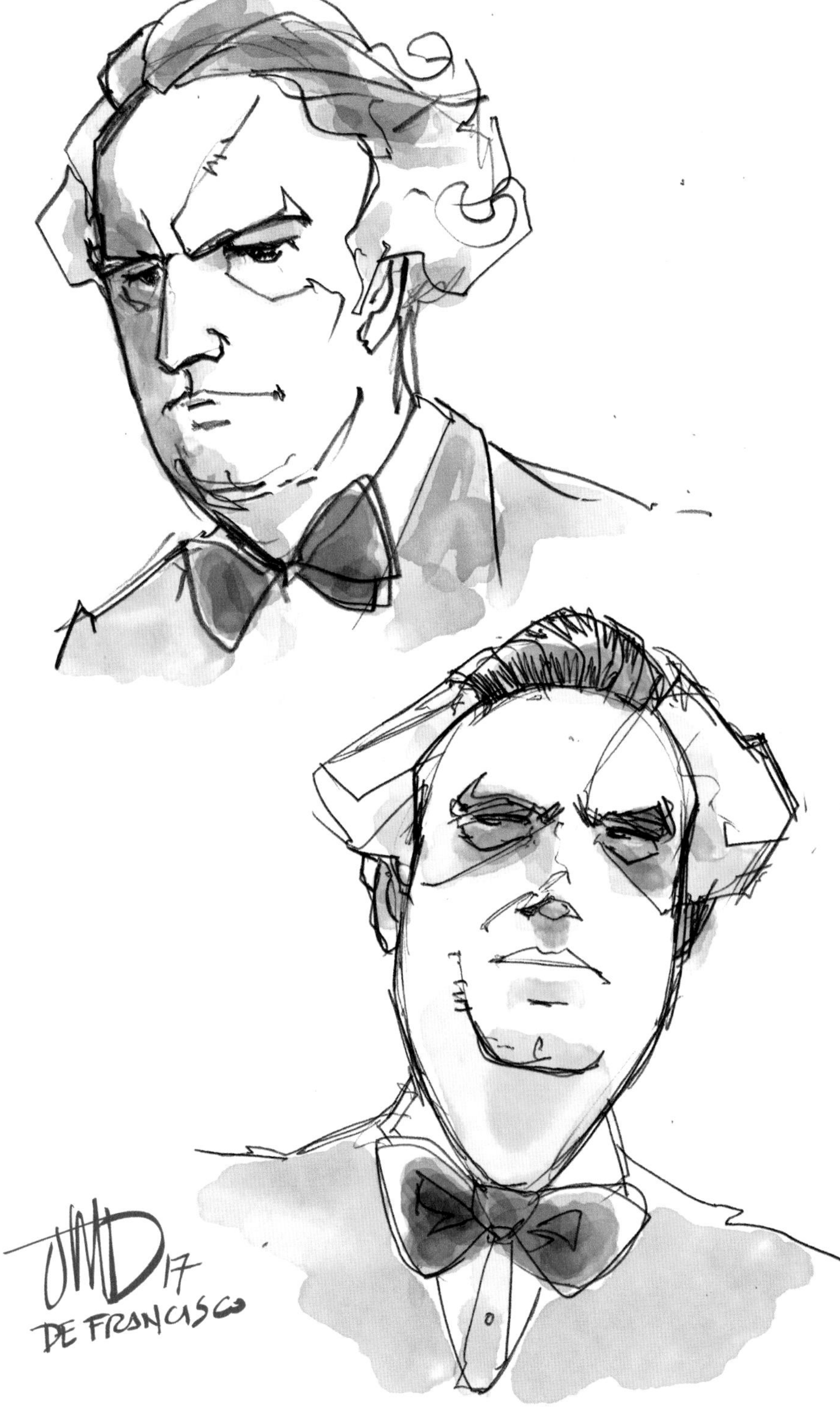
JMD 17
DE FRANCISCO

DE FRANCISCO

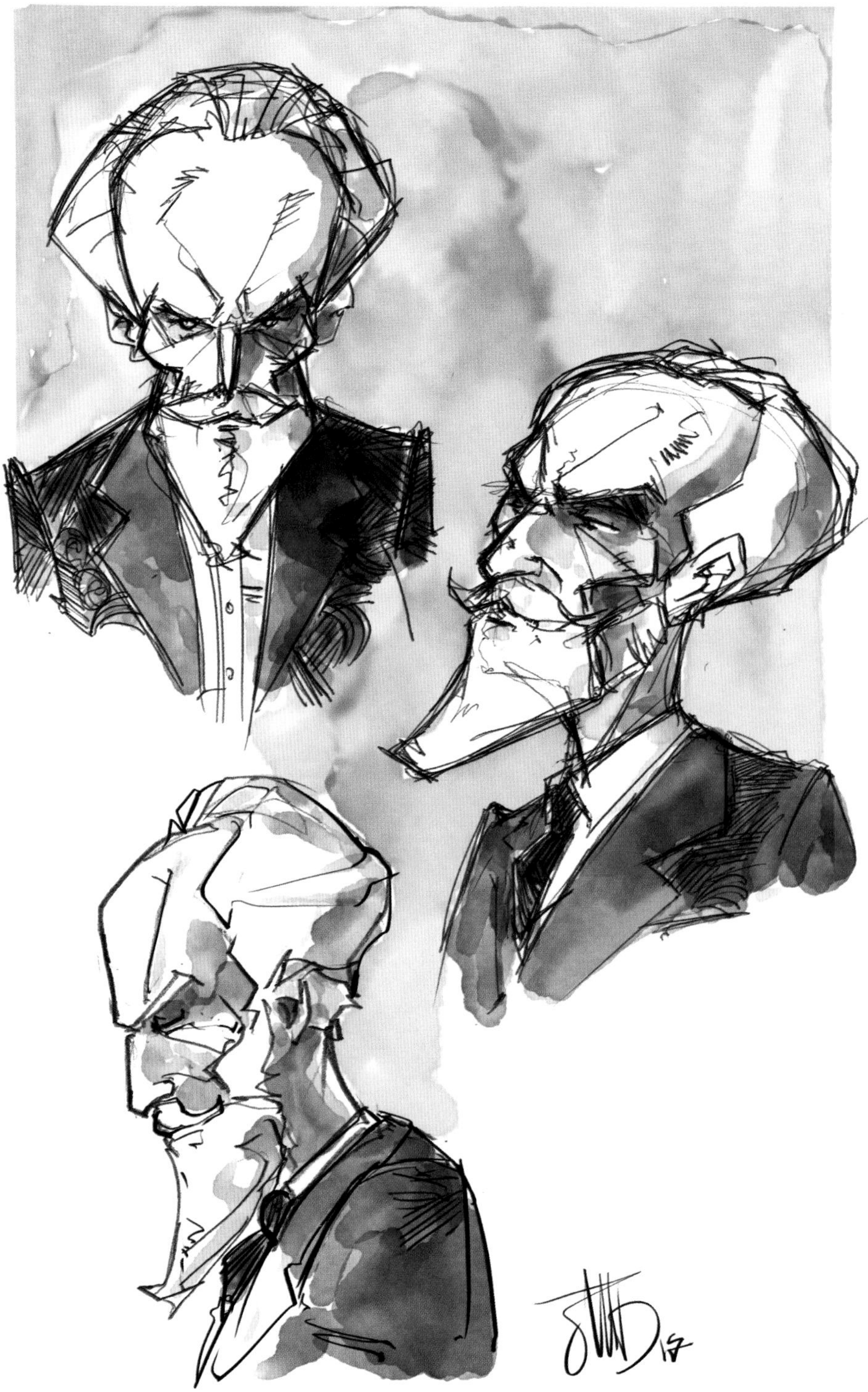

Publisher thanks: To Ami for bearing with me through all this.
To Andy for having such a brave daughter.
To Charlotte who was peerless.

Charlotte Salomon: Colors Of The Soul
© 2019 Ilaria Ferramosca & Gian Marco De Francisco
© BeccoGiallo S.r.l. 2019, for the original Italian edition
Translation made in arrangement with Am-Book (www.am-book.com)

© Fanfare / Ponent Mon 2020 for the English language edition

www.ponentmon.com

Translated by Noemi Milanesio
Edited by Stephen Albert
Layout by RG e HIJAS S.C.P.
ISBN: 978-1-912097-41-8
A CIP catalogue record for this book is available from the British Library.

Printed and bound in the European Union by Spauda, LT